Collins

Year 9, Additional Support Teacher's Pack

NEW MATHS FRAMEWORKING

Complete support for Mathematics at KS3

Keith Gordon

Contents

Assessment Tests

Introduction

This is the lowest level teaching text for Year 9. It accompanies *New Maths Frameworking* Year 9 Workbook and is for students working at National Curriculum Level 4. Students who are working above this level are catered for by Year 9 Pupil Books 1, 2 and 3 and Teacher's Packs 1, 2 and 3.

New Maths Frameworking has been based on the revised Mathematics Programme of Study for Key Stage 3 (KS3) and the renewed Framework for Teaching Mathematics: Year 9. Chapter 15, 'GCSE Preparation', draws on the new GCSE specification to help prepare students to make the transition to GCSE.

Lesson plans

- **Framework objectives** identify the key learning outcomes from the KS3 Frameworks.
- Engaging **Oral and mental starter** activities involve the whole class.
- **Main lesson activities** help you lead students into exercise questions.
- **Plenaries** offer guidance to round off the three-part lessons.
- **Answers** for Year 9 Workbook for easy access.

Extra teaching material

- **Photocopiable Masters** (available on the CD-ROM only) and **Overhead Transparencies** take the work out of lesson preparation.
- **National Test** style questions with separate answers, for Chapters 1–14, help your students to prepare fully for their Test.
- **Homework sheets** with separate answers for every lesson plan to consolidate classroom learning.
- **Assessment Tests** with separate answers help you to monitor progress and deliver Assessment for Learning.

PLUS

The **free, easy-to-use CD-ROM** contains Word documents as well as PDFs of all the material in this Additional Support Teacher's Pack. You can edit and customise your lessons, incorporate the material into your own scheme of work and print out the Homework sheets, Photocopiable Masters and Assessment Tests for your students.

New Maths Frameworking Year 9 Lesson Plans

For use with New Maths Frameworking Year 9 Workbook

Algebra **1** and **2**

Framework objectives – Mental addition and subtraction
Recall number facts, including positive integer complements to 100. Strengthen and extend mental methods of calculation.

Oral and mental starter

Resources required

Large 1–6 dice

- Students will find this exercise easier if they write their answers on a white board.
- Write pairs of numbers on the board, where the units digits total 10, such as 22 and 18, 13 and 27, 32 and 18, 34 and 16, 45 and 15.
- Ask students to write the **total** of these pairs of numbers on their white boards.
- Using a target board as shown, ask students to total a column or a row and write the answers on their white board.

23	16	4	43
14	7	26	47
17	33	9	59
54	56	39	

- Explain that students should look out for pairs of numbers where the units values have a **sum** of 10, for example 14 + 26 = 40. This method can be used to aid mental **addition**.

- Alternatively, use a target board, such as the one shown, and throw a dice.

57	86	74	63
72	94	56	48
23	48	21	22
18	32	13	27

- Write the number on the dice on the board, or ask what that number is multiplied by 10 and write this new value on the board.
- Select one of the numbers from the target board and ask students to **subtract** the value on the board from it.

Main lesson activity

Addition
- Following on from the Oral and mental starter, ask students how they could solve 16 + 82 in their heads.

- Encourage them to develop mental imagery of a blank **number line**, such as the one shown, or to break the problem down, for example 16 + 80 = 96, 96 + 2 = 98. Both methods are essentially the same.

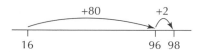

- Repeat with further examples, such as 36 + 17 (53), 124 + 63 (187), 148 + 207 (355).

Subtraction

- Ask students how they could solve 82 – 34 in their heads.
- Again, encourage them to develop mental imagery of a blank number line, such as the one below, or to break the problem down, for example 82 – 4 = 78, 78 – 30 = 48. Both methods are essentially the same.

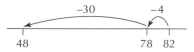

- Repeat with further examples, such as 86 – 23 (63), 124 – 63 (61), 203 – 127 (76).

- **The class can now do Exercise 1A from the Pupil Workbook.**

Exercise 1A   **Answers**

1 a 20   **b** 30   **c** 83   **d** 80   **e** 90   **f** 180   **g** 350   **h** 610   **i** 370
2 a 12   **b** 12   **c** 16   **d** 55   **e** 84   **f** 195   **g** 111   **h** 58   **i** 134
3 a 110   **b** 71   **c** 3   **d** –4   **e** 114   **f** 78
4 a 11   **b** 9   **c** 24   **d** 27   **e** 19   **f** 37
5 a 130 and 90   **b** 70 and 40   **c** 130 and 40

Plenary

Key words

- ☐ addition
- ☐ sum
- ☐ total
- ☐ subtraction
- ☐ difference
- ☐ number line

- Check on mental methods with a quick test.
- Students should write their answers on white boards if these are available.

    1 23 + 27 (50)
    2 34 + 26 (60)
    3 55 + 25 (80)
    4 26 + 44 (70)
    5 33 + 17 (50)
    6 45 – 21 (24)
    7 27 – 11 (16)
    8 54 – 24 (30)
    9 56 – 52 (4)
    10 21 – 13 (8)

LESSON 1.2

Framework objectives – Mental multiplication
Recall number facts, including multiplication facts up to 10 × 10.
Multiply integers.

Oral and mental starter

Resources required

Counting stick or metre rule
0 – 100 number cards
Multiplication table
 (if necessary)

- Use a counting stick marked with 10 divisions.
- Write the numbers from a **times-table**, for example the
  7 times-table, onto pieces of card (or use pre-prepared
  number cards), and attach to the counting stick as shown.

| 0 | 7 | 14 | 21 | 28 | 35 | 42 | 49 | 56 | 63 | 70 |

- Begin by asking the class to chant the table together, or ask an individual
  student to chant the table.
- It is useful to point to each number as it is chanted, to maintain a rhythm.
- Now take away one number, for example 14. Before removing the
  number ask students to concentrate on it and remember it.
- Now repeat the chanting of the table, pointing at the missing value.
- Continue, removing more numbers progressively, until all values are
  removed.
- When students find the table difficult to remember the chanting will
  become mumbled or out of rhythm.
- If this happens, put some values back on the counting stick and repeat.
- If time, repeat with other tables.

Main lesson activity

- This is a lesson on mental **multiplication**, but students may refer to a
  multiplication table if necessary.
- Discuss with the students which are the 'easiest' tables to remember or
  work out. They will probably respond with × 1, × 10, × 2, × 5.
- Do some quick checking of multiplication facts. It is better if students can
  recall these mentally but if they need to use a reference table allow them
  to do so.
- Now ask for the answer to 3 × 2 × 5 (30). Discuss how this may be
  worked out. Set more examples such as 2 × 2 × 6 (24), 3 × 4 × 4 (48), etc.
- Repeat with 3 × 40 (120). Discuss how this is found.
- Repeat with 4 × 60 (240), 6 × 70 (420), etc.
- Now ask students how they could work out 34 × 3 mentally.
- Encourage the mental imagery of splitting the double digit number into
  30 and 4, becoming

    3 × 30 + 3 × 4 = 90 + 12 = 102.

- Demonstrate this on the board if necessary.
- Repeat with further examples, such as 42 × 6 (252), 27 × 6 (162).
- **The class can now do Exercise 1B from the Pupil Workbook.**

Exercise 1B　Answers

1 a

×	4	3	7
2	8	6	14
5	20	15	35
10	40	30	70

b

×	7	8	9
4	28	32	36
6	42	48	54
7	49	56	63

2 a 12　**b** 35　**c** 24　**d** 24　**e** 54　**f** 56
3 a 24　**b** 30　**c** 42　**d** 80　**e** 80　**f** 162
4 a 210　**b** 240　**c** 350　**d** 720　**e** 320　**f** 490
5 a 28　**b** 38　**c** 46　**d** 54　**e** 39　**f** 63　**g** 51　**h** 75　**i** 102　**j** 48
　　k 76　**l** 92
6 a 42　**b** 60　**c** 150　**d** 320　**e** 88　**f** 240

Plenary

Key words

- ☐ **product**
- ☐ **times-table**
- ☐ **multiplication**

- Check on mental methods with a quick test.
- Students should write their answers on white boards if these are available.

1 3×4 (12)
2 4×5 (20)
3 5×7 (35)
4 6×7 (42)
5 5×8 (40)
6 3×15 (45)
7 4×12 (48)
8 5×21 (105)
9 6×13 (78)
10 9×16 (144)

LESSON 1.3

Framework objectives – Sequences
Describe integer sequences; generate terms of a simple sequence, given a rule.

Oral and mental starter

- Write '1, 2' on the board and ask a student to give the next number in a possible **sequence**.
- Ask another student to continue this sequence.
- If a student is unable to continue the sequence, either ask another student or ask for the rule.
- Possible rules are:

Add 1 each time	1, 2, 3, 4, 5, …
Double	1, 2, 4, 8, 16, …
Add one more each time	1, 2, 4, 7, 11, …
Add the two previous terms (Fibonacci)	1, 2, 3, 5, 8, 13, …

- Once one rule has been established, repeat the exercise using the same starting numbers, but asking for a different sequence, i.e. a different rule.
- If students cannot suggest further rules, prompt with extra numbers in the sequence.
- Make sure that they can describe the **term-to-term rule** each time.
- Repeat with two different starting numbers, such as 1, 5.

Main lesson activity

- Write a number on the board, for example 25.
- State, or ask a student to give, a term-to-term rule, for example add 3.
- Ask another student to continue the sequence for a further five terms.
- Repeat with another starting number and another rule.
- Make sure that some 'subtract' and 'multiply' rules are covered.
- Dividing by 2 or 3 can also be covered if suitable starting numbers are chosen, such as 64 or 81.
- Now state a more complex rule, such as multiply by 2 and subtract 1.
- For example, starting with 3, this rule produces the sequence 3, 5, 9, 17, 33, 65, … .
- Now ask students for the term-to-term rule in the following sequences.

    45, 40, 35, 30, 25, … (subtract 5)
    3, 6, 12, 24, 48, …   (multiply by 2)
    1, 3, 6, 10, 15, 21, … (add 2 then 3, etc.)
    256, 64, 16, 4, 1, …   (divide by 4)

- Repeat until the students are confident describing the term-to-term rules.

- **The class can now do Exercise 1C from the Pupil Workbook.**

Exercise 1C Answers

1 a 25, 29, 33, 37, 41 **b** −3, 4, 11, 18, 25 **c** 34, 28, 22, 16, 10
  d 16, 29, 42, 55, 68 **e** 55, 40, 25, 10, −5 **f** 9, 27, 81, 243, 729
  g 40, 121, 364 **h** 22, 46, 94 **i** 29, 83, 245
2 a add 3 **b** subtract 5 **c** subtract 2 **d** multiply by 2 (double) **e** add 9
  f subtract 7 **g** add 11 **h** subtract 20 **i** multiply by 3 **j** multiply by 10
  k divide by 2 (halve)
3 a 7, 11, 27 **b** 23, 51, 65 **c** 170, 90, 70 **d** 9, 288

Plenary

Key words

☐ **sequence**
☐ **term-to-term rule**

- Challenge the students to invent sequences.
- Explain that there must be a valid term-to-term rule and they should write down the first five terms.
- Once a student has completed a sequence, ask them to come and write it on the board.
- The rest of the class must decide on the next terms or describe the rule.

Framework objectives – Function machines

Know the meanings of the word function. Express simple functions in words. Generate coordinate pairs that satisfy a simple linear rule.

Oral and mental starter

● Tell the students that they are going to play the game 'Make me say …'.
● The aim of this game is that the students have to make you say a number that you give them in advance, for example 21.
● Tell students that you have a **rule** in your head. They give you a starting number, you apply the rule and tell them what the answer is.
● Using the rule 'add 4', the first student might say 7 and you reply with 11. The next student might say 13 and you reply with 17, and so on.
● Other rules could be: add, subtract, multiply, multiply and add (this is more difficult so jottings could be allowed), etc.
● The activity can be made easier by writing all of the **input** and **output** values on the board, but it is more challenging if no jottings are allowed.
● Repeat with different rules and 'Make me say …' numbers.

Main lesson activity

Simple function machines
● Draw a rectangle on the board.
● Draw four lines going into the rectangle and four lines exiting on the other side.
● Allocate a number to input on each line. You could ask the students to give you four numbers.
● Write a rule in the rectangle, such as Add 5.
● Ask students to give the corresponding output values for the chosen numbers.
● Repeat with other sets of numbers and rules. Suggested rules are Subtract 7, Multiply by 5, Divide by 3 (make sure the input values are multiples of 3).
● Draw on the board a function machine with the rule box and output column completed.

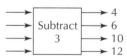

● Ask students to give the corresponding input values.
● Repeat with other rules.
● Now use one rectangle and give the input and output values.

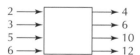

● Ask students to give the missing rule.
● Repeat with other sets of input and output values.

Complex function machines

- Draw two rectangles on the board with four input lines and four input numbers as shown.
- Write a rule in each rectangle.
- Ask students to give the final output value for the given inputs.
- Interim values can be written down if necessary.
- Repeat with different rules and input numbers.
- **The class can now do Exercise 1D from the Pupil Workbook.**

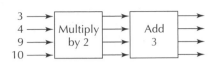

Exercise 1D **Answers**

1 a 16, 22, 45, 112 **b** 2, 24, 0, 114 **c** 42, 24, 78, 600 **d** 1, 3, 2, 6, 5, 15, 12, 36
2 a 4, 10, 17, 44 **b** 10, 13, 18, 40 **c** 2, 4, 8, 10 **d** 3, 9, 5, 10
3 a add 5 **b** add 20 **c** subtract 9 **d** multiply by 3 (treble)

Plenary

Key words

- input
- output
- rule

- Challenge the students to find the missing rules in this function machine.

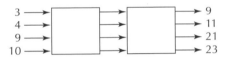

- The rules are Multiply by 2 and Add 3.
- If they cannot find the rule then the interim values can be written in.
- Repeat with other rules as time allows.

Framework objectives – Terms and expressions

Use letter symbols to represent unknown numbers. Understand that algebraic operations follow the rules of arithmetic.

Oral and mental starter

- Tell students that you will give them a rule, such as 'add 2'. You will then give them a number and they have to apply the rule to the number and reply with the answer. For example, if the rule is 'add 2' and you say to a student '7', the student should reply '9'.
- Work around the class using the same rule. After about 6 responses, say 'x' rather than a number. The students may be puzzled by this.
- Explain that the rule is 'add 2', so 7 gives 9, 20 gives 22 and so on, and ask again what x gives.
- It is sometimes useful to write on the board, $7 \rightarrow 7 + 2 = 9$, $20 \rightarrow 20 + 2 = 22$, $14 \rightarrow 14 + 2 = 16$. Then write $x \rightarrow$ and ask what to write next.
- If no students give the correct answer, tell them that it is $x + 2$.
- Explain that the difference between numbers and letters is that numbers give another number whereas letters give an **expression**.
- Repeat the activity with a simple subtract rule. This time use the letter z.
- Once again it may be useful to write some examples on the board and obtain the expression, for example, $z - 3$.
- Repeat with a multiplication rule and use the letter n. Emphasise that there is no need to include the multiplication sign in the expression. Although $2 \times n$ and $n \times 2$ are acceptable, $2n$ is better.
- Finally, repeat with a division rule and use the letter x. Emphasise that division can be written as, for example, $x \div 5$ or $\frac{x}{5}$.

Main lesson activity

- Write the expression $a - 5$ on the board and ask the students what the expression means.
- Ask them the value of the expression when $a = 8$.
- Repeat with other values for a.
- Now write the expression $b + 7$ on the board and ask a student what the expression means.
- Ask them the value of the expression when $b = -2$.
- Repeat with other values for b.
- Now write the expression $4c$ on the board and ask a student what the expression means.
- Ask them the value of the expression when $c = 2.5$.
- Repeat with other values for c.
- To complete this section, write the expression $d \div 2$ on the board and ask a student what the expression means.
- Ask them the value of the expression when $d = 6$.
- Repeat with other (even) values for d.

- Draw a **function machine**, a rectangle with four arrows going into it and four lines exiting on the other side, as shown.

$$3 \longrightarrow$$
$$7 \longrightarrow$$
$$12 \longrightarrow \boxed{n+3}$$
$$15 \longrightarrow$$

- Allocate a number to each line (or ask students to give you four numbers).
- Now write a rule in the rectangle, such as $n + 3$.
- Ask students to give the corresponding output values for the chosen numbers.
- Repeat with other sets of numbers and rules.

- **The class can now do Exercise 1E from the Pupil Workbook.**

Exercise 1E   Answers

1.
a number added to 6	$n + 6$
6 take away a number	$6 - n$
double a number	$2n$
2 times a number added to 1	$2n + 1$
a number minus 7	$n - 7$
divide a number by 2	$\frac{n}{2}$
a number added to 2	$n + 2$

2. **a** 8 **b** 6 **c** 10 **d** 6 **e** 16 **f** 8 **g** 14 **h** 9
3. **a** 8, 11, 16, 40
   b 0, 4, 12, 25
   c 8, 20, 40, 100
   d 7, 14, 35, 70
   e 2, 5, 10, 22
   f 4, 7, 13, 28

Plenary

Key words
- algebra
- expression
- function

- Challenge the students to find the output $(2x + 3)$ from this diagram.

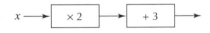

$$x \longrightarrow \boxed{\times 2} \longrightarrow \boxed{+ 3} \longrightarrow$$

- If students cannot find the output then the interim value $(2x)$ can be written in.
- Repeat with other sets of rules.

Framework objectives – Graphs from functions

Plot the graphs of simple linear functions, where y is given explicitly in terms of x

Oral and mental starter

Resources required

OHT 1.1 Coordinates
OHT 1.2 Coordinate grid
OHT 1.3 Lines

- Display OHT 1.1.
- Call out various letters and ask students to identify the coordinates of that letter.
- Ask the students to give the relationship between points A, B, C, D and E.
- They should identify that they are on a straight **line**.
- Write the coordinates of points A, B, C, D and E on the board: (2, 5), (3, 6), (4, 7), (5, 8), (6, 9).
- Ask students if they can identify a relationship between the coordinates.
- They may see that the second value (the y-value) is 3 more than the first value (the x-value) in all cases.
- If appropriate, explain that this could be written as $y = x + 3$, otherwise emphasise that points that make a straight line on a grid also have a connection between the x- and y-coordinates.
- Other relationships that could be explored are between points J, K and L ($y = 18$), N, G, Q and P ($y = x$), H, I and D ($x + y = 13$ or $y = 13 - x$) and M, S and K ($x = 8$).

Main lesson activity

- Put the following table on the board.

x	0	2	3	5
y				

- Now write up the rule $y = x + 6$ and ask students what this rule tells us.
- Emphasise that the rule says, 'The value of y is 6 more (or add 6) than the value of x'.
- Tell them that this is called an **equation** and is different to the expressions they have already met as it has an equals sign.
- Ask students to fill in the table.
- Write the values from the table as a set of coordinates (0, 6), (2, 8), (3, 9), (5, 11).
- **Plot** these points on OHT 1.2 or on a blank coordinate grid.
- Ask the students what the relationship is between the points on the grid.
- They should see that the points form a straight line.
- Join up the points.
- Label the line with the given equation.
- Explain that it is important to label lines on graphs.
- Repeat with more tables and rules. Include rules such as $y = 4 - x$, and $y = 3x - 1$. You may wish to work through an example from the Pupil Workbook.

- **The class can now do Exercise 1F from the Pupil Workbook.**

Exercise 1F — Answers

1 2, 4, 5, 7
2 5, 4, 2, 0
3 0, 3, 6, 9
4 3, 5, 7, 11
5 −1, 2, 5, 8, 11
Check that all coordinates are plotted correctly

Plenary

Key words

- Display OHT 1.3 and challenge the students to find the equations of the two lines shown.
- Prompt them to write down some of the points on the line and ask if they can find the connection between x and y.

Line A	(0,4), (1, 5), (2, 6), (3, 7)	$y = x + 4$
Line B	(0, 12), (1, 11), (2, 10), (3, 9), (4, 8)	$y + x = 12$

Key words:
- [ ] x-axis
- [ ] y-axis
- [ ] equation
- [ ] lines
- [ ] plotting

Number **1**

Framework objectives – Rounding
Round positive whole numbers to the nearest 10, 100 or 1000 and decimals to the nearest whole number or one decimal place.

Oral and mental starter

Resources required

Target board

- Use a target board such as the one shown.

6000	3	0.7	0.2	7
0.8	160	14	10	4.8
3000	0.5	3600	0.06	130
6.4	1500	12	1	2700

- Recall strategies for doubling and halving.
- Point to numbers and randomly select students to double them.
- Discuss the strategies again. For example:

$2 \times 6000 = 2 \times 6 = 12$

then add three zeros to the end to give 12 000.
- Point to further numbers and randomly select students to halve them.
- Discuss the strategies again. For example:

Half of 0.7 = 0.35

Main lesson activity

- Draw a number line on the board. Divide it into 10 segments. Mark one end with 0 and the other end with 10.

- Mark a point with an arrow, as shown. Ask the students to **estimate** the value of the number. (6.3) Ask what it is to the nearest whole number (**integer**).
- Repeat with other examples. Make sure that you give at least one number ending in 0.5, to practise the rounding-up rule.
- Change the scale to 0 to 100. Repeat, asking students to **round** numbers to the nearest 10.
- Change the scale to 0 to 1. Repeat, asking students to round numbers to the nearest one **decimal place**.
- Give some examples without using the scale. For example:

Round 546 to the nearest 10, 100, 1000.
Round 3098 to the nearest 10, 100, 1000.

Round 6.58 to one decimal place.
Round 9.321 to one decimal place.
Round 3.997 to one decimal place.

- Make sure students understand that the last example rounds to 4.0.
- **The class can now do Exercise 2A from the Pupil Workbook.**

Exercise 2A **Answers**

1 a 30 **b** 50 **c** 90 **d** 90 **e** 140 **f** 180 **g** 310 **h** 260 **i** 900
2 a 400 **b** 800 **c** 100 **d** 500 **e** 1300 **f** 2400 **g** 3900 **h** 5200 **i** 3900
3 a £123 000 **b** £175 000 **c** £189 000 **d** £205 000
4 a 4 **b** 6 **c** 9 **d** 9 **e** 15 **f** 36 **g** 7 **h** 4 **i** 7
5 a 5.7 **b** 1.3
6 a 4.6 **b** 9.8 **c** 3.3 **d** 6.2 **e** 14.3 **f** 0.5
7 a 2.4 **b** 4.2 **c** 0.9 **d** 9.9 **e** 16.3 **f** 8.9

Plenary

Key words
- approximately
- decimal place
- estimate
- integer
- round

- Write a variety of numbers on the board and ask the students to round them to various accuracies. For example:

3219   34.65   31.07   103.9   5244   829   0.632   3.438

to the nearest 1000, 100, 10, whole number.
- Discuss the techniques involved.

Framework objectives – Ordering decimals
Compare and order decimals in different contexts.

Oral and mental starter

Resources required

Student white boards
Various decimal number cards

- Using a target board such as the one shown, ask students to write down the largest number on the top (middle, bottom) row.

0.7	1.32	0.09	3.4
0.9	2.1	0.65	4.81
2.3	0.12	0.02	2.21
1.8	1.6	1.35	0.16

- Then ask for the smallest number on the top (middle, bottom) row.
- Repeat with columns.
- If there is time, you could ask individual students to mentally add (or subtract) the largest and smallest numbers in a particular row or column.

Main lesson activity

- Draw a table, as shown, on the board (or an OHT).

Units	Tenths	Hundredths	Thousandths

- Write on the board the following, or similar, numbers (or have prepared cards available):

    3.2   0.7   0.04   0.78   0.4   3.25   0.44   0.403   3.217

- Ask students to come to the board, select a number and write it into the table, using the appropriate place-value columns.
- Alternatively, ask each student to select the **largest** (or **smallest**) number and fill it in on the top line then continue to select the next largest (or smallest) as appropriate.
- When the table is completely filled in, discuss how to decide which number is largest.
- When comparing numbers, ensure that the concept of working from the left until the largest digit is encountered is understood.

- Repeat with:

  3.45   0.342   0.35   3   39   307   38

- Which of the numbers 3.5 and 3.47 is larger?
- Which of the numbers 4.111 and 4.118 is larger?
- Make sure students can identify the larger of two numbers with decimal places.

- **The class can now do Exercise 2B from the Pupil Workbook.**

Exercise 2B   **Answers**

1 3.02, 3.1, 3.15, 3.27, 3.32
2 **a** 0.7 **b** 4.4 **c** 12.6 **d** 10.9 **e** 4.3 **f** 8.7 **g** 9.38 **h** 4.75 **i** 4.63
   j 0.71 **k** 0.3 **l** 0.9 **m** 1.65 **n** 2.47 **p** 8.7
3 **a** 3.4, 4.3, 4.7, 7.4, **b** 0.6, 1.6, 6.0, 6.6 **c** 11.3, 13.3, 13.9, 19.3
   d 34.4, 34.6, 46.4, 63.4
4 **a** £0.88, £1.08, £1.80, £8.81 **b** £3.14, £3.41, £3.61, £4.13
   c £60.24, £60.40, £61.42, £64.04 **d** £0.58, £0.78, £0.85, £0.87

Plenary

Key words

- [ ] **difference**
- [ ] **largest**
- [ ] **smallest**

- Write pairs of numbers on the board (or have prepared cards available), such as 3.4 and 3.48, 7.1 and 7.34, 4.02 and 4.008.
- Ask students to put them together with a greater than or less than sign. For example:

  3.4 < 3.48

Framework objectives – Fractions and decimals
Convert terminating decimals to fractions. Recognise the equivalence of fractions and decimals.

Oral and mental starter

> **Resources required**
>
> Counting stick

- Use a number line drawn on the board or a counting stick divided into ten segments. State that one end is 0, the second division is 10.

0   10

- Ask the class to identify the rest of the marks on the line or stick.
- As a group, or with an individual student, count on in fives until they reach the end of the stick.
- Repeat the activity with the line or stick marked with 0 and 1, as shown, counting on in halves.

0   1

- When identifying the other points, use fractions rather than decimals (although the opportunity to link the equivalent fractions and decimals should be taken).
- Ask for the connection between this counting-on activity and the last one.
- Repeat with the line or the stick marked as shown.

0   25

- Repeat again with the line or the stick marked as shown.

0   $\frac{1}{4}$

- Establish the connection between these two counting-on activities.

Main lesson activity

- Following on from the Oral and mental starter ask the students to identify the divisions on this number line.

0   1

- Now ask them to identify the divisions on this number line.

0   0.1

- Recall column headings for whole numbers and extend this to fractional values.

Tens	Units	•	Tenths	Hundredths
	0	•	7	
	0	•	1	3

- Demonstrate, by filling in the table, that 0.7 is **equivalent** to $\frac{70}{100}$ which **cancels** to $\frac{7}{10}$ and that 0.13 is equivalent to $\frac{13}{100}$.
- Repeat with more examples.
- Similarly, show that $\frac{8}{10} = 0.8$ and that $0.07 = \frac{7}{100}$.
- Repeat with more examples.
- Ask the students to identify the divisions on this number line, both as fractions and decimals.

- Use this to show that $0.25 = \frac{1}{4}$, $0.5 = \frac{1}{2}$, $0.75 = \frac{3}{4}$ and so on.
- **The class can now do Exercise 2C from the Pupil Workbook.**

Exercise 2C **Answers**

1 a $\frac{1}{2}$, 0.5 b $\frac{1}{4}$, 0.25 c $\frac{3}{4}$, 0.75 d $\frac{1}{10}$, 0.1 e $\frac{1}{100}$, 0.01 f $\frac{1}{5}$, 0.2

2 a 0.1 b 0.3 c 0.7 d 0.01 e 0.03 f 0.19 g 0.43 h 1.9 i 2.43

3 a $\frac{1}{10}$ b $\frac{3}{10}$ c $\frac{9}{10}$ d $\frac{1}{100}$ e $\frac{7}{100}$ f $\frac{11}{100}$ g $2\frac{7}{10}$ h $1\frac{13}{100}$

4 a $0.5 = \frac{1}{2} = \frac{5}{10}$ b $0.25 = \frac{1}{4} = \frac{25}{100}$ c $0.75 = \frac{3}{4} = \frac{75}{100}$ d $0.2 = \frac{1}{5} = \frac{2}{10}$ e $0.6 = \frac{3}{5} = \frac{6}{10}$

Plenary

Key words

- [ ] **cancelling**
- [ ] **equivalent**

- Write fractions and decimals on the board (or have prepared cards) with tenths, hundredths, halves, quarters, and three-quarters.
- Ask the class to convert them to fractions or decimals as appropriate. Discuss the rules.
- Particularly focus on $\frac{1}{3}$ and $\frac{2}{3}$. One third is an important fraction but is difficult to convert according to the rules above.
- The students may know the equivalent decimals, but if not, they can be written as 0.33 and as 0.66 or 0.67. The actual values of 0.333 333… and 0.666 666… are obviously more accurate.

LESSON 2.4

Framework objectives – Equivalent fractions
Identify equivalent fractions.

Oral and mental starter

Resources required

OHT 2.1 Fraction grid 1
OHT 2.2 Fraction grid 2
OHT 2.3 Fraction grid 3
OHT 2.4 Fraction grid 4

- Relate to the previous Oral and mental starter (on page 18). The last activity was counting on in quarters.
- Display OHT 2.1, or draw the grid from this OHT on the board. Ask the class to count on and fill in the missing numbers until you have a complete grid (OHT 2.2).
- Ask them to study it for a few moments. Cover up the grid. Display OHTs 2.3 and 2.4, which are fragments of the whole grid. Ask the students to come to the board and fill in the missing numbers. Finally, reveal the grid to check the answers.z

$\frac{1}{4}$			1
		$1\frac{3}{4}$	
	$3\frac{1}{2}$		
			5

$\frac{1}{4}$	$\frac{1}{2}$	$\frac{3}{4}$	1
$1\frac{1}{4}$	$1\frac{1}{2}$	$1\frac{3}{4}$	2
$2\frac{1}{4}$	$2\frac{1}{2}$	$2\frac{3}{4}$	3
$3\frac{1}{4}$	$3\frac{1}{2}$	$3\frac{3}{4}$	4
$4\frac{1}{4}$	$4\frac{1}{2}$	$4\frac{3}{4}$	5

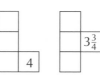

- This can be repeated with other grids, such as the one below.

$\frac{1}{8}$	$\frac{1}{4}$	$\frac{3}{8}$	$\frac{1}{2}$	$\frac{5}{8}$	$\frac{3}{4}$	$\frac{7}{8}$	1
$1\frac{1}{8}$	$1\frac{1}{4}$	$1\frac{3}{8}$	$1\frac{1}{2}$	$1\frac{5}{8}$	$1\frac{3}{4}$	$1\frac{7}{8}$	2

$7\frac{1}{8}$	$7\frac{1}{4}$	$7\frac{3}{8}$	$7\frac{1}{2}$	$7\frac{5}{8}$	$7\frac{3}{4}$	$7\frac{7}{8}$	8

Main lesson activity

- Draw the following diagram on the board.

$$\blacksquare\ =\ \blacksquare$$

- Ask students what they think it represents.
- They should establish that it shows $\frac{1}{2} = \frac{2}{4}$.
- Now write $\frac{1}{2} = \frac{...}{8}$ on the board and ask students for the missing number (4).
- Explain that these are called equivalent fractions.
- Explain that $\frac{1}{2}$ is a fraction in its simplest form and the rest can be cancelled down to $\frac{1}{2}$.
- Now write $\frac{1}{3}$ on the board and ask students if they can give an equivalent fraction.
- If necessary prompt by suggesting a new denominator such as 6 or 9.
- Now write $\frac{4}{5}$ on the board and ask students if they can give an equivalent fraction.
- Ask students what the connection is between the fraction in its simplest form and its equivalent fractions.
- Establish that both numerator and denominator of the simplest fraction are multiplied by the same number.

- Now write $\frac{2}{3} = \frac{}{15}$ and ask for the missing number (10).
- Ask how this can be done. It is unlikely that you will get a mathematical explanation but establish that 3 times 5 = 15 so you also multiply 2 by 5.
- Repeat with other examples including some where the numerator is given and the denominator has to be found such as $\frac{3}{7} = \frac{12}{}$.
- **The class can now do Exercise 2D from the Pupil Workbook.**

Exercise 2D   Answers

1 a $\frac{2}{4}, \frac{3}{6}, \frac{4}{8}, \frac{5}{10},$ b $\frac{2}{6}, \frac{3}{9}, \frac{4}{12}, \frac{5}{15}$ c $\frac{2}{10}, \frac{3}{15}, \frac{4}{20}, \frac{5}{25}$ d $\frac{4}{6}, \frac{6}{9}, \frac{8}{12}, \frac{10}{15}$
   e $\frac{6}{8}, \frac{9}{12}, \frac{12}{16}, \frac{15}{20}$ f $\frac{8}{10}, \frac{12}{15}, \frac{16}{20}, \frac{20}{25}$

2 a $\frac{9}{15}$ b $\frac{8}{14}$ c $\frac{8}{20}$ d $\frac{5}{30}$ e $\frac{21}{30}$ f $\frac{10}{18}$ g $\frac{15}{40}$ h $\frac{6}{33}$

3 a $\frac{15}{18},$ b $\frac{6}{16},$ c $\frac{40}{50}$ d $\frac{3}{21}$ e $\frac{24}{32}$ f $\frac{9}{30}$ g $\frac{18}{42}$ h $\frac{15}{36}$

4 $\frac{6}{9}, \frac{14}{21}, \frac{12}{18}$

5 $\frac{8}{10}, \frac{20}{25}$

Plenary

- Write $\frac{20}{25}$ on the board.
- Ask for the fraction that is in its simplest form equivalent to this ($\frac{4}{5}$).
- Ask students how they can do this easily.
- Establish that both numerator and denominator can be divided by 5.
- This is called the **highest common factor**.
- Repeat with other fractions that can be simplified.
- If the class are able enough, explain that this is called 'cancelling down' and demonstrate how this is normally written, i.e. $\frac{\overset{4}{\cancel{20}}}{\underset{5}{\cancel{25}}}$

Key words

- numerator
- denominator
- fraction in its simplest form
- equivalent fraction
- common factor

LESSON 2.5

Framework objectives – Comparing fractions
Use diagrams to compare two or more simple fractions.

Oral and mental starter

Resources required
Student white boards
2 dice (six- or ten-sided)

- Throw one dice to establish the **unit fraction**, i.e. if 5 is thrown the unit fraction is $\frac{1}{5}$.
- Throw the other dice to establish the integer, i.e. if 3 is thrown the integer is 3.
- Ask students how many of the unit fraction will divide into the integer, e.g. how many one fifths are there in 3.
- Repeat as many times as is necessary.

Main lesson activity

- Draw the following diagram on the board.

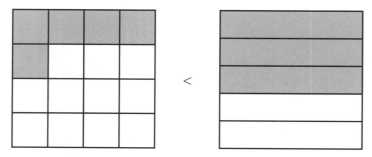

- Ask students what they think it represents.
- They should establish that it shows $\frac{5}{16} < \frac{3}{5}$.
- Ask if they can be sure that this is true.
- Establish that the shaded area is clearly bigger on the second 'unit'.
- Now draw the following diagram on the board.

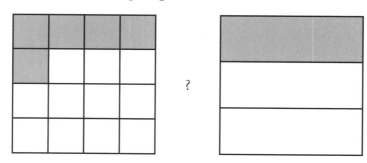

- Ask what sign <, > or = should go in the middle.
- You will probably get all three answers, so a method is needed to find the correct answer.
- Ask students to fill in the missing values from $\frac{5}{16} = \frac{}{48}$ and $\frac{1}{3} = \frac{}{48}$. This gives $\frac{15}{48}$ and $\frac{16}{48}$ so $\frac{1}{3}$ is bigger.
- Ask why 48 was chosen as the new denominator.
- Establish that it is 3 × 16 (= 48). Explain that this is always a way to find a common denominator.
- Now write $\frac{4}{5}$ and $\frac{7}{8}$ on the board and ask students to find which is the larger.

- Ask for the new denominator (40) and convert both fractions $\frac{32}{40}$ and $\frac{35}{40}$ to get $\frac{7}{8}$ as the larger.
- Repeat with other examples.
- **The class can now do Exercise 2E from the Pupil Workbook.**

Exercise 2E   Answers

1 a $\frac{3}{4}$ **b** $\frac{2}{3}$ **c** $\frac{1}{3}$ **d** $\frac{5}{6}$ **e** $\frac{4}{5}$ **f** $\frac{2}{5}$ **g** $\frac{2}{5}$ **h** $\frac{5}{6}$ **i** $\frac{4}{5}$ **j** $\frac{2}{3}$

2 a >   **b** =   **c** <   **d** =   **e** <   **f** =   **g** >   **h** <   **i** =   **j** <

3 a $\frac{4}{5}\left(\frac{28}{35}\right)$ is bigger than $\left(\frac{5}{7}\right)\frac{25}{35}$ **b** $\frac{5}{6}\left(\frac{20}{24}\right)$ is bigger than $\frac{3}{4}\left(\frac{18}{24}\right)$

    c $\frac{2}{3}\left(\frac{16}{24}\right)(16-24)$ is bigger then $\frac{5}{8}\left(\frac{15}{24}\right)$ **d** $\frac{4}{7}\left(\frac{32}{56}\right)$ is less than $\frac{5}{8}\left(\frac{35}{56}\right)$

    e $\frac{1}{6}\left(\frac{3}{18}\right)$ is less than $\frac{2}{9}\left(\frac{4}{18}\right)$ **f** $\frac{7}{8}\left(\frac{63}{72}\right)$ is less than $\frac{8}{9}\left(\frac{64}{72}\right)$

    g $\frac{3}{8}\left(\frac{9}{24}\right)$ is less than $\frac{5}{12}\left(\frac{10}{24}\right)$ **h** $\frac{13}{15}\left(\frac{26}{30}\right)$ is bigger than $\frac{7}{10}\left(\frac{21}{30}\right)$

    i $\frac{7}{9}\left(\frac{14}{18}\right)$ is less than $\frac{5}{6}\left(\frac{15}{18}\right)$ **j** $\frac{1}{4}\left(\frac{11}{44}\right)$ is less than $\frac{3}{11}\left(\frac{12}{44}\right)$

4 a <   **b** <   **c** >   **d** <   **e** >   **f** <   **g** <   **h** <   **i** >   **j** <

Plenary

Key words

- [ ] common denominator
- [ ] less than
- [ ] greater than

- Ask for $\frac{7}{12}$ compared to $\frac{5}{8}$. They will use 96 as the new denominator but demonstrate that it will work with 24 to give $\frac{14}{24}$ and $\frac{15}{24}$. This is because 96 is not the lowest common denominator although it can still be used to compare the fractions.
- Repeat with $\frac{5}{6}$ and $\frac{8}{9}$, and $\frac{7}{16}$ and $\frac{11}{24}$.

Framework objectives – Fractions and percentages
Recognise the equivalence of percentages and fractions.

Oral and mental starter

- Ask the class for all the factors of 100.
- Write them on the board as 1×100, 2×50, 4×25, 5×20 and 10×10. (Leave these displayed for the Main lesson activity.)
- Ask what 'per cent' means.
- Establish that it means 'out of 100'.
- Draw a number line on the board marked in tenths and label the ends 0 and 1.

- Ask for the percentages that go with 0 and 1 (0%) and (100%) and write these underneath the number line.
- Ask if any student knows what $\frac{1}{2}$ is as a percentage (50%).
- Mark these values on the number line.
- Now ask for $\frac{1}{10}$ as a percentage (10%).
- Mark these values on the number line.
- Use these values to fill in the rest of the fractions and the equivalent percentages.
- If time, do the twentieths as well.

Main lesson activity

- Explain that the lesson is directly connected to the Oral and mental starter and the students will be converting fractions to percentages and vice versa.
- Ask what the key number is in this (100).
- Establish that all fractions must be converted to an equivalent fraction with a denominator of 100.
- Now ask for the missing number in $\frac{3}{20} = \frac{}{100}$ (15).
- Ask how the calculations on the board help to do this.
- Explain that the factor pair 5×20 shows what number to multiply the numerator by.
- Ask the students what percentage is equivalent to $\frac{3}{20}$.
- Explain that 15% is the same as $\frac{15}{100}$.
- Now find the equivalent fraction with a denominator of 100 and thus the equivalent percentage to $\frac{7}{10}$ (70%), $\frac{6}{25}$ (24%), $\frac{7}{50}$ (14%), etc.
- Now write 60% on the board. Ask the students what this is as a fraction.
- The answer may be $\frac{60}{100}$ but show that this can be cancelled by a factor of 20 to $\frac{3}{5}$.
- Repeat with 30% ($\frac{3}{10}$), 66% ($\frac{33}{50}$), 65% ($\frac{13}{20}$), 8% ($\frac{2}{25}$), etc.

- **The class can now do Exercise 2F from the Pupil Workbook.**

Exercise 2F Answers

1 a $\frac{1}{2}$, 50% b $\frac{1}{4}$, 25% c $\frac{3}{4}$, 75% d $\frac{1}{10}$, 10% e $\frac{1}{100}$, 1% f $\frac{1}{5}$, 20%

2 a 100 b 50 c 25 d 5 e 10

3 a 10% b 70% c 50% d 20% e 75% f 90% g 40% h 23% i 35%
   j 28% k 82% l 25% m 80% n 55% o 18%

4 a $\frac{1}{5}$ b $\frac{1}{2}$ c $\frac{9}{10}$ d $\frac{17}{20}$ e $\frac{11}{25}$ f $\frac{3}{10}$ g $\frac{3}{20}$ h $\frac{2}{25}$ i $\frac{1}{4}$
   j $\frac{2}{5}$ k $\frac{9}{20}$ l $\frac{49}{50}$ m $\frac{1}{10}$ n $\frac{3}{4}$ o $\frac{1}{100}$

5 a < b > c = d < e = f > g = h < i = j <

Plenary

Key words

■ percentage

● Explain that because a decimal, a fraction and a percentage are all different ways of writing the same thing, we can sometimes make a calculation easier by using one of them instead of another.

Example 1 20% of 35. As 20% is $\frac{1}{5}$, this is the same as $\frac{1}{5} \times 35 = 7$.

Example 2 0.3×340. As 0.3 is 30%, this is the same as 30% of 340.
   10% of 340 is 34. So, 30% of 340 is $3 \times 34 = 102$.

Example 3 $\frac{3}{25}$ of 40. As $\frac{3}{25}$ is 0.12, this is the same as $0.12 \times 40 = 4.8$.

● Ask the class to rewrite each of the following, using an alternative to the percentage, decimal or fraction given, then work out the answers.

a 20% of 75 b $\frac{2}{25}$ of 60 c 25% of 19 d 60% of 550 e $\frac{3}{20}$ of 90
f 0.125×64 g $\frac{3}{5}$ of 7

(**Answers: a** 15 **b** 4.8 **c** 4.75 **d** 330 **e** 13.5 **f** 8 **g** 4.2)

Framework objectives – Percentages

Understand percentage as the 'numbers of parts per 100'; calculate simple percentages.

Oral and mental starter

- Recall fraction, percentage and decimal equivalences. This can be done with a linking diagram such as the one shown.

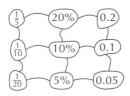

- Ask if the students know, or can work out, the fraction equivalent to 1%.
- Establish that this is $\frac{1}{100}$.
- Now ask what percentage is equivalent to 2%, 3%, etc. until the students understand that the fraction is just the percentage written over 100.

Main lesson activity

- This follows on from the Oral and mental starter.
- Ask students if they know what **percentage** means and establish that it means **out of one hundred**.
- Link this to the Oral and mental starter and establish that 47%, for example, can be written as $\frac{47}{100}$.
- Following the same rule, 25% can be written as $\frac{25}{100}$.
- Ask what is different about this fraction.
- Explain that some fractions can be cancelled down, but that using the idea of 'out of 100' makes some calculations easier.
- Give the following example.

  Find 4% of £200.
  First, work out 1%.   1% of 200 $= \frac{1}{100} \times 200 = 2$.
  Then multiply by 4. $4 \times 1\%$ of 200 $= 4\%$ of 200 $= 4 \times 2 = £8$.

- Repeat with other examples, such as 7% of 300 kg (21 kg), 15% of £400 (£60) and 80% of 2000 m (1600 m).
- Now explain what to do if the numbers are not so simple, for example 13% of 85 cm.
- Suggest that this is best done using a calculator, so 1% $= 85 \div 100 = 0.85$ and 13% $= 13 \times 1\% = 13 \times 0.85 = 11.05$.
- Decide on the best way to enter this into a calculator, i.e. $13 \div 100 \times 85$.
- Make sure students can key this into the calculator and get the correct answer.
- Repeat with other examples, such as 42% of 169 (70.98) and 61% of 350 (213.5).

- **The class can now do Exercise 2G from the Pupil Workbook.**

Exercise 2G (Answers)

1 a 15 **b** 34 **c** 93 **d** 7 **e** 20 **f** 3
2 a i £6 **ii** £21 **iii** £30 **iv** 20, £60 **v** 25, £75
  vi 80, £240
  b 7 kg **i** 7, 21 **ii** 7, 42 **iii** $30 \times 7 = 210$ **iv** $35 \times 7 = 245$
  c $2000 \div 100 = 20$ m **i** 20, 60 **ii** 20, 120 **iii** $25 \times 20 = 500$
  iv $40 \times 20 = 800$
3 a 21 **b** 28.8 **c** $68 \div 100 \times 80 = 54.4$ **d** $13 \div 100 \times 50 = 6.5$
  e $8 \div 100 \times 124 = 9.92$ **f** $73 \div 100 \times 52 = 37.96$

Plenary

Key words

- out of one hundred
- percentage

- Ask students how they would calculate 8% of 420 without a calculator.
- Suggestions may include 10% – 1% – 1%, or 8 × 1%.
- Ask students if they can find 1% of 420 (4.2).
- Now ask them to work out 8% of 420 without a calculator by any method.
- Give some other examples.

  13% of 540 (70.2)
  24% of 56 (13.44)
  48% of 96 (46.08)

LESSON 2.8

Framework objectives – Reducing ratios
Use ratio notation and simplify ratios.

Oral and mental starter

Resources required

OHT 2.5 Fish

● Using a target board such as the one shown, ask students to identify the equivalent fractions.

$\frac{1}{2}$	$\frac{9}{12}$	$\frac{2}{3}$	$\frac{6}{15}$
$\frac{5}{20}$	$\frac{9}{27}$	$\frac{5}{10}$	$\frac{4}{8}$
$\frac{1}{4}$	$\frac{8}{12}$	$\frac{1}{3}$	$\frac{2}{6}$
$\frac{2}{5}$	$\frac{3}{12}$	$\frac{6}{9}$	$\frac{3}{4}$

$(\frac{1}{2}, \frac{5}{10}, \frac{4}{8})$, $(\frac{3}{4}, \frac{9}{12})$, $(\frac{2}{3}, \frac{8}{12}, \frac{6}{9})$, $(\frac{2}{5}, \frac{6}{15})$, $(\frac{1}{4}, \frac{5}{20}, \frac{3}{12})$, $(\frac{1}{3}, \frac{9}{27}, \frac{2}{6})$

● Once all of the pairs or triples of equivalent fractions have been identified, ask students to give other equivalent fractions to the base fractions on the target board.

Main lesson activity

● Display OHT 2.5 and ask students to identify how many of each type of fish (striped, spotted, plain) there are. (2 spotted, 8 striped, 10 plain)
● Ask students to complete the sentences.

> For every spotted fish there are ...... striped fish.
> For every spotted fish there are ...... plain fish.
> For every 4 striped fish there are ...... plain fish.

● Explain that these sentences describe the **ratio** of, for example, spotted to striped fish.
● Explain that the actual numbers of spotted to striped fish are 2 : 8 (reminding the students of the colon notation for ratio), but in its **simplest form** this is 1 : 4.
● Ask students to explain the relationship between these.
● They should spot that one is double (or half of) the other.
● Repeat with ratios of spotted to plain (2 : 10 = 1 : 5) and striped to plain (8 : 10 = 4 :5).
● Ask students if they can write 2 : 6 in its simplest form and how they worked it out.
● They should say 1 : 3 and explain that they divided by 2.
● Repeat for 6 : 9 (2 : 3), 10 : 12 (5 : 6), 12 : 20 (3 : 5), etc.
● If students say 12 : 20 cancels to 6 : 10 explain that this is simplified but is not in the simplest form.
● Repeat with more examples until students can **cancel** using **common factors** with confidence.

● **The class can now do Exercise 2H from the Pupil Workbook.**

© HarperCollins*Publishers* Ltd 2008

Exercise 2H   Answers

1 6 : 2 and 3 : 1, 2 : 2 and 1 : 1, 2 : 4 and 1 : 2, 4 : 2 and 2 : 1, 2 : 6 and 1 : 3
2 a 1 : 2   **b** 2 : 1   **c** 1 : 1   **d** 3 : 1   **e** 2 : 3   **f** 3 : 1   **g** 5 : 1   **h** 3 : 7   **i** 1 : 4
   j 2 : 7   **k** 2 : 3   **l** 3 : 5
3 10 : 15, 2 : 3
4 12 : 15, 4 : 5
5 18 : 12, 3 : 2
6 14 : 14, 1 : 1
7 14 : 16, 7 : 8

Plenary

- Ask students to fill in the missing value from 2 : 3 = 1 : ... .
- They may feel that fractional values are not allowed.
- Explain that ratios can sometimes be written in the special form 1 : n, or n : 1.
- Ask students to fill in the missing values for the following: 2 : 7 = 1 : ... , 3 : 4 = 1 : ... , 7 : 10 = 1 : ..., 9 : 2 = ... : 1 and 10 : 4 = ... : 1.

Key words

- [ ] cancelling
- [ ] common factor
- [ ] ratio
- [ ] simplest form

Algebra 3

Framework objectives – Finding unknown numbers
Understand and use the rules of arithmetic and inverse operations in the context of positive integers.

Oral and mental starter

- Display OHT 3.1 and/or hand out PCM 3.1.
- Ask students to fill in the missing values for an answer of 60.
- If only using the OHT, students could write answers, one at a time, on white boards.

Resources required

Student white boards
PCM 3.1 60
OHT 3.1 60

Main lesson activity

- This follows on from the Oral and mental starter.
- Ask students what the value in the box should be for $\boxed{} + 7 = 20$.
- Repeat for the following: $\boxed{} + 8 = 20$, $\boxed{} + 9 = 20$.

    $25 - \boxed{} = 20$, $14 - \boxed{} = 8$.

    $\boxed{} \times 5 = 20$, $6 \times \boxed{} = 24$.

    $\boxed{} \div 4 = 7$, $24 \div \boxed{} = 6$.

    $3 + \boxed{} = 4 \times 5$, $6 \times \boxed{} + 3 = 27$.

- Discuss the methods used to solve these. You will need to remind students about the order of operations and may wish to write this on the board.
- Repeat with more examples until students are confident at finding missing values.

- **The class can now do Exercise 3A from the Pupil Workbook.**

Exercise 3A Answers

1 a 8 **b** 13 **c** 2 **d** 17 **e** 12 **f** 17 **g** 27 **h** 24 **i** 38
2 a 5 **b** 4 **c** 9 **d** 6 **e** 7 **f** 5 **g** 4 **h** 8 **i** 7
3 various answers
4 a 2 **b** 5 **c** 5 **d** 2 **e** 3 **f** 0

Plenary

Key words

☐ **solution**
☐ **variable**

- Ask students to find the value of x in $x + 8 = 20$.
- Discuss the connection with the problems covered in the Main lesson activity.
- Explain that sometimes letters are used to represent missing numbers.
- Ask students to solve $10 - y = 7$, $2 \times z = 8$, $12 \div p = 3$, ...

LESSON 3.2

Framework objectives – Calculating using rules
Use simple formulae from mathematics and other subjects.

Oral and mental starter

Resources required

OHT 3.2 Rules: Boat hire
OHT 3.3 Rules: Turkey cooking time
OHT 3.4 Rules: Car hire
OHT 3.5 Reverse rules

- Tell students that you are going to play a game called 'What is the rule?'.
- Say that you have a rule in your head. They give you a number; you apply the rule and tell them what the answer is.
- For example, if a student says 3, you say 7. If a student says 4, you say 8, and so on.
- Students can put up their hand at any time to give you a rule. In the case above it is Add 4.
- Other rules could be add, subtract, multiply and add (this is difficult so jottings could be allowed), add and multiply, etc.
- The activity can be made easier by writing all of the 'input' and 'output' values on the board, but it is more challenging if no jottings are allowed.

Main lesson activity

- This follows on from the Oral and mental starter.
- Display OHT 3.2 and explain that this shows the rule for calculating the cost of hiring a boat.
- Ask students to say how much the hire cost is for the examples shown.
- Give students some more times, such as 45 minutes and 3 hours 30 minutes.
- Now ask how many hours a boat was hired for if the total cost was £18, £15, etc.
- Display OHT 3.3 and explain that this is the rule for the cooking time for a turkey.
- Ask students to work out how long it would take to cook the examples shown.
- Students may need some practice calculating with time. Remind them that there are three lots of 20 minutes in 1 hour.
- Give students some more weights, such as 14 pounds and 12-and-a-half pounds.
- Now ask how much the turkey weighed if the total cooking time was 1 hour, 6 hours 20 minutes, etc.
- Display OHT 3.4 and explain that this is the rule for hiring a car.
- Ask students to work out the cost of hiring a car for the lengths of time shown.
- Give some more lengths of time such as 1 month and $3\frac{1}{2}$ days.
- Now ask how long the car was hired for if the total cost was £55, £115, etc.
- **The class can now do Exercise 3B from the Pupil Workbook.**

Exercise 3B **Answers**

1 a 140 miles **b** 350 miles
2 a £11 **b** £16 **c** £18
3 a £110 **b** £190
4 a i 120 **ii** 360 **iii** 1200
   b 5
5 a i 2 **ii** 5 **iii** 8
   b 12
6 a i £14 **ii** £21 **iii** £33
   b £22

Plenary

Key words

- Display OHT 3.5.
- Ask the students to work out the times the boat was hired for, the weight of the turkey and the length of car hire for the costs and times shown.
- Discuss the methods used to work these out.

☐ **formula**
☐ **inverse**
☐ **rule**

LESSON 3.3

Framework objectives – Simplifying terms and expressions

Simplify linear algebraic expressions by collecting like terms. Substitute positive integers into linear expressions.

Oral and mental starter

Resources required

PCM 3.2   Expressions 1

- Give a set of jigsaw cards made from PCM 3.2 to each pair, or small group.
- The aim is for the students to assemble the jigsaw as quickly as possible.
- If students have problems getting started, explain that the blank sides form the corners and edges.

Main lesson activity

- This follows on from the Oral and mental starter.
- Ask students to give you an easier way of writing $a + a + a$.
- They should say $3 \times a$, $a \times 3$ or $3a$.
- Explain that all of these are acceptable but that $3a$ is the best way of writing it.
- Emphasise that $3a$ means $3 \times a$ and that there is a rule in mathematics stating that a letter next to a number means that there is a hidden multiplication sign between them. All other signs are necessary, for example $3 + x$ must have the + sign, but $3x$ means $3 \times x$.
- Tell the students that the number in front of the letter is called the **coefficient**.
- Ask the students to give you the value of, for example, $3x$ when $x = 3$.
- Repeat for different values and different coefficients.
- If appropriate, explain the difference between the words **term** and **expression**.
- Now ask how to simplify expressions like $3a + 4a$ $(7a)$, $6a - a$ $(5a)$ and $6a + 3a + 2a$ $(11a)$.
- Now ask the students how to simplify $5a - 4a$. Students will often write $1a$, which is acceptable, but emphasise that a is better.
- Also ask for $4a - 4a$. Establish that the answer is 0 and not $0a$.
- Now ask how to simplify expressions like $a + a + a + b + b$ $(3a + 2b)$.
- Repeat with expressions such as $3a + 4b + 2a + 5b$ $(5a + 9b)$ and $5a + 6b - a - 3b$ $(4a + 3b)$.
- Repeat until the students are confident with these operations.
- **The class can now do Exercise 3C from the Pupil Workbook.**

Exercise 3C — Answers

1 a $3n$ **b** $4a$ **c** $2p$ **d** $5q$ **e** $4e$ **f** $3t$ **g** $6b$ **h** $2c$ **i** $7x$ **j** $3y$
2 a $5a$ **b** $12c$ **c** $17m$ **d** $2d$ **e** $4q$ **f** $5a$ **g** $3c$ **h** $2a$ **i** $6c$
3 a $3c + 2d$ **b** $2p + 4q$ **c** $j + 3k$ **d** $4s + 3t$ **e** $3a + 2b$ **f** $3g + 3h$
 g $3x + 4y$ **h** $2m + 4n$
4 a 3, 6, 12 **b** 10, 13, 14 **c** 7, 2, 17 **d** 16, 46, 96 **e** 9, 12, 21
 f 20, 50, 80

Plenary

Key words
- coefficient
- expression
- like terms

- Write the expression $10a$ on the board.
- Ask students to come to the board and write down an equivalent expression such as $9a + a$, $2 \times 5a$, $12a - 2a$, etc.
- Repeat with other expressions such as $8a + 6b$, or introduce a negative such as $3a - 2b$ for a more challenging task.

LESSON 3.4

Framework objectives – Formulae
Use formulae from mathematics and other subjects; substitute integers into simple formulae.

Oral and mental starter

- Give out a set of jigsaw cards made from PCM 3.3 to each pair, or small group.
- Write on the board $a = 3$, $b = 4$, $x = 7$ and $y = 10$.
- The aim is for the students to assemble the jigsaw as quickly as possible.
- If students have problems getting started, explain that the blank sides form the corners and edges.

Resources required

PCM 3.3 Expressions 2
OHT 3.6 Formulae 1
OHT 3.7 Formulae 2
OHT 3.8 Formulae 3

Main lesson activity

- This follows on from the Oral and mental starter.
- Display OHT 3.6 and ask students if they can identify the rule.
- The first is the perimeter of a square of side s.
- The second is the perimeter of a rectangle of width w and breadth b.
- Explain that these are **formulae**.
- Ask students if they can remember the difference between a formula and an **expression**.
- They should remember or realise that the formula has an equals sign.
- Ask students to work out the perimeter using the values given.
- Repeat for more squares and rectangles drawn on the board.
- Now display OHT 3.7 and ask students if they can identify the meaning of the letters and the formula.
- C is cost, d is days. Ask what the 50 represents. This is the basic charge.
- Ask students to work out the cost of hiring a car for the lengths of time shown.
- Give some more lengths of time such as 1 month and $4\frac{1}{2}$ days.

- **The class can now do Exercise 3D from the Pupil Workbook.**

Exercise 3D | Answers

1 **a** 36 **b** 60 **c** 180
2 **a** 13 **b** 27 **c** 44
3 **a** £8 **b** £17 **c** £35
4 **a** 36 **b** 42 **c** 36
5 15 − 7, 8
6 3 × 9, 27
7 7, 21, 23
8 3, 4, 6 + 8, 14

Plenary

Key words

- expression
- formula
- rule

- Display OHT 3.8.
- Ask students if they can identify the values of the sides, and number of days from the information given.
- Discuss how they worked out the answers.

Framework objectives – Equations
Construct and solve simple linear equations with integer coefficients (unknown on one side only) using an appropriate method (e.g. inverse operations).

Oral and mental starter

- Tell the students that they are going to play a game called 'Think of a number'.
- Say, 'I think of a number. I add 3. Then multiply by 2. The answer is 16. What is the number?'(5)
- Say, 'I think of a number. I multiply it by 5. Then I subtract 5. The answer is 30. What is the number?'(7)
- Repeat for different rules and different numbers.

Main lesson activity

- This follows on from the Oral and mental starter.
- Do a simple 'Think of a number' such as, 'I think of a number. I add 3. The answer is 10. What is the number ?' (7).
- Ask students if they can write this down mathematically.
- Some things may have to be explained, such as using a letter for a variable.
- Recalling some of the rules met in recent lessons, they should be able to establish the equation $x + 3 = 10$.
- Remind students that they have recently been solving things like this in the form

    $\square + 3 = 10$.

- Repeat with other rules to set up the equation, for example:

    'I think of a number. I multiply it by 3. The answer is 18. What is the number ?' (6)

- Now give the class an equation you have not used before, for example $x - 6 = 12$.
- Ask the students to put this into a 'Think of a number' problem.
- Discuss how they could do this.
- Tell them that they need to set out their working when solving equations, and outline the method as shown.

$$x - 6 = 12$$
$$\text{Add 6 to both sides} \quad x - 6 + 6 = 12 + 6$$
$$x = 18$$

- Repeat with other equations, outlining the steps.

    Example 1
    $x + 8 = 13$

$$x + 8 = 13$$
$$\text{Subtract 8 from both sides} \quad x + 8 - 8 = 13 - 8$$
$$x = 5$$

Example 2

$2x = 14$

$$2x = 14$$

Divide each side by 2 $\quad 2x \div 2 = 14 \div 2$

$$x = 7$$

- Work through more examples if necessary until students are confident using these operations.

- **The class can now do Exercise 3E from the Pupil Workbook.**

Exercise 3E **Answers**

1 **a** Subtract 4 from both sides; $x + 4 - 4 = 7 - 4$; $x = 3$
   b Subtract 9 from both sides; $x + 9 - 9 = 13 - 9$; $x = 4$
   c Subtract 7 from both sides; $x + 7 - 7 = 15 - 7$; $x = 8$
   d Subtract 5 from both sides; $x + 5 - 5 = 20 - 5$; $x = 15$
   e Subtract 1 from both sides; $x + 1 - 1 = 9 - 1$; $x = 8$
   f Subtract 8 from both sides; $x + 8 - 8 = 18 - 8$; $x = 10$
   g Add 5 to both sides; $x - 5 + 5 = 3 + 5$; $x = 8$
   h Add 2 to both sides; $x - 2 + 2 = 9 + 2$; $x = 11$
   i Add 3 to both sides; $x - 3 + 3 = 11 + 3$; $x = 14$
   j Add 7 to both sides; $x - 7 + 7 = 13 + 7$; $x = 20$
   k Add 8 to both sides; $x - 8 + 8 = 10 + 8$; $x = 18$
   l Add 4 to both sides; $x - 4 + 4 = 18 + 4$; $x = 22$
2 **a** Divide both sides by 3; $x = 12 \div 3$; $x = 4$
   b Divide both sides by 5; $x = 25 \div 5$; $x = 5$
   c Divide both sides by 4; $x = 8 \div 4$; $x = 2$
   d Divide both sides by 6; $x = 30 \div 6$; $x = 5$
   e Divide both sides by 3; $x = 18 \div 3$; $x = 6$
   f Divide both sides by 5; $x = 40 \div 5$; $x = 8$
   g Divide both sides by 7; $x = 21 \div 7$; $x = 3$
   h Divide both sides by 4; $x = 16 \div 4$; $x = 4$

Plenary

Key words

☐ **equation**
☐ **solution**

- Write the following equation on the board: $2x + 3 = 15$.
- Ask students to express it as a 'Think of a number' problem.
- Go through the process of solving the equation.

$$2x + 3 = 15$$

Subtract 3 from both sides $\quad 2x + 3 - 3 = 15 - 3$

$$2x = 12$$

Divide both sides by 2 $\quad\quad 2x \div 2 = 12 \div 2$

$$x = 6$$

- Repeat with other equations, asking students to supply the steps, for example $3x - 4 = 11$ and $3x + 2 = 17$.

Geometry and measures 1

Framework objectives – Properties of a triangle
Identify and use angle, side and symmetry properties of triangles.

Oral and mental starter

Resources required
PCM 4.1 Triangle grids
OHT 4.1 Triangle pattern
Triangular dotty paper
Tracing paper

- Ask students to brainstorm the types of triangles they know and the facts about them.
- Put these facts on the board in groups as shown below.

Equilateral triangle	Isosceles triangle	Right-angled triangle	Scalene triangle
All sides same length. All angles the same. All angles are 60°.	Two sides same length. Two angles the same.	One angle is 90°.	No sides same length. No angles the same.

Main lesson activity

- Use the 7-point triangular grid on PCM 4.1.
- Ask students to find two equilateral triangles, a right-angled triangle and an isosceles triangle by joining up three dots.
- Discuss whether rotations, reflections and translations are different.
- Establish that there are four different answers that are congruent to:

- Discuss what each type of triangle is and the symmetries of each triangle (**rotational** and **line symmetry**).
- Repeat for the 10-point grids. This time there are four equilateral triangles, three isosceles triangles, two right-angled triangles and four scalene triangles.
- The answers are congruent to those below.

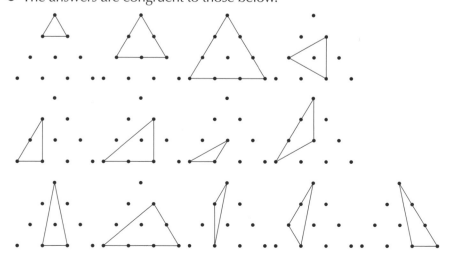

- Discuss what each type of triangle is and the symmetries of each triangle (rotational and line symmetry).

- **The class can now do Exercise 4A from the Pupil Workbook.**

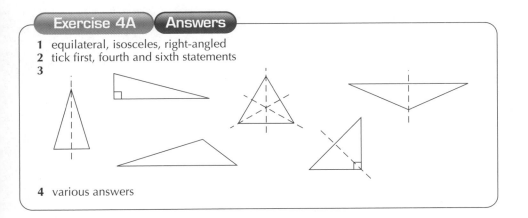

Exercise 4A **Answers**

1 equilateral, isosceles, right-angled
2 tick first, fourth and sixth statements
3

4 various answers

Plenary

- Display OHT 4.1 and discuss:
  - the type of triangle in the pattern;
  - the symmetries.

Key words

- equilateral
- isosceles
- right-angled
- scalene
- line symmetry
- rotational symmetry

LESSON
4.2

Framework objectives – Angles on a straight line
Know the sum of angles on a straight line.

Oral and mental starter

Resources required

PCM 4.2 Measuring angles
PCM 4.3 Angles on a straight line
Protractors

- This is not strictly an Oral and mental starter because, as protractors are to be used in the Main lesson activity, students will need practice in using these.
- Ask students to recall how to use a protractor, i.e. centre of the protractor over the centre of the angle, zero line of the protractor over one of the arms of the angle.
- Using PCM 4.2 practise measuring angles ($a = 60°$, $b = 116°$, $c = 40°$, $d = 108°$, $e = 130°$, $f = 85°$, $g = 24°$, $h = 105°$).

Main lesson activity

- Using PCM 4.3, ask students to measure the angles shown, write them down and add each pair of values ($a = 50°$, $b = 130°$, $c = 160°$, $d = 20°$, $e = 45°$, $f = 135°$, $g = 100°$, $h = 80°$, $i = 40°$, $j = 140°$, $k = 65°$, $l = 115°$, total should be 180° in each case).
- After they have done this, ask if they can see a relationship between them.
- The measurements may not be exact but they should appreciate that the sum of the angles is about 180°.
- Ask why it should be exactly 180°.
- Establish that the angle on a straight line is 180°.
- Put this diagram on the board.

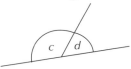

- Ask what the relationship is between c and d (add up to 180° or $c + d = 180°$).
- Cross out d and replace with 50°.
- Ask for the value of c and how it can be calculated ($180 - 50 = 130$).
- Cross out c, replace with 108° and cross out 50° and replace with d.
- Ask for the value of d and how to work it out ($180 - 108 = 72$).
- Repeat for other values of c and d.
- Finally draw this diagram on the board.

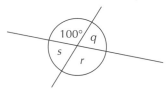

- Ask for the values of q, r and s and how to work them out (80°, 100° and 80°).
- Write these values on the diagram.
- Ask students if they can see any relationships.
- They may identify that opposite angles are the same.

- **The class can now do Exercise 4B from the Pupil Workbook.**

Exercise 4B   Answers

1 $a = 80°$, $b = 110°$, $c = 60°$, $d = 128°$, $e = 133°$, $f = 82°$
2 $a = 65°$, $b = 68°$, $c = 50°$, $d = 72°$, $e = 68°$, $f = 54°$
3 $a = 120°$, $b = 60°$, $c = 120°$, $d = 50°$, $e = 130°$, $f = 50°$, $g = 122°$, $h = 58°$, $i = 122°$,
    $j = 38°$, $k = 142°$, $l = 38°$, $m = 91°$, $n = 89°$, $o = 91°$, $p = 65°$, $q = 115°$, $r = 65°$

Plenary

Key words

☐ **opposite angles**
☐ **straight line**

- Put the following diagram on the board.

- Ask students for the value of a (60°).
- Discuss how this can be worked out (180 ÷ 3).
- Ask students if they can give an algebraic relationship ($3a = 180$).
- Recall the processes for solving equations met in Chapter 3.
- Now put the following diagram on the board.

- Ask students for the value of b (50°) and for an algebraic relationship
  ($2b + 80 = 180$).

.

LESSON 4.3

Framework objectives – Angles at a point
Know the sum of angles at a point.

Oral and mental starter

Resources required

PCM 4.4 Estimating angles
PCM 4.5 Angles around a point
Small squares of paper
Protractors

- Ask students to fold a small square of paper in half and then in half again.

```
360° | 0°
-----|-----
270° | 90°
     |
     | 180°
```

- Tell them to press hard along the folded edges to get sharp creases.
- Ask them to open out the paper and write 0° on one of the creases.
- Ask them what angles should be written on the other lines (going clockwise).
- They should say 90°, 180° and 270°. (360° could also be written by the zero line.)
- This guide can then be used in the starter activity which is 'Estimation superstar'.
- Hand out copies of PCM 4.4 and ask students to estimate the angles shown and write them in the 'guess' column of the table.
- When all angles have been estimated give the correct answers and scores.
- Students can fill these in.
- Add up the scores to see who is the 'Estimation superstar'.

Angle	Actual (10pts)	Difference (7pts)	Difference (5pts)	Difference (2pts)
a	67°	≤ ±3°	≤ ±5°	≤ ±10°
b	126°	≤ ±3°	≤ ±5°	≤ ±10°
c	31°	≤ ±3°	≤ ±5°	≤ ±10°
d	145°	≤ ±3°	≤ ±5°	≤ ±10°
e	97°	≤ ±3°	≤ ±5°	≤ ±10°
f	85°	≤ ±3°	≤ ±5°	≤ ±10°

Main lesson activity

- Using PCM 4.5, ask students to measure the angles shown, write them down and add each set of values ($a = 90°$, $b = 120°$, $c = 150°$, $d = 70°$, $e = 125°$, $f = 165°$, $g = 60°$, $h = 105°$, $i = 195°$, $j = 140°$, $k = 105°$, $l = 115°$, total should be 360° in each case).
- After they have done this, ask if they can see a relationship between them.
- The measurements may not be exact but they should appreciate that the sum of the angles is about 360°.
- Ask why it should be exactly 360°.
- Establish that the angle around a point or a full turn is 360°.
- Put this diagram on the board

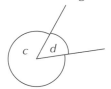

- Ask what the relationship is between c and d (add up to 360° or $c + d = 360°$).
- Cross out d and replace with 50°.

- Ask for the value of *c* and how it can be calculated (360 – 50 = 310).
- Cross out *c*, replace with 302° and cross out 50° and replace with *d*.
- Ask for the value of *d* and how to work it out (360 – 302 = 58).
- Repeat for other values of *c* and *d*.
- Finally draw this diagram on the board.

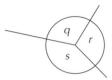

- Ask what the relationship is between *q*, *r* and *s* (add up to 360° or $q + r + s = 360°$).
- Cross out two of the letters and replace with appropriate angles.
- Ask for the value of the third angle and how it can be calculated (360 – *q* – *r*).
- Repeat for other values for two of the angles.

- **The class can now do Exercise 4C from the Pupil Workbook.**

Exercise 4C   Answers

1 $a = 50°$, $b = 296°$, $c = 135°$, $d = 264°$, $e = 288°$, $f = 109°$
2 $a = 70°$, $b = 162°$, $c = 147°$, $d = 53°$, $e = 23°$, $f = 73°$
3 $a = 120°$, $b = 130°$, $c = 90°$, $d = 55°$, $e = 60°$, $f = 180°$, $g = 45°$, $h = 90°$

Plenary

Key words

☐ **full turn**
☐ **angles at a point**

- Put the following diagram on the board.

- Ask students for the value of *a* (72°).
- Discuss how this can be worked out (360 ÷ 5)
- Ask students if they can give an algebraic relationship ($5a = 360$).
- Recall the processes for solving equations met in Chapter 3.
- Now put the following diagram on the board.

- Ask students for the value of *b* (65°) and for an algebraic relationship ($3b + 165 = 360$).

Framework objectives – Finding unknown angles
Know the sum of angles in a triangle. Use angle properties of a quadrilateral.

Oral and mental starter

Resources required

PCM 4.6 Quadrilaterals
Protractors

- Draw the following triangle on the board.

- Ask the students:
  - what type of triangle is this? (scalene)
  - what is the smallest angle? (20°)
  - what is the biggest angle? (100°)
- Students may need to be reminded of the fact that the angles in a triangle add up to 180°.
- Draw this triangle on the board.

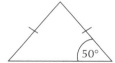

- Ask the students:
  - what type of triangle is this? (isosceles)
  - what is the smallest angle? (40°)
  - what is the biggest angle? (70°)
- Establish how this angle was found.
- Draw this triangle on the board.

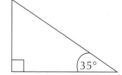

- Ask the students:
  - what type of triangle is this? (isosceles)
  - what is the smallest angle? (50°)
  - what is the biggest angle? (80°)
- Establish how this angle was found.
- Finally, draw this triangle on the board.

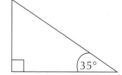

- Ask the students:
  - what type of triangle is this? (right-angled)
  - what is the smallest angle? (35°)
  - what is the biggest angle? (90°)
  - what is the third angle? (55°)
- Establish how this angle was found.

Main lesson activity

- Hand out copies of PCM 4.6 and ask students to measure the four angles in each quadrilateral and write them down. Ensure that students measure obtuse angles correctly.
- After they have done this ask them to add up the total of the four angles.
- The measurements will not be exact but they should appreciate that the total is about 360°, within a degree or two.
- Draw the following quadrilateral on the board.

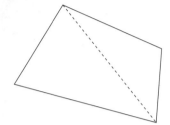

- Ask students to explain how this diagram links to the quadrilaterals and the work done in the Oral and mental starter.
- Make sure students are clear that the angles in a quadrilateral add up to 360°.
- Draw the following quadrilateral on the board.

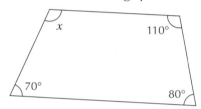

- Ask the students to explain how they could find the value of x (100°).
- Repeat with more examples.

- **The class can now do Exercise 4D from the Pupil Workbook.**

Exercise 4D   **Answers**

1 **a** $a = 50°$ **b** $b = 50°$ **c** $c = 20°$ **d** $d = 40°$ **e** $e = 110°$ **f** $f = 40°$
2 **a** $a = 70°$ **b** $b = 40°$ **c** $c = 75°$, $d = 30°$ **d** $e = 45°$, $f = 90°$ **e** $g = 50°$, $h = 50°$
3 **a** 125° **b** 90° **c** 55° **d** 90° **e** 30° **f** 140°
4 90°

Plenary

- Draw a pentagon on the board as shown.

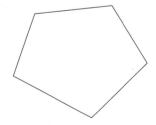

- Ask students if they know what the angles in a pentagon add up to (540°).
- Give clues by drawing in diagonals to show three triangles if necessary.
- Repeat with a hexagon.

Statistics 1

Framework objectives – Data collection sheets
Design data collection sheets. Construct frequency tables for gathering discrete data, grouped where appropriate in equal class intervals.

Oral and mental starter

Resources required

PCM 5.1 Data

- Play hangman using the following words: STATISTICS, DATA, SURVEY, TALLY and FREQUENCY.
- After each word is found ask students if they know the meaning of the word. Establish that:

    Statistics is the study of information.
    Data is a generic term for information.
    A **survey** is what is done to find out information.
    Tally is a means of recording survey results.
    Frequency is a term for the total of the tally marks.

- Discuss what kinds of things appear in surveys, for example how people will vote in an election or what types of drinks people prefer.
- Discuss how these surveys could be carried out, for example questionnaires or collecting information from the Internet.

Main lesson activity

- Using PCM 5.1, explain that Mary is an Office manager who is looking for a new assistant. She has spoken to a recruitment agency and asked them to send her details of potential candidates. The agency has sent her a sheet with the details of 20 candidates on it.
- Using the sheet, ask students questions such as:

    Who is the oldest candidate? (Heledd)
    Who is the youngest candidate? (Hariette)
    What is the most common notice period? (4 weeks)
    How many candidates gave reading as their hobby? (6)
    What is the longest time any candidate has spent in their current job? (34 months)

- Discuss with students ways of representing some of the data. They should mention bar charts, pie charts and frequency tables.
- Decide on a category, for example 'Year of birth', and use a tally chart to collect the data.

Year of birth	Tally	Frequency
1971	I	1
1972		0
1973	I	1
1974	II	2
1975	HHI	5
1976	IIII	4
1977	HHI	5
1978	II	2

● Ask students if they think this makes it easier to answer questions like those above.
● Pick another category, for example 'Notice period', and make a further tally chart/frequency table.

Notice period	Tally	Frequency
1 week	HHI	5
4 weeks	HHI HHI III	13
8 weeks	I	1
12 weeks	I	1

● Discuss ways to represent this data.
● If there is time, draw a bar chart or similar.
● Finally, tell students that, after interviewing, Mary chose a female candidate who was born in 1976, had a 1-week notice period and had been in her current job more than a year. Who was it? (Glenda)

● **The class can now do Exercise 5A from the Pupil Workbook.**

Exercise 5A **Answers**

1

Score	Tally	Frequency
1	HHI II	7
2	HHI	5
3	IIII	4
4	III	3
5	HHI I	6
6	HHI	5
	Total	30

2

Method	Tally	Frequency
car	HHI I	6
walk	HHI HHI	10
bus	HHI HHI II	12
cycle	II	2

3 Frequencies are 14, 7, 3, 2, 0, 2

Plenary

● Using PCM 5.1, ask students to describe a candidate without using their name and see if the rest of the class can name him/her.

Key words

- [ ] data
- [ ] frequency
- [ ] survey
- [ ] tally chart
- [ ] statistics

LESSON 5.2

Framework objectives – Two-way tables
Construct two-way tables for recording discrete data.

Oral and mental starter

> **Resources required**
>
> OHT 5.1   Two-way tables
> PCM 5.2   Two-way tables

- Use OHT 5.1. Explain that it shows the eye colour of boys and girls in a class.
- Ask the students questions such as:
  - How many boys have brown eyes? (9)
  - How many more boys have brown eyes than girls? (2)
  - How many girls are there in the class altogether? (16)
  - What fraction of the girls have blue eyes? ($\frac{6}{16} = \frac{3}{8}$)
  - What percentage of the pupils with green eyes are boys? (25%)
  - How many pupils are in the class altogether? (30)

Main lesson activity

- Explain that the table used in the Oral and mental starter is a two-way table.
- Two-way tables show two variables. One goes horizontally and the other goes vertically.
- Use PCM 5.2 which shows two two-way tables.
- The first table shows the number of people and cars in 50 houses in a street.
- Use this to ask various questions, e.g.
  - How many houses have 2 people and 2 cars? (11)
  - How many houses have just 1 car? (16)
  - How many houses have 3 or more people living in them? (24)
  - How many houses are there altogether? (50) At this stage, if it has not already been suggested, it is a good idea to add up the columns and rows to get the total.
  - How many houses have the same number of people and cars? (17)
  - What fraction of the houses with 1 car have 3 people? $\frac{2}{16} = \frac{1}{8}$
  - What percentage of the houses with 4 people in them have 1 car? (20%)
  - What percentage of the houses with 2 cars have 3 people? (36%)
- If the class are able enough you can ask for the total number of people, and how to work it out, ($6 \times 1 + 20 \times 2 + 14 \times 3 + 10 \times 4 = 128$) and the total number of cars. (84)

- **The class can now do Exercise 5B from the Pupil Workbook.**

Exercise 5B **Answers**

1 a yellow **b** blue **c** $\frac{1}{4}$
2 a 8 **b** Sunday **c** Friday **d** £31.50
3 a 16, 16, 22, 10 **b** 32 **c** $\frac{1}{4}$ **d** 60%
4 9N own 16, 9N don't own 12, 9M own 24, 9M don't 8
5 a Capetown **b** Rome **c** Rome (46°) **d** Miami (27°)

Plenary

Key words

- Use PCM 5.2 and look at the second table.
- This shows the distance on the motorway network between 5 cities.
- This is not in the usual style of a two-way table but these are quite common and often difficult to read.
- Explain how the table works, i.e. Bristol to London is 120 miles, etc.
- Ask questions such as:
  - How far is it from London to Leeds? (201)
  - How far is it from London to Birmingham if you go via Bristol? (210)

☐ **two-way table**
☐ **row**
☐ **column**
☐ **totals**

LESSON 5.3

Framework objectives – Statistical diagrams

Construct diagrams to represent data, including bar-line graphs.

Oral and mental starter

Resources required

OHT 5.2 Bar charts
OHT 5.3 Bar-line graphs
PCM 5.3 Dice scores
1–6 dice

- Display OHT 5.2 (with the bottom half covered up) and explain that the **bar chart** shows how students in a class get to school. Ask questions similar to:

> What is the most common way of coming to school? (walk)
> How many more students walk than cycle? (11)
> How many students are in the class altogether? (30)
> Is it true that over half the students walk to school? (no)

- Now reveal the second half of the OHT and ask if students can match the method of transport to the speech bubble. (Order of bubbles is walk, cycle, bus, car, other (train).)

- Now display OHT 5.3 (with the bottom half covered up) and explain that this **bar-line graph** shows the choices for a school trip. Ask questions similar to:

> What is the most popular choice? (Alton Towers)
> How many more students would rather visit a town than Alton Towers? (11)
> How many students are in the class altogether? (33)

- Now reveal the second half of the OHT and ask if students can match the choice to the speech bubble. (Order of bubbles is Blackpool, Alton Towers, London, Bath, Calais.)

Main lesson activity

- Collect the same data as on OHT 5.2 and 5.3 for the class. Categories for the trip could be changed but restrict choices to a maximum of five venues.
- Draw a bar chart and bar-line graph for each of these.
- Discuss things that need to be considered such as the vertical scale, i.e. how big the graph/chart needs to be.
- Hand out copies of PCM 5.3 and divide the students into pairs.
- One student should roll the dice and the other should keep a tally. When the data has been collected they should draw a bar chart to show the results.
- Once all bar charts have been drawn, discuss the differences.
- If they have rolled the dice fairly, the last chart should be more evenly distributed.
- Take this opportunity to discuss the reliability of experimental results and explain that the more trials that are done, the more accurate the results.

- **The class can now do Exercise 5C from the Pupil Workbook.**

Exercise 5C — Answers

1 Frequencies are 34, 8, 25, 10, 20, 12

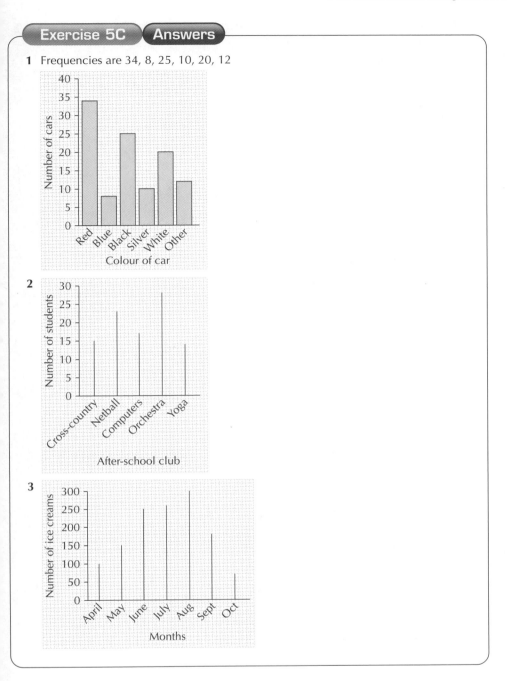

Plenary

- Ask the class what they think the reasons are for carrying out the types of questionnaire discussed today. The reasons could include, for example, traffic monitoring, the number of buses allocated to the various routes, whether a crossing is needed for people walking to school and whether the bike sheds are still needed.
- Who might be asking these questions? Parents, school governors, head teacher, director of transport, police chief, safety officers.
- Finish with a short discussion on the size of the sample. Is it any use asking just one class or should the whole school be asked? The larger the sample the better, but a single class can still indicate the trend in a school.

Key words

- [ ] **bar chart**
- [ ] **bar-line graph**
- [ ] **frequency**

Framework objectives – Range, mode, mean and median

Calculate statistics for small sets of discrete data.

Oral and mental starter

- Use a target board, as shown below.

8	5	2	9	8
4	3	5	6	8

- Ask the class to give you the 10 numbers in ascending order.
- Now ask the class to give you the most common number and the difference between the highest and lowest values.
- Now show them a three-by-three target board, as shown below.

4	7	2
4	9	5
3	3	8

- Ask the students to give you the nine numbers in ascending order.
- Now ask the class to give you the most common number (there isn't one) and the difference between the highest and lowest values.
- Ask them to tell you, without repeating all the numbers, which is the third number when the numbers are in ascending order.
- Repeat this for the fifth number, for example, as necessary.

Main lesson activity

- Tell the class that the aim of the lesson is to work out the range, mode, median and mean of a set of data.
- Ask the students if they can recall the meaning of these terms.
- Establish the definitions and write them on the board.

   Range: Difference between highest and smallest values.
   Mode: Most common value.
   Median: Middle value when arranged in order.
   Mean: Total of values divided by number of values.

- Using the second target board from the Oral and mental starter, ask for the range, mode, median and mean for the nine numbers and show how they are obtained.

   (Range is 7 (9 – 2), mode is undefined (3 and 4 both occur twice), median is 4 and mean is 5.)

- Emphasise that there may not always be a mode.
- Now use the values from the first target board in the Oral and mental starter and, again, ask for the range, mode, median and mean and show how they can be obtained.

   (Range is 7 (9 – 2), mode is 8, median is 5.5, mean is 5.8.)

- Emphasise that the median may not always be an actual value, if there are an even number of pieces of data the mid-value of the two middle values is taken.
- Repeat with other small sets of **discrete data**, for example those below.

Data	Range	Mode	Median	Mean
3, 6, 2, 8, 6	6	6	6	5
8, 9, 2, 5, 7, 8, 3, 6	7	8	6.5	6

- **The class can now do Exercise 5D from the Pupil Workbook.**

Exercise 5D   **Answers**

1 a £8   **b** 52   **c** 0.6, 0.7   **d** $4\frac{1}{2}$, 5   **e** None
2 a 7   **b** 43   **c** 16   **d** 6   **e** 7   **f** 16
3 a Range 7, mean 7
  b Range 15, mean 10.6
  c Range 0.5, mean 2.64
  d Range £3.92, mean £3.30
4 a Mean for Team A is 147 kg, mean for Team B is 155 kg
  b Team B because they have a heavier mean weight and will pull harder

---

Plenary

Key words

- discrete data
- mean
- median
- mode
- range

- Write the following set of data on the board 3, 7, 3, 5, 8, 6, 9, 50, 3, 6.
- Ask the class for the range (47), mode (3), median (6) and mean (10).
- Discuss which of the three averages best represents the data.
- The mode is too low, the mean is too high as it is affected by the large value of 50, so the median is probably best.

LESSON 5.5

Framework objectives – Pie charts
Construct pie charts.

Oral and mental starter

Resources required

PCM 5.4 Pie charts 1
PCM 5.5 Pie charts 2

- Down the left-hand side of the board, or on an OHT, write 10, 20, 30, 40 and 50.
- Ask the class to give you three numbers that add up to 10. For example: 2, 5 and 3. Write the numbers on the board or the OHT (2 + 5 + 3 = 10).
- On the next line write, for example, 4, 10 and 6 (4 + 10 + 6 = 20).
- Ask the class to give you the third line (6 + 15 + 9 = 30).
- Repeat this with different sets of numbers.
- Now write on the board, or OHT, three or four *even* numbers that add up to 20. For example: 2 + 6 + 8 + 4 = 20.
- Ask the class to scale the numbers down so that they add up to 10 (1 + 3 + 4 + 2 = 10).
- Now give the class multiples of three which add up to 30. For example: 12 + 6 + 9 + 3 = 30.
- Again, ask the class to scale down the numbers so that they add up to 10 (4 + 2 + 3 + 1 = 10).
- Write 360 on the board. Then write 1 × 360 = 360, and ask the class to give you other products which give an answer of 360. Tell them that 36 is a clue to working these out. When they have finished, write the products on the board: 1 × 360, 2 × 180, 3 × 120, 4 × 90, 5 × 72, 6 × 60, 8 × 45, 10 × 36, 12 × 30, 15 × 24, 18 × 20. Some students may need help with some of these.

Main lesson activity

- Explain that in this lesson they will be drawing **pie charts** from data that has already been collected for them, and that this type of data is called *secondary* data.
- Draw a circle on the board or on an OHT. Explain that the circle has 10 sectors.
- Now present some quantities which add up to 10. Take, for example, the different types of cereal eaten regularly by 10 students:

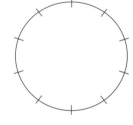

Cereal	Popcorn	Muesli	Corn flakes	Porridge
Number of students	2	3	4	1

- Remind the class how to draw a pie chart to represent this data, labelling the **sectors** clearly (see diagram).
- Now produce another table. For example, take the numbers of different types of house on a small estate:

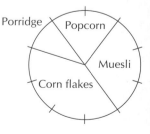

Type of house	Frequency	Number of sectors on pie chart
Terraced	8	
Bungalow	4	
Semi-detached	6	
Detached	2	
Total	**20**	**10**

- Note that the total number of houses is 20 but there are only 10 sectors on the pie chart.
- Prompt the class to tell you to scale down the **frequencies**, as in the Oral and mental starter.
- Complete the table.
- Draw the pie chart on a 10-point circle.

- **The class can now complete PCM 5.4.**

- Explain that they are now going to draw a pie chart where the total is not a multiple of 10.
- Ask how many degrees are in a full circle.
- Write the first table on the right on the board.
- Point out that the numbers add up to 360, so to put this information into a pie chart the angles would be 100°, 150°, 50° and 60°, as these add up to 360°. Sketch a pie chart on the board with these angles and **label** the sectors A, B, C and D.
- Now draw the second table on the board. Tell the class that the total this time is 180.
- Ask the class by what number they would have to multiply 180 to get 360 (2). Point out that this means that each value has to be multiplied by two to get the angles on the pie chart to add up to 360°. Complete the table as shown and then sketch the pie chart and label the sectors A, B, C and D.

- **The class can now complete PCM 5.5.**

- **The class can now do Exercise 5E from the Pupil Workbook.**

A	100
B	150
C	50
D	60

A	40
B	60
C	50
D	30

		Angle
A	40	$40 \times 2 = 80°$
B	60	$60 \times 2 = 120°$
C	50	$50 \times 2 = 100°$
D	30	$30 \times 2 = 60°$
		Total = 360°

Exercise 5E   Answers

1 a 8 students; number of sectors 1, 3, 3, 2, 1   **b** Number of sectors, 1, 2, 4, $2\frac{1}{2}$, $\frac{1}{2}$

2 a 10°; size of sector 180°, 90°, 60°, 30°   **b** 20°; size of sector 20°, 40°, 120°, 180°

Plenary

- Point out to the class that the pie charts they have been working on have generally had three, four or five sectors. Ask them why a pie chart with, for example, 20 sectors would not be that useful. Prompt the class to tell you that it would be difficult to interpret, or difficult to measure the angles accurately, if there were many small sectors.
- Now sketch a four-sector pie chart without labels on the board. Ask them to criticise it. Stress the importance of labels and titles.
- Finally, show the class the three main ways of labelling: labelling on the sectors; using a key and shading; labelling outside the sectors. Ask them why you might use different ways of labelling. Discuss the amount of space required for a label and why the information is sometimes easier to read with a key.

Framework objectives – Interpreting statistical diagrams
Interpret diagrams and graphs

Oral and mental starter

- There is no Oral and mental starter as the main activity requires students to work together to produce a display of information.

Main lesson activity

- This is a lesson on comparing data.
- Students should work in small groups.
- Using PCM 5.6 ask students how they would produce a display of the data.
- Ask students to produce a poster or display in their groups, using bar charts, pie charts or pictograms.

- **If there is time, the class can now do Exercise 5F from the Pupil Workbook.**

Exercise 5F **Answers**

1 a 7 **b** 8 **c** 30
2 a Blue **b** 5 **c** 20 **d** 50
3 a £385 **b** 10 **c** No **d** Majorca, Lanzarote **e** Orlando

Plenary

- Ask students to show their work to the rest of the class.
- Discuss the good and bad points of the displays.

Key words

☐ **comparison**
☐ **criticise**
☐ **interpret**

Geometry and measures 2

Framework objectives – Imperial and metric measures
Choose and use units of measurement. Know rough metric equivalents of imperial measures in common use.

Oral and mental starter

- Brainstorm units with students.
- Group these into **Length**, **Mass** and **Capacity**. List any other units under 'other'.
- Point out to students that the correct term is **mass** rather than the colloquial term weight. This is the term that will be used in the National Test paper.

Length	Mass	Capacity
miles, feet, yards, metres, centimetres, kilometres.	pounds, ounces, kilograms, grams.	litres, millilitres, pints, gallons.

Resources required

Objects with masses of
1 pound (jar of jam),
1 kilogram (bag of sugar),
1 ounce, 5 grams (20p coin)
Containers with a capacity
of 1 gallon and 1 litre
(mineral water bottle)
Ruler marked in inches
and centimetres

- Ask students if they can identify which of the units are **imperial** and which are **metric**, and discuss which countries commonly use each type of measure.
- Mark the units with I or M, or group them together.
- If available, pass around a jar of jam (or object), which has a mass of 1 pound and a bag of sugar which has a mass of 1 kilogram. Ask students to estimate how many times heavier the sugar is than the jam (twice as heavy).
- Also pass around a 20p coin, which has a mass of 5 grams. (Alternatives are a 50p coin, which has a mass of 8 g, a £1 coin, which has a mass of 9.5 g, or a £2 coin, which has a mass of 12 g.) Then pass around an object with a mass of 1 ounce. (Science departments often have old weights which are no longer used.) Ask students to estimate how many 20p coins would have the same mass as the ounce (5 or 6).
- If available, show a gallon container and a 1-litre container. Ask students to estimate how many litres would fit into a gallon (4 or 5).
- Finally, pass around a ruler marked with centimetres and inches. Students will see that 12 inches (1 foot) is equivalent to 30 cm.

Main lesson activity

- Explain to the class that the lesson is about the imperial system of measurement, which is still commonly used in Britain, even though a gradual change to the metric system is happening.
- Tell the class that these units have been used in Britain for centuries and that, in comparison, the metric system is fairly recent. (The metric system was developed in the time of Napoleon at the start of the nineteenth century. Some of today's imperial units were used in Roman times. For example, 'oz' is the abbreviation for 'onza', the Latin word for ounce, and 'mile' is derived from the Latin word 'milia', a thousand paces.)
- Following on from the Oral and mental starter, establish the relationships between the imperial and metric units.
- 1 pound ≈ 500 g (actually 454 g), 1 kilogram ≈ 2 pounds (actually 2.2 pounds), 12 inches = 1 foot ≈ 30 cm, 1 gallon ≈ 4.5 litres, 5 miles ≈ 8 kilometres, 1 yard ≈ 1 metre, 1 ounce ≈ 30 grams.

- These should be written on the board or students should write them in their exercise books.
- Ask students to give approximate equivalences to the following:

  3 kilograms in pounds (6 or 6.6)   20 miles in kilometres (32)
  4 ounces in grams (120)   180 grams in ounces (6)   2 gallons in litres (9)

- Give more examples, ensuring that students are using the correct and appropriate conversion method.

- **The class can now do Exercise 6A from the Pupil Workbook.**

Exercise 6A   Answers

1 **a** cm or mm **b** litres **c** m² **d** kg or tonnes
2 **a** 500 g **b** 2.5 cm **c** 4.5 litres **d** 8 km **e** 1 m

3

miles	km
5	8
10	16
15	24
20	32
50	80
100	160

20 km

4

pints	litres
1.75	1
3.5	2
5.25	3
7.0	4
8.75	5
17.5	10

20 litres

5

Flapjacks	
butter	120 g
sugar	60 g
oats	150 g
flour	30 g
syrup	2 tablespoons

6

Height	Height
65 in ≈ 162.5 cm = 1.625 m	71 in ≈ 177.5 cm = 1.775 m
Weight	**Weight**
130 lbs ≈ 65 000 g = 65 kg	165 lbs ≈ 825 00 g = 82.5 kg

Plenary

- Divide the class into teams and, using a prepared answer sheet, ask the following 10 questions. (The teams are allowed to confer. You may repeat each question.)

  1 How many inches in 3 feet?
  2 How many feet in 4 yards?
  3 How many ounces in 2 pounds?
  4 How many pounds in 3 stones?
  5 How many pints in 5 gallons?
  6 Approximately how many centimetres make 1 inch?
  7 Approximately how many feet make 1 metre?
  8 Approximately how many grams make 1 ounce?
  9 Approximately how many grams make 1 pound?
  10 Approximately how many litres make 1 gallon?

Plenary Answers: **1** 36 **2** 12 **3** 32 **4** 42 **5** 40
6 2.5 **7** 3 **8** 30 **9** 500 **10** 4.5

Imperial units of length

12 inches	= 1 foot (ft)
3 feet	= 1 yard (yd)
1760 yards	= 1 mile

Imperial units of mass

16 ounces	= 1 pound (lb)
14 pounds	= 1 stone (st)
2240 pounds	= 1 ton

Imperial units of capacity

| 8 pints (pt) | = 1 gallon (gal) |

Units of length conversions

1 in ≈ 2.5 cm
1 foot ≈ 30 cm
1 yard ≈ 1 m
5 miles ≈ 8 km

Units of mass conversions

1 oz ≈ 30 g
1 lb ≈ 500 g
2 lbs ≈ 1 kg

Units of capacity conversions

1.75 pints ≈ 1 l
1 gallon ≈ 4.5 l

Key words

- **Imperial units:** feet, inches, yards, miles, pounds, ounces, gallons, pints
- **Metric units:** metres, litres, grams
- **Prefixes:** kilo, centi, milli

Framework objectives – Area of rectangles and compound shapes
Know and use the formula for the area of a rectangle; calculate the area of shapes made from rectangles.

Oral and mental starter

Resources required
OHT 6.1 Rectangles 1
OHT 6.2 Rectangles 2
PCM 6.1 Compound shapes

- Display OHT 6.1 and ask the students to give the area of each shape.
- The first two shapes can be done by counting squares if necessary but for later examples students will need to use the rule.
- Establish the rule with students. Make sure they know the **formula** $A = l \times w$.
- Display OHT 6.2 and ask students to give the missing side lengths.
- Discuss the method used to do this.

Main lesson activity

- This lesson revises Year 8 work on calculating the **area** of a **rectangle** and calculating the area of a **compound shape** made up of rectangles. This is necessary in order to lead in to the work on areas of triangles and areas of compound shapes made up of triangles and rectangles.
- Using PCM 6.1, ask students to find the area of the compound shapes.
- The first two examples can be done by counting squares.
- When the class have finished, go through the answers and discuss the methods.
  (**PCM 6.1 Answers: a** 21 cm² **b** 26 cm² **c** 34 cm² **d** 21 cm² **e** 74 mm² **f** 96 m²)
- It is very important that they realise that a compound shape must be divided into two rectangles and the area of each rectangle calculated.
- It is also important that they realise that the lengths of each rectangle must be calculated carefully.
- Work through the following example. All bold items on the diagram, and the dotted line, should be added at the correct stage in the instructions.

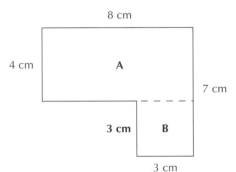

1 Split the shape (dotted line).
2 Label each part A and B.
3 Work out length of shape B (3 cm).

Area shape A = 4 × 8 = 32 cm²
Area shape B = 3 × 3 = 9 cm²
Total area = 41 cm²

- The shape could also be split into a 3 × 7 cm and a 4 × 5 cm rectangle.
- Encourage students to set out their working as above.
- **The class can now do Exercise 6B from the Pupil Workbook.**

Exercise 6B · Answers

1 **a** $7 \times 3 = 21$ cm² **b** $5 \times 5 = 25$ cm² **c** $6 \times 10 = 60$ cm² **d** $8 \times 4 = 32$ cm²
   e $11 \times 3 = 33$ cm² **f** $10 \times 3.5 = 35$ cm²

2

l	*w*	*A*
7 cm	11 cm	77 cm²
4 m	15 m	60 m²
10 cm	25 cm	250 cm²
13 km	4 km	52 km²
12 cm	32 cm	384 cm²

3 **a** $8 \times 4 + 3 \times 3 = 32 + 9 = 41$ cm² **b** $5 \times 2 + 7 \times 3 = 10 + 21 = 31$ cm²
   c $12 \times 4 + 8 \times 5 = 48 + 40 = 88$ cm²
   d Missing side is 8 cm, $10 \times 8 + 4 \times 5 = 80 + 20 = 100$ cm²
   e Missing side is 8 cm, $8 \times 4 + 3 \times 2 = 32 + 6 = 38$ cm²
   f $4 \times 10 + 4 \times 10 + 3 \times 4 = 40 + 40 + 12 = 92$ cm²
4 **a** 3 cm **b** 6 cm **c** 8 cm **d** 9 cm

Plenary

● Ask students to work out the shaded area in this shape.

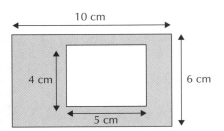

● They should come up with the idea of subtracting the two separate areas:

   $10 \times 6 - 4 \times 5 = 60 - 20 = 40$ cm².

● Ask how this method could be used to work out the area of a compound shape, such as the example shown.

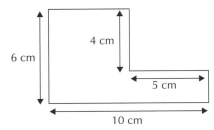

LESSON 6.3

Framework objectives – Area of triangles

Derive and use the formula for the area of a triangle.

Oral and mental starter

Resources required

PCM 6.2 Area of triangles
Gummed paper
Scissors

- Use four congruent right-angled triangles cut from card.
- Put onto an OHP.
- Ask individual students to come to the OHP to arrange two or four triangles into an isosceles triangle, rectangle, trapezium, parallelogram, rhombus, larger right-angled triangle (see diagram).

Main lesson activity

- Using PCM 6.2, ask students to find the area of each triangle by counting squares. Then ask them to fill in the table.
- Once the table is completed ask students if they can see a relationship between the **base**, height and **area**.
- They should see that the area is half of the product of base and height.
- Give out coloured card, or gummed paper, and scissors.
- Ask the class to cut out two triangles which are exactly the same. Cut both triangles into two, as in the diagram on the right.
- Arrange the four triangles to form a rectangle, which shows that the area of the triangle is equal to half the area of the rectangle:

    Area 1 = Area 2 and Area 3 = Area 4

The length of the base and the height of the triangle are defined as in the diagram below the rectangle. The height of the triangle is sometimes referred to as the **perpendicular height**.

The area of a triangle is given by the **formula**:

$$A = \tfrac{1}{2} \times b \times h = \tfrac{1}{2}bh$$

- Show the class an example.

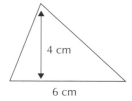

In the diagram above, $b = 6$ cm and $h = 4$ cm.

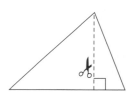

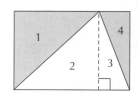

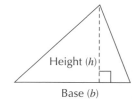

So $A = \frac{1}{2} \times 6 \times 4 = 12$ cm^2. Explain that this calculation can be worked out in different ways. For example: $(6 \div 2) \times 4 = 12$ or $(6 \times 4) \div 2 = 12$.

- Work through another example with the class, involving individual students where you can. For example, find the area of a right-angled triangle where the sides enclosing the right angle measure 5 cm and 8 cm.
- Work through more examples as necessary.

- **The class can now do Exercise 6C from the Pupil Workbook.**

Exercise 6C　Answers

1 a 1 cm^2　**b** 2 cm^2　**c** 4 cm^2　**d** 2 cm^2　**e** 3 cm^2
2 a 8 cm^2, 4 cm^2　**b** 12 cm^2, 6 cm^2　**c** 16 cm^2, 8 cm^2　**d** 10 cm^2, 5 cm^2
3 a $\frac{1}{2}$ of $5 \times 4 = 10$ cm^2　**b** $\frac{1}{2}$ of $8 \times 6 = 24$ cm^2
　c $\frac{1}{2}$ of $8 \times 8 = 32$ cm^2　**d** $\frac{1}{2}$ of $7 \times 10 = 35$ cm^2
　e $\frac{1}{2}$ of $2 \times 7 = 7$ cm^2　**f** $\frac{1}{2}$ of $5 \times 3 = 7.5$ cm^2
4 a $\frac{1}{2}$ of $4 \times 3 = 6$ cm^2　**b** $\frac{1}{2}$ of $8 \times 2 = 8$ cm^2
　c $\frac{1}{2}$ of $9 \times 6 = 27$ cm^2　**d** $\frac{1}{2}$ of $10 \times 4 = 20$ cm^2
　e $\frac{1}{2}$ of $8 \times 6 = 24$ cm^2　**f** $\frac{1}{2}$ of $3 \times 10 = 15$ cm^2

Plenary

- Show students the following diagram.

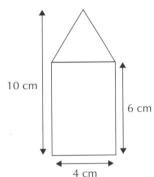

- Ask them if they can work out the area of this compound shape.
- They should realise that the shape can be split into a rectangle and a triangle.
- The rectangle is $4 \times 6 = 24$ cm^2.
- The triangle is $\frac{1}{2} \times 4 \times 4 = 8$ cm^2.
- The total area of the shape is $24 + 8 = 32$ cm^2.
- Repeat with other compound shapes such as the one shown below.

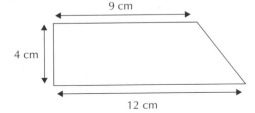

LESSON 6.4

Framework objectives – Area of parallelograms
Derive and use the formula for the area of a parallelogram.

Oral and mental starter

Resources required

PCM 6.3 Area of
              parallelograms
Gummed paper
Scissors

- The purpose of this starter activity is to revise the names and spelling of the different types of quadrilateral.
- First, ask the students to sketch, on their white boards or on paper, all of the different types of quadrilateral they can remember. Then ask them to write the name of each one below their sketches.
- Ask individual students to show their answers on their white boards, or to write their answers on the board. Check their spelling.
- The following quadrilaterals should be covered: square, rectangle, parallelogram, rhombus, kite and trapezium.

Main lesson activity

- Using PCM 6.3, ask students to find the area of parallelograms by counting squares and to then fill in the table.
- When the table is completed ask students if they can see a relationship between the base, height and area.
- They should see that the area is the product of base and height.
- Give out coloured card, or gummed paper, and scissors.
- Ask the class to cut out a parallelogram.

- Then ask them to cut off a triangle, as shown in the diagram above, and place it at the other side. This shows that the area of a parallelogram has the same area as a rectangle, which has the same length of **base** (*b*) and **height** (*h*). Hence, the **area** of a **parallelogram** is given by:

$$A = b \times h = bh$$

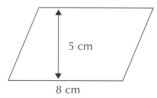

Height (*h*)

Base (*b*)

- Show the class an example. In the diagram below, *b* = 8 cm and *h* = 5 cm. So, $A = 8 \times 5 = 40$ cm².

5 cm

8 cm

- Work through more examples as necessary.

- **The class can now do Exercise 6D from the Pupil Workbook.**

Plenary

- Give students a revision exercise to make sure that they know the **formulae** for the area of different quadrilaterals.
- Draw the following quadrilaterals on the board or on an OHT: square, rectangle and parallelogram.
- Ask the students to write in their books the formula to find the area of each of the quadrilaterals.
- Check their answers by asking individual students to write the formula for each quadrilateral on the board.

Key words

- ☐ area
- ☐ parallelogram
- ☐ formula
- ☐ base
- ☐ perpendicular height

Number **2**

Framework objectives – Powers of 10
Multiply and divide integers and decimals by 10, 100, 1000 and explain the effect.

Oral and mental starter

Resources required

PCM 7.1 Powers of 10
Student white boards
1–100 number cards
(optional)

- For this activity you will need number cards to 100, or you could write numbers on the board.
- Show students a whole number between 1 and 100, such as 68 or 82, and a **power of 10**, such as 10 or 100.
- Ask students to combine two of the cards (one of each) and multiply the number by the power of 10.
- Students could write the answer on white boards.
- Repeat as necessary.
- Discuss the ways of doing this mentally.

Main lesson activity

- This lesson follows on from the Oral and mental starter.
- On the board, write a problem such as 6.3×100. Ask students for the answer (630) and to explain how they worked it out. They are likely to talk about moving the decimal point. In the context of this lesson this may be the best way to see what is happening but students should be reminded that it is the digits that are actually moving.
- Now write a problem such as 7.8×10^2. Ask students for the answer (780) and also what connection there is with the previous example. (Establish that the power and number of zeros are the number of places that the decimal point moves.)
- Repeat with 0.32×1000 and 0.32×10^3 (320).
- On the board, write a problem such as 67.2×10^5. Ask students for the answer (6 720 000) and ask them to explain their method.
- Explain the convention of leaving a space between every three digits, working from the right, for numbers with five or more digits. This is to make them easier to read.
- Discuss any similarities with previous examples. They should realise that multiplying by a power of 10, written as a power (e.g. 10^3) or as an ordinary number (e.g. 1000), is the same process and depends on the power or the number of zeros.
- Work through more examples if necessary.

- **The class can now do PCM 7.1 followed by Exercise 7A from the Pupil Workbook.**

Exercise 7A Answers

1 **c** 100 **d** 1000 **e** $10 \times 10 \times 10 \times 10 = 10\,000$ **f** $10 \times 10 \times 10 \times 10 \times 10 = 100\,000$
   g $10 \times 10 \times 10 \times 10 \times 10 \times 10 = 1\,000\,000$

2 One: 10^0, one thousand: 10^3, ten thousand: 10^4, one hundred thousand: 10^5,
   one hundred: 10^2, ten: 10^1, one million: 10^6

3 **a** 300 **b** 70 000 **c** $4 \times 1000 = 4000$ **d** $2 \times 100\,000 = 200\,000$
   e $8 \times 1000 = 8000$ **f** $9 \times 1\,000\,000 = 9\,000\,000$

4 **a** Three hundred **b** Seventy thousand **c** Four thousand
   d Two hundred thousand **e** Eight thousand **f** Nine million

5 **a** 3400 **b** 170 **c** $8.8 \times 10\,000 = 88\,000$ **d** $2.3 \times 1\,000\,000 = 2\,300\,000$
   e $3.7 \times 100 = 370$ **f** $2.9 \times 10 = 29$

Plenary

- Reverse the starter activity.
- Put a number on the board such as 640. Ask students to write it as a multiplication using a number between 1 and 10 and a power of 10, for example 6.4×100.
- Repeat with other numbers such as 8900, 53, 510 000, etc.

Key words

- ☐ power of 10
- ☐ place value

LESSON 7.2

Framework objectives – Addition of whole numbers and decimals

Use efficient written methods to add whole numbers and decimal numbers with up to two decimal places.

Oral and mental starter

Resources required

PCM 7.2 Adding decimals

- Draw the target board shown on the right on the board or on an OHT. Tell the class that the aim of this game is to make 24 (or any target number given) by using adjacent numbers and any of the four operations. The numbers may be vertically, horizontally or diagonally adjacent.

- For example, 24 can be made in the following ways, using adjacent numbers as shown:

  8×3 6×4 $6 \times 5 - 6$

- Students can work on this individually or in pairs. The winning team is the one with the most correct answers at the end of the activity.

8	3	1	5
6	6	5	2
7	4	6	1
9	3	2	1

Main lesson activity

- Ask students how they could work out 18 + 46 mentally.
- Some students may be able to do this 'in their head' but should be encouraged to mentally view a blank number line.

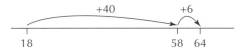

- Repeat with 47 + 126.

- Repeat with 1.2 + 3.6.

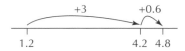

- Repeat with 7.6 + 4.9.

- Repeat with 8.1 + 2.73.

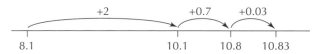

- PCM 7.2 may be used to demonstrate the carrying process.
- Students will already have made progress in formalising the process of adding whole numbers and decimals.
- Extend and revise this process by more formal methods. The column method is shown opposite.

- Emphasise the need to line up the **decimal points** and to fill in gaps with zeros.

$$
\begin{array}{r} 18 \\ + 46 \\ \hline 64 \\ \hline 1 \end{array}
\qquad
\begin{array}{r} 47 \\ + 126 \\ \hline 173 \\ \hline 1 \end{array}
\qquad
\begin{array}{r} 1.2 \\ + 3.6 \\ \hline 4.8 \end{array}
\qquad
\begin{array}{r} 7.6 \\ + 4.9 \\ \hline 12.5 \\ \hline 1 \end{array}
\qquad
\begin{array}{r} 8.10 \\ + 2.73 \\ \hline 10.83 \\ \hline 1 \end{array}
$$

- Emphasise the carried digits.

- **The class can now do Exercise 7B from the Pupil Workbook.**

Exercise 7B **Answers**

1 a 446 **b** 1075 **c** 1287 **d** 1934 **e** 249 **f** 927
2 a 8.98 **b** 13.37 **c** 24.02 **d** 6.3 **e** 10.05 **f** 33.57
3 various answers

Plenary

Key words

☐ decimal point
☐ column methods

- Ask students what the missing number is in this calculation:
  $0.2 + \ldots = 1$ (0.8).
- Now ask for the missing number in $0.37 + \ldots = 1$ (0.63).
- Repeat with other examples such as $0.52 + \ldots = 1$ (0.48),
  $0.85 + \ldots = 1$ (0.15).
- Ask students if they can see a quick way of working this out. They should refer to complements of 10, 100 and 1000.
- Test understanding with $0.642 + \ldots = 1$ (0.358).

LESSON 7.3

Framework objectives – Subtraction of whole numbers and decimals

Use efficient written methods to subtract whole numbers and decimal numbers with up to two decimal places.

Oral and mental starter

Resources required
PCM 7.3 Subtracting decimals OHTs and pens or   A3 paper and felt-tip pens

- Divide the students into small groups. Hand each group an OHT and some OHP pens, or a large sheet of paper and some felt-tip pens.
- Give each group the same five numbers, for example 2, 4, 5, 7 and 10 (use just four values if necessary). In a timed session (5 or 10 minutes), ask them to write down as many calculations as possible using these numbers. Rules can be flexible to suit the group. For example:

    Answers such as 24 + 5 = 29 are acceptable.
    All the numbers must be used individually, for example 2 × 4 + 5 = 13.
    Not all of the numbers need to be used, for example 2 × 5 − 7 = 3.
    All the numbers must be used, for example 2 + 4 + 5 − 7 + 10 = 14.

    Answers, however, must always be shown.

- Also give the students a target number, for example 80. Ask them to make a calculation using all the numbers with 80 as the answer. For example: (2 × 7 − 10) × 4 × 5.
- After the given time, ask students to stop and then award themselves a score of 1 point for every calculation, and 5 points for each calculation that gives the target number. Record their scores, but do not check anything yet. (Sheets may be collected.)

Main lesson activity

- Ask students how they could calculate 54 − 28 mentally.
- Some students may be able to do this 'in their head' but should be encouraged to mentally view a blank number line.

- Repeat with 134 − 57.

- Repeat with 3.6 − 1.2.

- Repeat with 7.6 − 4.9.

● Repeat with 8.1 – 2.73.

● PCM 7.3 may be used to demonstrate the carrying process.
● Students will already have made progress in formalising the process of subtracting whole numbers and decimals.
● Extend and revise this process by more formal methods such as **column methods**.
● Emphasise the need to line up the **decimal points** and to fill in gaps with zeros.

$$\begin{array}{r} 4\overset{1}{5}4 \\ -\ 28 \\ \hline 26 \end{array} \qquad \begin{array}{r} \overset{12}{1}\overset{1}{3}4 \\ -\ 57 \\ \hline 77 \end{array} \qquad \begin{array}{r} 3.6 \\ -1.2 \\ \hline 2.4 \end{array} \qquad \begin{array}{r} 6\overset{1}{7}.6 \\ -4.9 \\ \hline 2.7 \end{array} \qquad \begin{array}{r} 7\overset{10}{8}.\overset{1}{1}0 \\ -2.73 \\ \hline 5.37 \end{array}$$

● Emphasise the borrowing and carried digits.

● **The class can now do Exercise 7C from the Pupil Workbook.**

Exercise 7C   Answers

1 a 223   **b** 438   **c** 284   **d** 277   **e** 999   **f** 1108
2 a 14.2   **b** 15.4   **c** 1.89   **d** 4.99   **e** 21.56   **f** 53.17   **g** 116.94
   h 19.55   **i** 45.21

Plenary

● Display the students' OHTs or pin up their pieces of paper. Check each set of answers for accuracy and correct use of BODMAS. Score each sheet. Check with the score recorded for each group earlier. Deduct 5 when a total is wrong. Add 5 when a total is correct. Declare a winning group.

Key words

☐ **decimal point**
☐ **column methods**

Framework objectives – Multiplication of whole numbers and decimals

Multiply decimals with one or two places by single-digit whole numbers.

Oral and mental starter

Resources required

PCM 7.4 Tables

- This starter is best done when there is work for the students to get on with, as they will finish at different times. Alternatively, introduce the main lesson activity and introduce a 'mental break' halfway through the lesson.
- Ask the class to draw a 10 × 10 grid or hand around PCM 7.4.
- Using PCM 7.4 as an OHT, ask one student to give you the numbers from 1 to 10 in any order. Write these across the top of the grid.
- Ask another student to give you the numbers from 1 to 10 in a different order. Write these down the side of the grid.
- Fill in the top row of products in the grid, on the OHT, as a class.
- At a given signal, the students should fill in the rest of the multiplication grid.
- The time taken to do this should be recorded.
- Some will finish in a couple of minutes, while others will take much longer. It is best to fix a time limit of, for example, 10 minutes.
- The aim is to improve on the time (or number of answers filled in) the next time the activity is given.

Main lesson activity

Example 1   Multiply 437 by 3.
- Students may have a variety of methods, all of which can be discussed. The likely methods are:

Box method
(partitioning)

×	400	30	7	
3	1200	90	21	1311

Column method
(expanded working)

```
      437
   ×    3
     1200    (400 × 3)
       90    (30 × 3)
       21    (7 × 3)
     1311
        1
```

Column method
(compacted working)

```
      437
   ×    3
     1311
       1 2
```

Example 2   Multiply 3.572 by 7.
- Demonstrate using compacted **column method**.

```
    3 . 5 7 2
  ×         7
   2 5 . 0 0 4
      4   5 1
```

- Emphasise the carried digits.

Example 3   Multiply 4.46 by 6.
- First estimate the answer, 5 × 6 = 30.

- Demonstrate using expanded column method.

$$
\begin{array}{r}
4.46 \\
\times \quad\quad 6 \\
\hline
24.00 \\
2.40 \\
0.36 \\
\hline
26.76 \\
\hline
\end{array}
$$

- Emphasise that the decimal points must line up, and that the estimate can be used to put the point in the right place.

Example 4   Multiply 2.068 by 8.
- First estimate the answer, $2 \times 8 = 16$.
- Demonstrate using the **box method**.

	2000	0	60	8
8	16 000	0	480	64

$$
\begin{array}{r}
16\,000 \\
480 \\
64 \\
\hline
16.544 \\
\hline
{\scriptstyle 1}
\end{array}
$$

- Emphasise that the calculation is treated as 2068×8 and the estimate used to put the decimal point in the right place.

- **The class can now do Exercise 7D from the Pupil Workbook.**

Exercise 7D   **Answers**

1 a 245   **b** 3424   **c** 3072   **d** 26 184   **e** 295.2   **f** 19.65   **g** 211.59   **h** 24.48
2 a 228   **b** 621   **c** 1422   **d** 2048   **e** 9920   **f** 47.6 **g** 137.94   **h** 3677.6
  i 288.72
3 various answers

Plenary

- Using the multiplication square from the starter activity, discuss strategies for filling it in quickly. For example:

  First, complete the 1 times-table (across and down), then the 10 times-table, then the 5 times-table, then the 2 times-table, possibly the 9 times-table. Look for columns (or rows) where the neighbouring column (or row) is easy to calculate. For example 6 × next to 3 ×, so it is double the previous entry; or 4 × next to 2 ×, so it is double the previous entry.

Key words

- column method
- box method
- tables
- product

Framework objectives – Division of whole numbers and decimals

Divide decimals with one or two places by single-digit whole numbers.

Oral and mental starter

- Use a target board like the one shown below.

57.3	36.9	27.4	63.8
72.1	39.4	46.8	18.6
35.6	38.5	78.2	22.6
12.9	52.9	33.9	67.2

- Ask students to estimate the answer when a chosen number is divided by an integer less than 10.
- Students will not always be able to round to the nearest 10.
- Explain that they will need to round to a value in the times-table of the **divisor**.

  e.g. $38.5 \div 7 \approx 35 \div 7 = 5$, $38.5 \div 6 \approx 36 \div 6 = 6$, etc.

Main lesson activity

Example 1   135 students are to be seated in rows of six chairs. How many rows will be needed?

- Do this by taking away in chunks:

$$
\begin{array}{r}
135 \\
10 \times 6 - 60 \\
\hline
75 \\
10 \times 6 - 60 \\
\hline
15 \\
2 \times 6 - 12 \\
\hline
3
\end{array}
$$

Try each time to take away the largest multiple you can.

Multiples of 2 and 10 are always easy to find.

There are $10 + 10 + 2 = 22$ sixes in 135 with 3 left over. That means that 23 rows will be needed.

Example 2   Divide 3.92 by 7.
- This is demonstrated using the **column method**.
- Emphasise the position of the decimal point.

$$
\begin{array}{r}
0\,.\,5\;6 \\
7\overline{)\,3\,.\,{}^3 9\,{}^4 2}
\end{array}
$$

Example 3   Divide 44.7 by 6.
- First estimate the answer, $42 \div 6 = 7$.
- This is demonstrated using the **chunking** method.

$$
\begin{array}{rl}
4\;4\,.\,7 & \\
-\;\;\;2\;4\,.\,0 & \quad 40 \times 6 \\
\hline
2\;0\,.\,7 & \\
-\;\;\;1\;8\,.\,0 & \quad 30 \times 6 \\
\hline
2\,.\,7 & \\
-\;\;\;\;\;\;2\,.\,4 & \quad 4 \times 6 \\
\hline
0\,.\,3 & \quad 74 \times 6
\end{array}
$$

- Using the estimate, the answer is 7.4 remainder 0.3.
- Emphasise that the decimal points line up, or that the estimate can be used to put the point in the right place.

Example 4   Divide 2.072 by 8.
- First estimate the answer $2 \div 8 = 0.25$.
- This is demonstrated using the standard **column method**.

$$\begin{array}{r} 0.259 \\ \hline 8)\,2.{}^20^47^72 \end{array}$$

- Emphasise the lining up of the decimal point, or using the estimate to place the point in the correct place.
- Work through more examples if necessary.

- **The class can now do Exercise 7E from the Pupil Workbook.**

Exercise 7E   **Answers**

1 a 14   **b** 15   **c** 14   **d** 13   **e** 27   **f** 32
2 a 23   **b** 57   **c** 118
3 a 13 r 2   **b** 21 r 3   **c** 21 r 3   **d** 13 r 3   **e** 15 r 6   **f** 33 r 3
4 a 13 r 4   **b** 76 r 3   **c** 57 r 5
5 a 1.3   **b** 1.4   **c** 1.3   **d** 2.3   **e** 5.3   **f** 0.59   **g** 0.12   **h** 0.77   **i** 0.101

Plenary

- Put the following problem on the board: $8 \times 8.9 = 71.2$
- Ask students for the answer to the following:

    $71.2 \div 8$ (8.9)
    $7.12 \div 8$ (0.89)
    $712 \div 8$ (89)
    $712 \div 89$ (8)

- Discuss the connections and the importance of estimating answers.

Key words
- column method
- repeated subtraction
- chunking
- tables
- divisor

LESSON 7.6

Framework objectives – Real-life problems

Identify the necessary information to understand or simplify a context or problem.
Represent problems, making correct use of symbols. Use appropriate procedures.

Oral and mental starter

- Copy the menu for a local, fast-food takeaway onto an OHT (or produce photocopies for the whole class).
- Either read out an order for food and ask students to mentally add the costs, or nominate one student as the customer and another as the waiter.
- If the menu is too complicated, reproduce a simplified version with fewer choices.

<table>
<tr><td colspan="2">Resources required</td></tr>
<tr><td>PCM 7.5</td><td>Problem 1</td></tr>
<tr><td>PCM 7.6</td><td>Problem 2</td></tr>
<tr><td>PCM 7.7</td><td>Problem 3</td></tr>
<tr><td>PCM 7.8</td><td>Problem 4</td></tr>
<tr><td>PCM 7.9</td><td>Problem 5</td></tr>
<tr><td>PCM 7.10</td><td>Problem 6</td></tr>
<tr><td>PCM 7.11</td><td>Problem 7</td></tr>
<tr><td>PCM 7.12</td><td>Problem 8</td></tr>
<tr><td>PCM 7.13</td><td>Problem 9</td></tr>
<tr><td colspan="2">OHP pens</td></tr>
</table>

Main lesson activity

- Copy the PCMs onto acetates.
- Divide the class into pairs or small groups.
- Give one of the PCMs and an OHP pen to each pair or group.
- There are nine of these so there should be enough for each group to have a different one.
- Some **problems** are easier than others. Care should be taken to match the problem to the ability of the group.
- Ask students to solve the problem, writing their **solution** onto the acetate.
- Later, each group should be asked to come to the OHP and show their solution to the rest of the class, and to talk through it.
- Make sure that the appropriate **methods** have been used and that the answers are correct.
- Encourage the rest of the class to comment on methods and answers.
  Answers
  Problem 1: Mr Smith 864 mints, Mr Jones 945 mints, 81 mints more
  Problem 2: 126 cm wide, 16.2 m long
  Problem 3: 1.765 kg or 1765 g, 2 .77 l or 277 cl
  Problem 4: 9.6 km or 9600 m, 4.83 kg or 4830 g
  Problem 5: Yes he has 256 biscuits and 224 are needed, £1.88
  Problem 6: £1445, £6.78
  Problem 7: 1.89, 18.69, 17.41 − 7.85 = 9.56
  Problem 8: £11.11, Jack has £10.23, he has to borrow 88p
  Problem 9: 0.34 kg of flour (2.16 kg needed), 1.065 kg of sugar
              (0.435 kg needed); no, not enough flour.

- **The class can now do Exercise 7F from the Pupil Workbook.**

Exercise 7F Answers

1 746 − 389 = 357
2 139 + 276 = 415
3 365 × 4 = 1460 days
4 318 ÷ 6 = 53 boxes
5 9 × 375 = 3375 m
6 1.4 − 0.56 = 0.84 kg
7 **a** £2.79 + £1.27 = £4.06   **b** £3.20 + £2.09 = £5.29
  c £5.29 − £4.06 = £1.23

Plenary

● As the class has been demonstrating their solutions there is no plenary, although this time could be used to discuss answers to any of the problems from the exercise.

Key words
- strategy
- problem
- solution
- method

Algebra **4**

Framework objectives – Divisibility and multiples
Recognise and use multiples.

Oral and mental starter

Resources required

PCM 8.1 100 grids
PCM 8.2 Number grids
20-sided dice

- Write the numbers 1 to 20 across the board.
- Put a different letter from the alphabet under each number (avoiding J, X, Y, Z).
- Roll a 20-sided dice (or take numbers from a hat). Ask students at random, or in order, to give a mathematical word containing the corresponding letter.
- A rule can be used to restrict certain groups of words, for example numbers (one, two, three, …), which are not allowed. Students can be given 'lives' or the class can be split into two teams. Other students or the other team may challenge whether a word is mathematical, repeated or very similar to a previous word (such as division and divide).

Main lesson activity

- Using PCM 8.1, ask students to shade in multiples of 2, 3, 4, 6, 7 and 9. (It may be necessary to recall the definition of **multiple**.)
- Now use PCM 8.2, which shows number grids of different widths, that is grids with rows 1–7, 8–14, 15–21, …, or rows 1–5, 6–10, 11–15, … .

1	2	3	4	5
6	7	8	9	10

1	2	3	4	5	6	7
8	9	10	11	12	13	14

- Ask the students to shade in the multiples of 2, 3, 4, 6 and 9 on the different grids.
- The results always form a pattern. The shaded grids can be used as a display.
- Ask how you can tell if a number divides by 2, and so is a multiple of 2 (ends in 0, 2, 4, 6, 8).
- Ask how you can tell if a number is a multiple of 3 (sum of digits is a multiple of 3).
- Ask how you can tell if a number is a multiple of 5 (ends in 0 or 5).
- Ask how you can tell if a number is a multiple of 10 (ends in 0).
- Optional: Ask how you can tell if a number is a multiple of 4 (last two digits are a multiple of 4).

- Put a list of numbers on the board such as:

  44   57   80   95   72   100   112   115   34   33   18   30

- Ask the students to identify the multiples of 2, 3, 5, 10, 4 (optional).

- **The class can now do Exercise 8A from the Pupil Workbook.**

Exercise 8A   Answers

1 a 3, 6, 9, 12, 15   **b** 5, 10, 15, 20, 25   **c** 6, 12, 18, 24, 30
  d 8, 16, 24, 32, 40   **e** 13, 26, 39, 52, 65   **f** 20, 40, 60, 80, 100
  g 35, 70, 105, 140, 175   **h** 51, 102, 153, 204, 255
2 56, 60
3 60, 72
4 14
5 22
6 Shade 63, 108, 9, 72, 45, 81, 18, 99 to give letter F
7 33; multiple of 3 or 11

Plenary

Key words

- [ ] multiple
- [ ] digit
- [ ] divisible
- [ ] even
- [ ] odd

- Write a set of numbers on the board such as:

  15   18   22   27   31   45   50   90

- Ask the students to identify which are **divisible** by 2, 3, 5, 10, 4 (optional).

- Discuss the methods used.

Framework objectives – Factors of numbers
Recognise and use factors.

Oral and mental starter

Resources required

PCM 8.3 Factors 1
1–6 dice
Student white boards

- Throw three 1–6 dice.
- Write the numbers on the board, for example 2, 4, 6.
- Ask students to multiply them together, for example
  $2 \times 4 \times 6 = 48$. Answers could be written on white boards.
- Students may make jottings if necessary.
- Repeat several times.

Main lesson activity

- Write 24 on the board.
- Ask the students to give numbers that 'go into' 24.
- Create a factor diagram, as shown below.

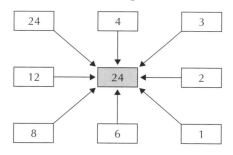

- Repeat with 30, 16, 13, 20, 10, 18.
- Recall (or define for the first time) the idea of a **factor**.
- Ask the students to think of some rules. For example:

    1 is always a factor.
    The number itself is a factor.
    Factors always occur in pairs (except for square numbers like 16).
    Square numbers always have an odd number of factors.
    Some numbers have only two factors.

- Recall ways to find factors: know tables, use test of **divisibility**.

- **The class can now do PCM 8.3 followed by Exercise 8B from the Pupil Workbook.**

Exercise 8B   Answers

1 **a** $1 \times 8, 2 \times 4$ **b** $1 \times 21, 3 \times 7$ **c** $1 \times 12, 2 \times 6, 3 \times 4$
   d $1 \times 24, 2 \times 12, 3 \times 8, 4 \times 6$
2 **a** 1, 2, 4, 5, 10, 20   **b** 1, 2, 3, 5, 6, 10, 15, 30
   c 1, 2, 3, 4, 6, 9, 12, 18, 36
3 20
4 8
5 Shade 1, 3, 7, 4, 14, 6, 50, 5, 2, 12, 10, 25, 8, 24 to leave letter S
6 4, 9, 14, 27

Plenary

Key words

☐ **factor**
☐ **divisibility**

● Put a list of numbers on the board such as:

     15   22   35   80

● Find the factors of each.
● Discuss the methods used.

LESSON 8.3

Framework objectives – Highest common factors and lowest common multiples

Recognise and use highest common factors and lowest common multiples in simple cases.

Oral and mental starter

Resources required

PCM 8.4 LCM and HCF
Number fans or student
white boards

- The students should use a number fan or a white board on which to write their answers.
- They should not hold these up until requested so that weaker students have time to think, and do not copy.
- Ask for an example of an even number; a multiple of 6; a factor of 12; a prime number; a square number; a number that is a multiple of both 3 and 4; a triangle number; etc.
- Go around the class for each example, checking each student's answer.
- If necessary, discuss and define what was required.
- Particularly emphasise factors and multiples, as these will be used in the Main lesson activity.

Main lesson activity

- Ask the students if they know a number that is a multiple of both 3 and 4 (see Oral and mental starter).
- On the board write all the answers given.
- Ensure that the number 12 is included in the list. Ask students what is special about this number.
- Emphasise that it is the **lowest common multiple** or **LCM** of 3 and 4.
- Repeat for a common multiple of 4 and 5.
- Now ask for the lowest common multiple of 3 and 5.
- Then ask for the lowest common multiple of 4 and 6. Many students will answer 24, as they will have spotted that previous answers were the product of the two numbers in question.
- Make sure they understand that the LCM of 4 and 6 is 12, not 24 which is the product.
- The students should be encouraged to write out the multiples for the two numbers and to look for the first common value in each list. For example, for the LCM of 4 and 5:

    4   8   12   16   ⑳   24   28   ...

    5   10   15   ⑳   25   30   35   ...

- Now ask them to give a number that is a factor of 12 and 18.
- Once again, write on the board all the numbers shown. It is likely that all possibilities will be shown (1, 2, 3, 6) plus a few that are incorrect.
- Ensure that the class has understood the concept and, if any factors are missing, ask what numbers are needed to complete the set.
- Ask what is special about 6. Emphasise that it is the **highest common factor** or **HCF**.
- Repeat for the common factors of 30 and 50.
- Now ask for the highest common factor of 16 and 20.

- Repeat for 15 and 30. (5 is a likely answer here – make sure they understand that the HCF is 15.)
- Students should be encouraged to write the factors and look for the highest common value.

- **The class can now do PCM 8.4 followed by Exercise 8C from the Pupil Workbook.**

Exercise 8C **Answers**

1 1, 2, 4, 8; 1, 2, 5, 10; 1 and 2; 2
2 1, 2, 3, 4, 6, 12; 1, 2, 4, 5, 10, 20; 1, 2 and 4; 4
3 8, 12, 24 in red; 6, 12, 15, 24, 27, 30 in blue; 12 and 24
4 10, 15, 45, 25, 30 in red; 10, 38, 16, 30 in blue; 10 and 30
5 2, 4, 6, 8, 10, 12; 3, 6, 9, 12, 15, 18; 6 and 12; 6
6 4, 8, 12, 16, 20, 24, 28, 32, 36, 40; 5, 10, 15, 20, 25, 30, 35, 40, 45, 50; 20 and 40; 20

Plenary

Key words

- highest common factor (HCF)
- lowest common multiple (LCM)

- Write numbers on the board (or use prepared cards), such as:

    1, 2, 3, 4, 6, 8, 10, 12, 15, 20, 24, 25, 30, 35, 40, 48

- Ask students to pick out one number or card and then:
  - When a low value is chosen, ask for the first ten multiples.
  - When a high value is chosen, ask for all the factors.
- Then ask students to pick out two numbers or cards. Ask for the LCM when both are a low value. Ask for the HCF when both are a high value, or ask for the product (or quotient and remainder) if one is high and one low.
- Alternatively, ask for a card that is the lowest common multiple of 5 and 6, or the highest common factor of 15 and 20, for example.

Framework objectives – Prime numbers

Recognise and use prime numbers less than 100.

Oral and mental starter

Resources required

PCM 8.5 Factors 2

- Using a target board such as the one shown, point to a number and ask for the **factors**.

15	16	5	6
14	2	1	4
13	8	3	9
12	11	10	7

- Recall rules for factors: one is always a factor, the number itself is always a factor, factors come in pairs.

Main lesson activity

- Hand out copies of PCM 8.5 and ask the class to shade in the squares where the numbers across the top are **factors** of the number at the side.
- When they have done this, ask students to count the number of factors of each number and fill in the last column.
- Then ask them to list all of the numbers which have only two factors.
- Explain that such numbers are **prime** numbers, i.e. they do not have any factors other than themselves and 1.
- List all of the prime numbers up to 100. (2, 3, 5, 7, 11, 13, 17, 19, 23, 29, 31, 37, 41, 43, 47, 53, 59, 61, 67, 71, 73, 79, 83, 89, 97)
- **The class can now do Exercise 8D from the Pupil Workbook.**

Exercise 8D   Answers

1 Unshaded numbers are 2, 3, 5, 7, 11, 13, 17, 19, 23, 29, 31, 37, 41, 43, 47, 53, 59, 61, 67, 71, 73, 79, 83, 89, 97
2 2, odd, factors
3 4, 8, 9, 16
4 Prime only 2, 7, 17; greater than 20 only 25, 27, 33, 40; 23 and 31 in the intersection
5 **a** 2×2 **b** 2×3 **c** 3×3 **d** 2×5 **e** 2×7 **f** 3×5 **g** $2 \times 2 \times 2$
   h $2 \times 2 \times 3$ **i** $2 \times 3 \times 3$ **j** $2 \times 2 \times 5$

Plenary

Key words

- [ ] **prime**
- [ ] **factors**

- Go back to PCM 8.5.
- Ask students to list the numbers that have an odd number of factors.
- These should be 1, 4, 9, 16, 25 and 36. Write these as a list.
- Ask students to predict the next number that would have an odd number of factors by looking at the number pattern. They may predict 49 as the difference is 3, 5, 7, 9, 11, etc.
- Ask students to remember these numbers, as they will need them in the next lesson.

LESSON 8.5

Framework objectives – Square numbers
Use squares.

Oral and mental starter

Resources required

Counters
Calculators

- Recall the Plenary from the previous lesson.
- The numbers with an odd number of factors were 1, 4, 9, 16, 25 and 36.
- Write these on the board.
- Ask students to continue the sequence and explain the term-to-term rule.
- They should say something like, increases by 2 each time, i.e. the difference is 3, 5, 7, 9, 11 and so on.
- Using this rule, write down the next four values: 49, 64, 81, 100.
- Now ask if they could work out the 20th number in the sequence.
- Ask if there is any other way that this sequence can be expressed.
- Students may realise that the numbers can be written as squares although they do not always see this.
- Explain that you will give them a clue in the Main lesson activity.

Main lesson activity

- Place four counters on the OHP.
- Ask an individual student to come to the OHP and make a pattern with the counters.
- Repeat until a 2×2 square is made.
- Leave this pattern to one side of the OHP or draw it on the board.
- Repeat with nine counters. Obtain a 3×3 square.
- Repeat with 16 counters. Obtain a 4×4 square.
- Now ask students how many counters would be in the next pattern (25).
- Ask them how they worked this out.
- They may link this to the Oral and mental starter, so once again ask if they could now say how many counters would be in the 20th pattern. They may not be able to do the calculation mentally but they should be able to explain how to work it out (20×20).
- Explain that these are **square numbers**. They have this name because they can be formed into square patterns.
- Explain the square notation, for example $9^2 = 9 \times 9 = 81$.
- Emphasise that square means 'multiply by itself'. Students often just multiply by 2.
- Using calculators, explain how to use them to work out squares. This can be done by a simple calculation such as 12×12, or the square key can be used. Make sure students are able to square numbers using a calculator.

- **The class can now do Exercise 8E from the Pupil Workbook.**

Exercise 8E   Answers

1 4
    $3 \times 3 = 9$
    $4 \times 4 = 16$
    $5 \times 5 = 25$
    $6 \times 6 = 36$
    $7 \times 7 = 49$
    $8 \times 8 = 64$
    $9 \times 9 = 81$
    $10 \times 10 = 100$
    $11 \times 11 = 121$
    $12 \times 12 = 144$
2 a 36 **b** Eleventh **c** 81
3 Yellow – 36, 100, 4, 64; red – 1, 81, 9, 49, 25; green – all other numbers
4 a 38 **b** 99

Plenary

● Revise all of the square numbers up to 15×15.
● List them and encourage students to learn them.

Key words

☐ **square numbers**

Framework objectives – Square roots
Use positive square roots.

Oral and mental starter

Resources required

Calculators

- On the board write 4, 9 and 16. Invite the students to say something about these numbers.
- They should recall from the last lesson that these are **square numbers**.
- Revise the square numbers up to 12×12, using the square patterns of dots if necessary.
- Reinforce the concept by stating that when we multiply any number by itself, the answer is called the square of the number or the number squared. This is because the answer is a square number.
- Now show the class the sequence of square numbers from 1 to 144. Ask them, either as a class or individually, to read out the sequence.
- Try to get the class to memorise the sequence. Cover numbers in the sequence one or two at a time.
- Repeat for as long as necessary.

Main lesson activity

- Following on from the Oral and mental starter, tell the class that 49 is a square number and ask them which number you have to square to get 49.
- It is likely that the students will identify 7.
- Then move on to the concept that the opposite of the square number is its **square root**, represented by the symbol: $\sqrt{}$. So, in this case, $\sqrt{49} = 7$.
- Ask for a few more examples such as: $\sqrt{16}$, $\sqrt{36}$, $\sqrt{81}$ and $\sqrt{100}$.
- Write out a list of the square roots up to $\sqrt{144}$.
- Many students have difficulty recalling these, so encourage them to write the list down for reference.
- Using calculators, introduce the **square root key**.
- Make sure students know how to use this. For example, on some calculators the number is entered first, then the square root key is pressed, on others the square root key is pressed first.
- Use calculators to find square roots of 1764 (42) and 12.25 (3.5).
- Work through more examples if necessary.

- **The class can now do Exercise 8F from the Pupil Workbook.**

Exercise 8F Answers

1 $3 \times 3 = 9$, square root of 9 is 3
   $4 \times 4 = 16$, square root of 16 is 4
   $5 \times 5 = 25$, square root of 25 is 5
   $6 \times 6 = 36$, square root of 36 is 6
   $7 \times 7 = 49$, square root of 49 is 7
   $8 \times 8 = 64$, square root of 64 is 8
   $9 \times 9 = 81$, square root of 81 is 9
   $10 \times 10 = 100$, square root of 100 is 10
   $11 \times 11 = 121$, square root of 121 is 11
   $12 \times 12 = 144$, square root of 144 is 12
2 **a** 6 **b** 5 **c** 10 **d** 9 **e** 1 **f** 8 **g** 3 **h** 2 **i** 7 **j** 4 **k** 11 **l** 12
3 **a** 56 **b** 42 **c** 28 **d** 29 **e** 44 **f** 33

Plenary

Key words

☐ **square number**
☐ **square root**
☐ **square root key**

● Revise the concept of square numbers and their square roots, including a reminder about root notation.
● Conduct a quick recall test of square numbers and square roots.

1 What is the square root of 64?
2 What is 10 squared?
3 What is 3 squared?
4 What is the square root of 81?
5 What is the square root of 100?
6 What is 5 squared?
7 What is the square root of 121?
8 What is 2 squared?
9 If $x^2 = 16$, what is the value of x?
10 What is the value of x if $x^2 = 25$?

Answers **1** 8 **2** 100 **3** 9 **4** 9 **5** 10 **6** 25 **7** 11 **8** 4 **9** 4 **10** 5

Framework objectives – Cube numbers
Use cube numbers.

Oral and mental starter

Resources required

PCM 8.6 Cube tower
Calculators

- Using PCM 8.6, ask students to describe what they see.
- Students will hopefully recognise that it is a tower of cubes made up of unit cubes.
- Ask them to tell you how big each of the cubes forming the tower is.
- Students should recognise that the bottom cube is $5 \times 5 \times 5$ and the next $4 \times 4 \times 4$ and so on.
- Ask how many smaller cubes are in each of the larger cubes.
- Students should work out that there are 125, 64, 27, 8 and 1 respectively.
- Ask other questions like 'How many faces are grey?', 'How many faces are shaded with the spot pattern?'.

Main lesson activity

- This follows on from the Oral and mental starter.
- On the board write the sequence found earlier, i.e. 1, 8, 27, 64, 125.
- Ask if students know how each of these can be worked out.
- They should recall that they are $1 \times 1 \times 1$, $2 \times 2 \times 2$, $3 \times 3 \times 3$, ...
- Demonstrate this by writing:

$$1 \times 1 \times 1 = 1$$
$$2 \times 2 \times 2 = 8$$
$$3 \times 3 \times 3 = 27$$
$$4 \times 4 \times 4 = 64$$
$$5 \times 5 \times 5 = 125$$

- Ask for the next line of the pattern and the value. Calculators may be used.
- Continue the pattern until the first 10 **cube numbers** are obtained, i.e. 216, 343, 512, 729, 1000.
- Explain the notation $4^3 = 64$, $7^3 = 343$, for example.
- Emphasise that cube means 'multiply by itself twice'. Students often multiply by 3.
- Using calculators, explain how to use them to work out cubes. This can be done by a simple calculation such as $12 \times 12 \times 12$, or the **power key** can be used. This last option may be too confusing for students as this is often a second function key.

- **The class can now do Exercise 8G from the Pupil Workbook.**

Exercise 8G   Answers

1 8
   $3 \times 3 \times 3 = 27$
   $4 \times 4 \times 4 = 64$
   $5 \times 5 \times 5 = 125$
   $6 \times 6 \times 6 = 216$
   $7 \times 7 \times 7 = 343$
   $8 \times 8 \times 8 = 512$
   $9 \times 9 \times 9 = 729$
   $10 \times 10 \times 10 = 1000$
2 **a** 343 **b** 8 **c** 64 **d** 125 **e** 1000 **f** 729 **g** 1 **h** 216 **i** 27
3 **a** 125 **b** 512 **c** fourth **d** 1000
4 100
5 **a** 1331 **b** 1728 **c** 2744 **d** 5832 **e** 8000 **f** 15 625 **g** 64 000
   h 125 000 **i** 1 000 000

Plenary

● Revise all cube numbers up to $5 \times 5 \times 5$, and $10 \times 10 \times 10$.
● List them and encourage students to learn them.

Key words
☐ **cube numbers**
☐ **powers**
☐ **power key**

Framework objectives – Cube roots
Use cube roots.

Oral and mental starter

> **Resources required**
>
> Calculators

- Write the numbers 1, 8, 27, 64 on the board. Remind students that they were dealing with these numbers in the last lesson. Ask students to give the next number in the sequence (125).
- Ask how they found the number. It is unlikely that they 'counted on'.
- Make sure they understand that these are **cube numbers** and ask for 10^3.
- Ask how to find the cube numbers missing from the sequence. They may use a calculator.
- Work out 6^3 (216), 7^3 (343), 8^3 (512) and 9^3 (729).
- Explain that students are expected to know and recognise the cubes of 1, 2, 3, 4, 5 and 10.

Main lesson activity

- Following on from the Oral and mental starter ask what is a if $a^3 = 8$.
- It is likely that students will identify 2.
- Introduce, or ask if students know, the notation $\sqrt[3]{8}$.
- Explain the meaning of **cube root**.
- Ask for a few more examples such as $\sqrt[3]{27}$, $\sqrt[3]{1000}$, … .
- Write out a list of the cube roots up to $\sqrt[3]{125}$.
- Students often have difficulty recalling these, so it is helpful to write the list in their books.
- The list can be left on the board or rubbed off before students do the exercise.
- Using calculators, introduce the **cube root key**.
- Make sure students know how to use this. For example on some calculators the number is entered first, then the cube root key is pressed, on others the cube root key is pressed first. On calculators without a cube root key the **power key** with a **power** of one-third (entered as a fraction) must be used. This can be confusing for students.
- Use calculators to find cube roots of 3.375 (1.5) and 35 937 (33).
- Work through more examples if necessary.

- **The class can now do Exercise 8H from the Pupil Workbook.**

Exercise 8H **Answers**

1 $3 \times 3 \times 3 = 27$, cube root of 27 is 3
  $4 \times 4 \times 4 = 64$, cube root of 64 is 4
  $5 \times 5 \times 5 = 125$, cube root of 125 is 5
  $6 \times 6 \times 6 = 216$, cube root of 216 is 6
  $7 \times 7 \times 7 = 343$, cube root of 343 is 7
  $8 \times 8 \times 8 = 512$, cube root of 512 is 8
  $9 \times 9 \times 9 = 729$, cube root of 729 is 9
  $10 \times 10 \times 10 = 1000$, cube root of 1000 is 10
2 **a** 2 **b** 4 **c** 1 **d** 10 **e** 5 **f** 7 **g** 3 **h** 8 **i** 6 **j** 9
3 **a** 4 **b** 10 **c** 7 **d** 8
4 **a** 11 **b** 15 **c** 16 **d** 12 **e** 13 **f** 19 **g** 20 **h** 21 **i** 25

Plenary

- Revise the concept of cube numbers and their cube roots, including a reminder about root notation.
- Conduct a quick recall test of cube numbers and cube roots.

  1 What is the cube root of 8?
  2 What is 10 cubed?
  3 What is 3 cubed?
  4 What is the cube root of 125?
  5 What is the cube root of 1?
  6 What is the cube of 4?
  7 What is the cube of 1?
  8 What is the cube of 5?
  9 What is the cube root of 1000?
  10 What is twenty cubed?

Answers **1** 2 **2** 1000 **3** 27 **4** 5 **5** 1 **6** 64 **7** 1 **8** 125 **9** 10 **10** 8000

CHAPTER 9

Statistics 2

LESSON 9.1

> **Framework objectives – Probability scales**
> Use vocabulary and ideas of probability, drawing on experience.
> Understand and use the probability scale from 0 to 1.

Oral and mental starter

> **Resources required**
> PCM 9.1 Spinner
> Counters
> Bag or large envelope
> 1–6 dice

- For this you will need a bag containing 20 counters in three different colours, in different amounts, for example 10 red, 5 blue and 5 green.
- Ask a student to take a counter from the bag without looking inside. Write the colour chosen on the board. Replace the counter.
- Shake the bag and repeat the activity 10 times.
- The results on the board should be similar to: R, B, R, G, G, R, R, G, B, R.
- Tell the class that there are 20 counters in the bag.
- Ask the students to write down how many counters of each colour they think are in the bag.
- Show the class the counters.
- Discuss how they decided how many counters of each colour there were.
- Emphasise chance and expectation.

Main lesson activity

- Ask the class to explain the term **chance** by giving everyday examples. Write them on the board. For example, the chance of getting a 6 when throwing a normal dice, the chance of rain tomorrow, the chance of winning the lottery.
- Draw the **probability scale** on the board:

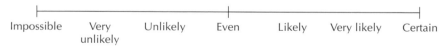

Impossible   Very unlikely   Unlikely   Even   Likely   Very likely   Certain

- Ask the class to give examples of **events** which are described by any of the above terms.
- Explain that **probability** is the mathematical way of describing the chance that something will happen.
- Ask what other terms they know that describe probability, for example fair chance, 50-50 chance, uncertain.
- Tell the class that to describe probability more accurately we use a scale from 0 to 1:

0 $\frac{1}{2}$ 1

- Throw a coin. Ask the class to write down all of the possible ways the coin can land.
  Each way is called an **outcome of the event**. For throwing a coin, the outcomes are:
      Head (H) or Tail (T).

Each outcome is **equally likely** to happen because the coin is **fair**.

Since there are two equally likely outcomes, the probability of getting a Head is 1 out of 2. This is written as:

$$P \text{ (Head)} = \tfrac{1}{2} \text{ or } P \text{ (H)} = \tfrac{1}{2}$$

- Probability is usually written as a fraction or a decimal, although percentages can be used, as in weather forecasts. Probability fractions sometimes cancel down.
- Throw a 1–6 dice. Ask the class to write down all the equally likely outcomes (1, 2, 3, 4, 5, 6). Hence:

$$P \text{ (6)} = \tfrac{1}{6} \text{ and } P \text{ (1 or 2)} = \tfrac{2}{6} = \tfrac{1}{3}$$

- **The class can now do PCM 9.1.** Discuss the differences in the bar charts.
- **The class can now do Exercise 9A from the Pupil Workbook.**

Exercise 9A   **Answers**

1 a Likely b Likely c Impossible d Even e Unlikely
  f Certain g Likely (various)
2 a $\tfrac{1}{2}$ b 0 c $\tfrac{1}{4}$ d 1 e $\tfrac{3}{4}$
3 a $\tfrac{6}{10} = \tfrac{3}{5}$ b $\tfrac{3}{10}$ c $\tfrac{1}{10}$ d 0 e $\tfrac{4}{10} = \tfrac{2}{5}$

Plenary

- Use another bag of counters with 12 red, 5 blue and 3 green.
- Show the students the 'results' of an experiment, which involves taking out counters at random.

	Red	Blue	Green
After 10 tries	5	2	3
After 100 tries	55	29	16
After 2000 tries	1196	508	296

- Ask the students if they think there are any black counters in the bag.
- Could they be absolutely sure?
- Ask the students to estimate how many counters of each colour are in the bag.
- Ask which row of the table they used to work this out.
- Discuss the reliability of the results.
- Show the students how many counters were in the bag.

Key words

- certain
- chance
- even chance
- equally likely
- event
- outcome
- fair
- likely
- possible
- impossible
- probability
- probability scale

LESSON 9.2

Framework objectives – Calculating probabilities
Find and justify probabilities based on equally likely outcomes in simple contexts.

Oral and mental starter

Resources required

OHT 9.1 Complements to 1
PCM 9.2 Play your cards right
Counting stick

- Write 10 fractions and/or decimals on the board or use OHT 9.1.
- Ask the class what is needed to make each one add up to 1. Write the correct answer on the board or the OHT. To help them, you may wish to use a number line drawn on the board, or a 'counting stick' with 10 divisions marked on. Mark it at one end with 0 and at the other end with 1.

0 ———————————————————————— 1

- Discuss methods for working out the **complement** of a fraction.

Main lesson activity

- Ask the class to give you an example of an event for which you can predict the probability, for example, getting a head with a coin.
- Write the suggestions on the board and, if possible, write down the probability, for example throwing a six with a dice $\frac{1}{6}$, or winning a raffle.
- Now put the following word on the board:

STATISTICS

- Ask the class to imagine that the letters are in a bag and that you are going to take one out at random.
- Explain that 'at random' means without looking or that each letter has an equal chance of being picked.
- Ask the class to give you the probability of picking the letter T $(\frac{3}{10})$.
- Ask the class to give you the probability of picking the letter I $(\frac{2}{10} = \frac{1}{5})$.
- Ask them for the probability of picking a vowel $(\frac{3}{10})$.
- Now ask them for the probability of picking a consonant $(\frac{7}{10})$.
- Ask if there is a connection between the last answers.
- They should see that vowel and consonant are all the possible outcomes and that the probabilities add up to 1.
- Now explain to the class that one letter (C) has been taken away and not replaced.
- What is the probability of getting a T now $(\frac{3}{9} = \frac{1}{3})$?
- Remind the class of the method used to calculate probabilities:

$$\text{Probability of an event } (P) = \frac{\text{Number of outcomes in the event}}{\text{Total number of all possible outcomes}}$$

- **The class can now do PCM 9.2.**
- **The class can now do Exercise 9B from the Pupil Workbook.**

Exercise 9B   Answers

1 $\frac{3}{7}$

2 $\frac{7}{10}, \frac{3}{10}$

3 $\frac{5}{8}, \frac{3}{8}$

4 $\frac{2}{5}, \frac{3}{5}$

5 $\frac{1}{8}, \frac{7}{8}$

6 $\frac{1}{2}, \frac{1}{2}$

7 $\frac{1}{6}, \frac{3}{6} = \frac{1}{2}$

8 $\frac{3}{10}, \frac{7}{10}$

9 $\frac{2}{11}, \frac{4}{11}, \frac{7}{11}$

10 $\frac{5}{100} = \frac{1}{20}$

Plenary

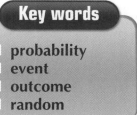

Key words

- ☐ **probability**
- ☐ **event**
- ☐ **outcome**
- ☐ **random**

- Emphasise the fact that the probability of all events is 1.
- Emphasise that probabilities can never be greater than 1.
- Emphasise that probabilities can never be less than 0.
- Ask what the probability of a certain event is (1) and that of an impossible event (0).

Framework objectives – Experimental probability 1
Estimate probabilities by collecting data from a simple experiment and recording it in a frequency table.

Oral and mental starter

- Write five colours on the board or on an OHT.
- Ask the students to each choose one of the colours but not to reveal it. They could write it down on a white board.
- Now ask them to hold up their boards to reveal their colours.
- Count up each colour.
- Ask the class how you could record these results.
- Encourage them to suggest alternative methods, for example tally charts, or counting and recording the frequencies.
- Make a table of the class results.
- Now lead onto probability by asking the students whether it is possible to predict the colour that someone entering the room would choose.
- Point out that although the most popular colour has the best chance of being chosen, the person may choose one of the others.

Main lesson activity

- Explain that you are going to ask all the students to throw a dice 6 times and record the results.
- Before they do that, ask the students how many times they would expect to get a 1 or 2, etc.
- They should appreciate that there should be one of each value in 6 throws.
- Ask them if this will happen. Ask why not.
- Explain that chance is random (any result is possible) and that 6 sixes is a possibility.
- Now give each student a dice and ask them to throw it 6 times and record the results (throwing the dice on an exercise book makes this a much quieter activity).
- Once this is done set up a table on the board like this:

Score

Number of throws	1	2	3	4	5	6
6						
12						
30						
60						
All class						

- Choose one student and fill in their results in row 1.
- Choose two students and put their combined results in row 2.
- Repeat with 5 sets of collected results, then 10, then the whole class.
- Discuss whether the results are what is expected.
- Keep a record of the results for the next lesson.

- **The class can now complete Exercise 9C from the Pupil Workbook.**

Exercise 9C   Answers

1 Own investigation – results may vary
2 a i 10 ii 10
  b Own experiment – results may vary
  c Own experiment – results may vary
3 a i 10 ii 10 iii 10 iv 10 v 10 vi 10
  b Own experiment – results may vary
  c Own experiment – results may vary

Plenary

● Choose one of the experiments from Exercise 9C.
● Discuss the results.
● Ensure that students know that the outcomes of experiments will not always be the same.

Key words

☐ repeated experiment
☐ different outcomes

LESSON 9.4

Framework objectives – Experimental probability 2
Compare experimental and theoretical probabilities in simple contexts.

Oral and mental starter

Resources required

PCM 9.3 Biased dice
PCM 9.4 Toast
Drawing pins
Coins

- Use two boards marked with grids, as shown on the right.
- The letters could be replaced by colours: R, red; B, blue; G, green; Y, yellow.
- Hold up the first grid and ask the students which colour there is most of, and which there is least of.
- Now repeat with the second grid.
- You could now increase the level of difficulty by putting one grid below the other, as shown, and counting the colours out of 20. Then, by covering columns, there could be, say, 16 colours and so on.
- Write the following words, in random order, on the board.

    Impossible   Very unlikely   Unlikely   Even chance   Likely   Very likely   Certain

    Ask the class to give you a sentence using these words. For example:

    'There is an even chance of picking red for the first grid.'
    'It is impossible to pick yellow for the first grid.'

- Repeat for each colour on each grid.

R	R	R	R	R
B	B	B	G	G

R	R	R	R	B
G	G	G	Y	Y

Main lesson activity

- Put the results of the last lesson's experiment with rolling dice on an OHP. Show this to the class.
- Ask what the probability is of throwing a 1 with a dice.
- Point out that this is 0.1666 as a decimal.
- Compare this with the probability of a 1 from the first row of just 6 throws.
- Then compare this with the experimental probabilities from the other rows.
- Hopefully, the final row will give the most accurate results.
- Ask why the final row will give the most reliable results.
- Explain to the class that you want to be able to predict whether, for example, the next person who comes through the door watches 'Eastenders'. Ask how they would collect the information needed.
- Note on the board any key words that are given. For example: tally, observation sheet, survey, sample.
- Conduct a survey of the class by recording data about their hair colour.
- Now use the results to obtain the experimental probability. Allow the class time to put this information into their books.
- Discuss if the results for hair colour would be useful for predicting the hair colour of the whole school.
- Ask students how many people should be surveyed to get a reliable estimate of hair colour of the school (30 or 10%).
- Tell the students that they will often be asked to criticise an experiment. One common criticism is that there were not enough **trials**.
- Tell them that experimental results may be unreliable.

© HarperCollins*Publishers* Ltd 2008

- Now ask them to explain the word **fair**. Discuss the meaning in the context of a dice or spinner.
- Introduce the word **bias**. Encourage the students to associate the words fair and biased (not fair).

- **The class can now do PCM 9.3.** Discuss the results of the experiment.
- **The class can now do PCM 9.4 followed by Exercise 9D from the Pupil Workbook.**

Exercise 9D **Answers**

Own experiments – results may vary

Plenary

- Discuss the outcomes of Question 2 in Exercise 9D and collect together all the results for the class for a Head and a Tail.
- Hopefully these will be just about equal.
- Remind the class that experiments are prone to errors, but that the more trials carried out, the more reliable the results tend to be.

Key words
- fair
- bias
- repeated experiment
- trials
- different outcomes
- estimate

Geometry and measures 3

Framework objectives – Line symmetry and reflection
Understand and use the language and notation associated with reflections.
Identify the line symmetry of 2-D shapes.

Oral and mental starter

Resources required

PCM 10.1 Reflections
OHT 10.1 Line symmetry
Mirrors (these can be made
  with silver tape and card)
Tracing paper
Shapes cut from paper
  (see below)

- Prepare a kite, square, rectangle, isosceles triangle, equilateral triangle, regular hexagon, regular octagon, oval and circle on sheets of A4 paper and cut them out.
- Fold them once or twice along lines of symmetry.
- Explain to the class that you will be showing them shapes that have been folded once or twice.
- Show the folded shapes to the class and ask them to name the shape they will see when it is unfolded. For example:

 could be a square or an isosceles triangle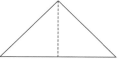

- Open out the shapes to see if the students were correct.
- Ask if they know the correct name for the fold (**line of symmetry**).

Main lesson activity

- Give students mirrors, if available, and tracing paper.
- Tell the students that they are going to use a mirror to see a **reflected** shape. Explain how to hold a mirror vertically along the mirror line, then look into it at an angle.
- Now tell students that they are going to use tracing paper to find a reflected shape. Explain how to trace the shape and the mirror line, then fold the paper along the mirror line.

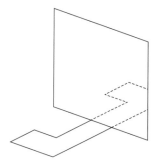

- **The class can now do PCM 10.1.**

- Use OHT 10.1 together with three square pieces of card, cut to the same size as the squares on the OHT.
- Ask students to come to the OHP and add one, two or three pieces to the diagram to make a shape with a line of symmetry.

- **The class can now do Exercise 10A from the Pupil Workbook.**

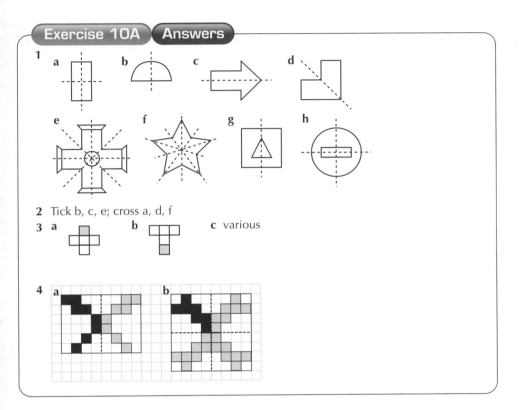

Exercise 10A **Answers**

1 a   b   c   d

e   f   g   h

2 Tick b, c, e; cross a, d, f

3 a   b   c various

4 a   b

Plenary

- Discuss some of the key facts about reflections.

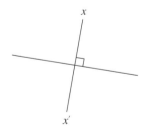

- Ask students how far a point (x) and its **image** (x') are from the mirror line (same distance).
- Ask students what angle the line joining a point and its image makes with the mirror line (right angle).

Framework objectives – Rotation symmetry
Understand and use the language and notation associated with rotations.
Identify the rotational symmetry of 2-D shapes.

Oral and mental starter

Resources required

OHT 10.1 Line symmetry
OHT 10.2 Alphabet
PCM 10.2 Rotations
Tracing paper

- Display OHT 10.2 and ask students which letters have line symmetry.
- Identify each one and ask how many lines of symmetry each has.

    A (1), B (1), C (1), D (1), E (1), H (2), I (2), M (1), O (2),
    T (1), U (1), V (1), W (1), X (2), Y (1)

- Ask students which letters would look the same if the OHT was turned through half a turn.

    H, I, N, O, S, X, Z

- Explain that this is called **rotation symmetry**.

Main lesson activity

- Distribute tracing paper and PCM 10.2.
- Explain how to use tracing paper to find rotation symmetry.
- The first shape has rotation symmetry of **order** 4.
- Explain the terminology, 'order of …', and notation, ↻ 4.
- Ask students what the order of the second shape is.
- They may say 'It hasn't got any' or 'none' or 'one'. All of these answers are correct. There is no recognised method of describing rotation symmetry for shapes without any. To avoid confusion agree to call such shapes 'of order 1'.
- Ask the class to find the order of symmetry of the rest of the shapes.
- Some of the latter shapes do not have a **centre** marked on them.
- Students should decide for themselves where the centre is.
- Use OHT 10.1 together with three square pieces of card, cut to the same size as the squares on the OHT.
- Ask students to come to the OHP and add one, two or three pieces to the diagram to make a shape with rotation symmetry.
- **The class can now do Exercise 10B from the Pupil Workbook.**

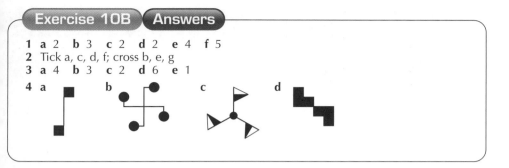

Exercise 10B   Answers

1 a 2 **b** 3 **c** 2 **d** 2 **e** 4 **f** 5
2 Tick a, c, d, f; cross b, e, g
3 a 4 **b** 3 **c** 2 **d** 6 **e** 1
4 a   **b**   **c**   **d**

Plenary

- Discuss some of the key facts about rotations.
- Ask students what you must have for rotation symmetry (a centre).
- Ask students what angle the shape rotates through to look the same, if it has rotation symmetry of order 4 (90°).
- Ask them if they could make this shape into a shape with rotation symmetry of order 4.

- These diagrams show possible answers using four cut-out shapes.

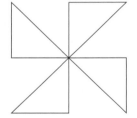   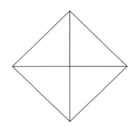

Key words
- [ ] **rotation**
- [ ] **rotation symmetry**
- [ ] **centre**
- [ ] **order**

LESSON 10.3

Framework objectives – Scale drawings
Make and interpret scale drawings.

Oral and mental starter

Resources required

PCM 10.3 Scale drawings
Metre rulers and/or tape
  measures
Ordnance Survey map
Student white boards

- This starter will give practice in estimating length.
- Students will need rulers and possibly a tape measure for this activity. It is best done using individual white boards, but students can give their answers orally.
- Ask a student to select an object in the classroom.
- Ask the rest of the class to estimate the length of the object and to write their answer on their white boards.
- Ask the first student to measure the actual length of the object.
- The students can now show their estimates on their white boards. Some discussion of the units used may be a useful exercise.
- The student whose estimate is closest to the actual length wins a point.
- The activity can be repeated with a different student selecting another object.

Main lesson activity

- Explain to the class that the lesson is about using and making **scale drawings**.
- Draw on the board, or OHT, a scale drawing to show the dimensions of a room in school, for example a classroom, the school hall or gym.
- You could provide a tape measure or metre rule and ask a student to measure this room for you.

8 m

6 m

Scale: 1 cm to 2 m

- Explain to the class the importance of choosing a sensible **scale**. It might be worth pointing out that if you double the scale, the scale drawing is halved in size.
- Show the class how to find the actual length and width of the room by using the scale.

- **The class can now do PCM 10.3 followed by Exercise 10C from the Pupil Workbook.**

Exercise 10C (Answers)

1 Reading clockwise from top 10 cm, 6 cm, 8 cm, 4 cm, 2 cm

2

Length of line on scale drawing	Actual length of line
2 cm	6 cm
5 cm	15 cm
10 cm	30 cm
7 cm	21 cm
4 cm	12 cm
6 cm	18 cm
1 cm	3 cm
20 cm	60 cm

3 $D = 20$ cm, $d = 15$ cm, $h = 40$ cm, $L = 70$ cm, $w = 20$ cm
4 Measure size of student drawings

Plenary

Key words

- plan
- scale
- scale drawing

- Show students an Ordnance Survey map. Ask them if they know what it is.
- They should be familiar with these from Geography but if not explain that it is a section of a huge map of Great Britain.
- Ask them if they know the scale.
- Show them the scale on the cover. A standard OS map is 1 : 50 000 or 2 cm to 1 km.
- To put this in context show them a millimetre on a ruler. On the map this would represent 50 metres.
- Ask students how they would make a scale drawing of their bedroom.
- Students should describe a process such as the following:

  1 Sketch a rough **plan**. (A student could be asked to sketch their bedroom on the board.) Point out that only the walls and door are needed, not the furniture.
  2 Measure all of the lengths.
  3 Decide on a scale.
  4 Make a scale drawing.

- Emphasise the need to measure accurately and to pick a sensible scale.
- You could mention that this task will be the homework.

LESSON 10.4

Framework objectives – Coordinates in all four quadrants
Generate points in all four quadrants.

Oral and mental starter

Resources required

OHT 10.3 Coordinates 1
OHT 10.4 Coordinates 2
OHT 10.5 Coordinates 3
PCM 10.4 Coordinates 4
2 different coloured OHT pens

- Display OHT 10.3 and divide the class into two teams, or pick two individuals.
- Choose one student as the marker and ask each team (or student) to read out a pair of coordinates.
- The marker uses a red pen to mark, for example, a cross on the coordinates for team A.
- Check that points are plotted correctly and that the convention of x followed by y is used.
- Team B now chooses a pair of coordinates.
- The first team with three crosses in a line wins.
- Note that 'in a line' can include examples such as those shown on the right.
- Now display OHT 10.4 and explain that this is a coordinate grid marked in tenths.
- Indicate points on the grid and ask students to give the coordinates.
- Repeat until students can give coordinates using decimals accurately.

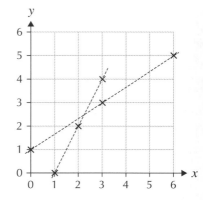

Main lesson activity

- Remind the students that **coordinates** are used to locate a point on a **grid**. Draw, on the board or on an OHT, the grid shown on the right, or use OHT 10.3.
- Establish the meaning of **axes**, the **x-axis**, the **y-axis** and the **origin** and that coordinates are written in the form (x, y).
- Remind the students that the first number is the **x-coordinate**, which is the number of units across the grid and the second number is the **y-coordinate**, which is the number of units up the grid. Use the point A as an example.
- The point A has coordinates $(4, 3)$ and can be written as A$(4, 3)$.
- Plot other points on the grid and ask the class to write down their coordinates.
- Emphasise the need to plot coordinates using a cross.
- Explain that the grid can be extended to use negative numbers.
- Draw on the board the grid shown on the right or use OHT 10.5.
- Explain that the grid is divided into four **quadrants**.
- Explain how to write down the coordinates of the four points:

    A$(4, 2)$, B$(-4, 2)$, C$(-4, -2)$ and D$(4, -2)$.

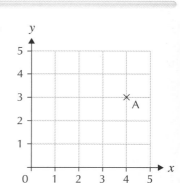

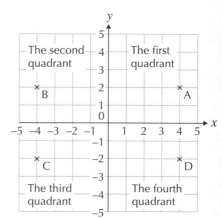

- Plot other points on the grid and ask the class to write down their coordinates.
- Emphasise that the x value is given first, followed by the y value.

- **The class can now do PCM 10.4. Check accuracy of reading scales and estimations.**

- **The class can now do Exercise 10D from the Pupil Workbook.**

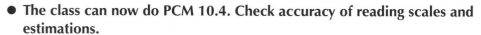

Exercise 10D **Answers**

1 a C **b** A **c** G **d** B **e** E **f** D **g** F **h** H **i** J

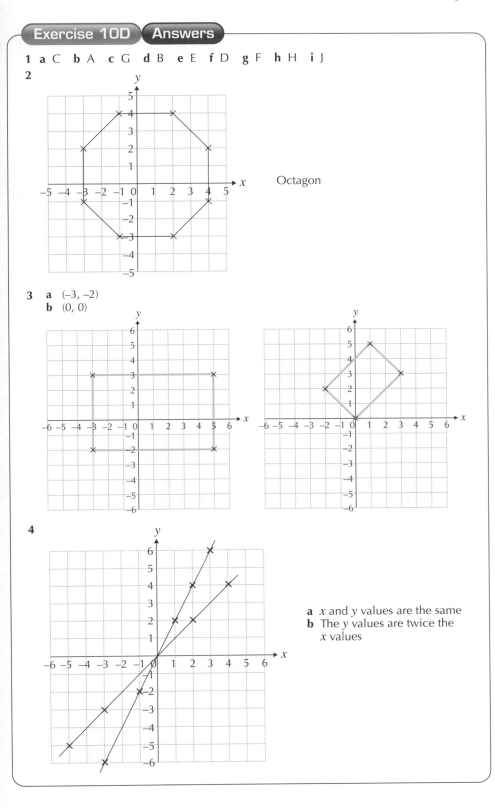

2

Octagon

3 a (–3, –2)
  b (0, 0)

4

a *x* and *y* values are the same
b The *y* values are twice the *x* values

Plenary

● Display OHT 10.4 or 10.5 and ask the class to write down the coordinates of the points as you point to them.

Key words

☐ **axis**
☐ **axes**
☐ **coordinates**
☐ **grid**
☐ **origin**
☐ **quadrant**
☐ ***x*-axis**
☐ ***y*-axis**
☐ ***x*-coordinate**
☐ ***y*-coordinate**
☐ **decimals**

Algebra 5

Framework objectives – BODMAS
Use the order of operations, including brackets.

Oral and mental starter

Resources required

OHT 11.1 BODMAS
PCM 11.1 BODMAS

- Write the following operations on the board, or display the relevant part of OHT 11.1.

$+5$ ⟩ $×2$ ⟩ -4 ⟩ $÷2$ ⟩

- Ask the students to arrange the **operations** in any **order**.
- Ask them to pick a number and work through the operations in the order they have chosen, then subtract their original number. For example, the order as above, starting with 7, gives:

$$7 \rightarrow 12 \rightarrow 24 \rightarrow 20 \rightarrow 10 \rightarrow 3$$

(Note that there are 24 possible arrangements of the operations, but only seven answers: –3, –1.5, 0.5, 1, 2, 3, 6.)

- Discuss whether the order of the operations matters. For the four operations above, for example, the answer is always 1 if $÷ 2$ and $× 2$ are consecutive.

Main lesson activity

- This is a revision lesson on BODMAS, covered in Year 7.
- Recall the meaning of BODMAS and what it implies using Examples 1 and 2 below.

> **Example 1** Work out the value of
> $2 × 3 + 4$ (10) $2 × (3 + 4)$ (14)
> $2 + 3 × 4$ (14) $2 + 3^2$ (11)

> **Example 2** Put brackets into these to make them true.
> $2 × 5 + 4 = 18$ $(2 × (5 + 4) = 18)$ $5 + 2^2 × 2 = 18$ $((5 + 2^2) × 2 = 18)$

- Emphasise the important rules, and that addition and subtraction are of equal worth if there are no other operations in the calculation; the same is true for multiplication and division. For these calculations work from left to right.
- Work through some more complex examples, such as those below.

> $4 × 2^2 – 12 ÷ 4$
> Firstly, work out the **power** $4 × 4 – 12 ÷ 4$
> Secondly, the division and the multiplication $16 – 3$
> Finally, the subtraction 13

© HarperCollins*Publishers* Ltd 2008

$(5 + 4)^2 \times 4 \div 6$

Firstly, work out the **bracket**	$9^2 \times 4 \div 6$
Secondly, the power	$81 \times 4 \div 6$
Thirdly, the multiplication	$324 \div 6$
Finally, the division	54

Point out that the order in the last two steps is decided by working from left to right.

● Work through more examples as necessary.

● **The class can now do PCM 11.1 followed by Exercise 11A from the Pupil Workbook.**

Exercise 11A **Answers**

1 a $6 + 12 = 18$ b $44 + 4 = 48$ c $36 - 24 = 12$ d $50 - 35 = 15$ e $15 - 8 = 7$
  f $18 - 9 = 9$
2 a $15 + 12 = 27$ b $25 - 21 = 4$ c $32 - 4 = 28$ d $5 + 8 = 13$ e $7 + 16 = 23$
  f $27 - 9 = 18$
3 a $21 \div 7 = 3$ b $3 \times 6 = 18$ c $3 \times 8 = 24$ d $25 \times 6 = 150$ e $30 \div 3 = 10$
  f $10 \times 16 = 160$
4 a $7 + 15 + 4 = 26$ b $18 - 8 + 2 = 12$ c $4 \times 4 + 3 = 16 + 3 = 19$
  d $19 + 7 \times 5 = 19 + 35 = 54$

Plenary

Key words

- bracket
- order
- power
- operation
- priority

● Ask the class, 'Which operation comes first: multiplication or division? What about addition or subtraction?' Make sure students understand that neither operation takes precedence within these pairs, but when there is a choice between them, they must work from left to right.

● Write a complex calculation on the board, such as:

$$(5^2 - 2) \times 4 + (8 - 6) \div (2^2 \div 16)$$

● Discuss the order of operations and evaluate the above in order (or ask students if they can do it):

Firstly, the powers inside the brackets	$(25 - 2) \times 4 + (8 - 6) \div (4 \div 16)$
Secondly, each bracket	$23 \times 4 + 2 \div \frac{1}{4}$
Thirdly, multiplication and division	$92 + 8$
Finally, the addition	100

Framework objectives – Expanding brackets
Begin to multiply a single term over a bracket (integer coefficients).

Oral and mental starter

> **Resources required**
>
> PCM 11.2 Perimeters and areas

- Ask the class if they can divide 420 by 5 in their heads, without writing anything down.
- It is most unlikely that anyone can. The answer is 84. If anyone is able to give the answer, ask that student to tell the class how they did it.
- Explain that this can be done in two ways. One way is to split 420 into, for example, 400 and 20. $400 \div 5 = 80$, $20 \div 5 = 4$, $80 + 4 = 84$. The other way is to divide by 10 (42) and double the answer.
- Ask them to divide the following numbers by 5.

  320 (64)   180 (36)   220 (44)

- Now reverse the process. Ask students to work out the answer to 5×56 mentally (280).
- Once again if anyone can do this ask them to explain how they did it.
- Explain that the calculation can be split into $5 \times 50 + 5 \times 6 = 250 + 30 = 280$.
- They may also realise that the value can be halved (28) then multiplied by 10.
- Repeat with 5×48 (240), 5×38 (190) and 5×26 (130).

Main lesson activity

- Write on the board $5(3 + 4)$ and ask the class what value this has. When someone suggests 35, ask them how they calculated it (they should say 5×7).
- Now show them that each **term** could have been multiplied out separately:

  $5 \times 3 + 5 \times 4$, which is $15 + 20 = 35$

  So, we can see that $5(3 + 4) = 5 \times 3 + 5 \times 4$.
- Repeat with:

  $4(9 + 2) \ = \ 4 \times 11$ or $4 \times 9 + 4 \times 2$ (44)
  $3(5 + 7) \ = \ 3 \times 12$ or $3 \times 5 + 3 \times 7$ (36)
  $4(7 - 2) \ = \ 4 \times 5$ or $4 \times 7 - 4 \times 2$ (20)

- Emphasise where the minus sign goes in the expansion.
- This process is called **expanding** or **multiplying out** a bracket. Work through a few more examples like this, such as:

  $2(4 + 5) = 2 \times 4 + 2 \times 5 = 18$ (Check: $2 \times 9 = 18$)

- Show how to use this technique to simplify an **expression**, such as $4(m + 3)$:

  $4(m + 3) = 4 \times m + 4 \times 3 = 4m + 12$

- Explain that, unlike in previous numerical examples, when working with letters we get an expression which cannot be simplified.
- Repeat with $3(2m - 7) = 6m - 21$ and $5(3p + 2) = 15p + 10$.

- Work through more examples as necessary.

- **The class can now do Exercise 11B from the Pupil Workbook with PCM 11.2 being used for more practice if necessary.**

Exercise 11B   **Answers**

1 **a** $6 + 12 = 18$ **b** $15 + 25 = 40$ **c** $28 - 20 = 8$ **d** $30 - 25 = 5$
   e $4 \times 3 + 4 \times 6 = 12 + 24 = 36$ **f** $5 \times 4 - 5 \times 2 = 20 - 10 = 10$
   g $3 \times 2 + 3 \times 7 = 6 + 21 = 27$ **h** $4 \times 6 - 4 \times 2 = 24 - 8 = 16$
2 **a** $5a$ **b** $7b$ **c** $9c$ **d** $4m$ **e** $2n$ **f** $8j$
3 **a** $4a + 20$ **b** $3b + 6$ **c** $2c - 6$ **d** $3 \times d + 3 \times 4 = 3d + 12$
   e $5 \times e + 5 \times 6 = 5e + 30$ **f** $3 \times f - 3 \times 7 = 3f - 21$

Plenary

Key words

- Ask the class what is meant by the word expression. Request some examples. Ensure that none includes an equals sign.
- Then ask what is meant in algebra by the word expand. Ask for an example of a term outside a bracket and the process involved in multiplying out the bracket.
- Put two or three expressions on the board, all containing brackets. Ask the class to tell you how to simplify them.

- bracket
- expand
- expression
- term
- multiply out

Framework objectives – Solving equations

Construct and solve simple linear equations with integer coefficients (unknown on one side only) using an appropriate method (e.g. inverse operations).

Oral and mental starter

Resources required

OHT 11.2 Steps

- Put this diagram on the board or use OHT 11.2.

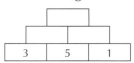

| 3 | 5 | 1 |

- Explain that the numbers in two adjacent blocks are added together and the total put in the box directly above. Do this with the class to end up with the diagram:

```
      14
   8      6
 3    5    1
```

- Ask the class what numbers you could start with in order to get 20 at the top. Let them try to work this out, either on their own or in pairs.
- There will be several different answers, one of which is:

```
      20
   5     15
 1    4    11
```

- Now ask them what numbers you could start with in order to get 25 at the top, but this time there must be an 8 somewhere in the bottom row.
- Again, there will be several different solutions, two of which are:

```
      25                      25
  12     13               10      15
 4    8    5             8    2    13
```

- You could continue with similar problems, such as getting 30 on top with 10 in the bottom row.

Main lesson activity

- Tell the class that, in this lesson, they will use mappings to help solve equations.
- Ask the class how $3x + 2 = 23$ might be written as a mapping.
- Explain that we call x the **unknown**.
- Go through how to solve this:

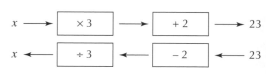

$$3x + 2 = 23$$

Subtract 2 from both sides $\quad 3x + 2 - 2 = 23 - 2$

$$3x = 21$$

Divide both sides by 3 $\quad x = 21 \div 3$

$$x = 7$$

- Go through another example: $5x + 3 = 18$.

- Establish the mapping and inverse mapping.
- Go through how to solve this:

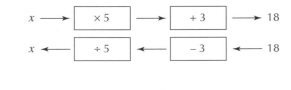

Subtract 3 from both sides $5x + 3 - 3 = 18 - 3$

$$5x = 15$$

Divide both sides by 5 $x = 15 \div 5$

$$x = 3$$

- Work through another equation: $6x - 1 = 23$.
- Establish the mapping:
- Go through how to solve this:

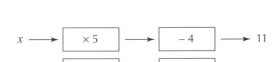

$$6x - 1 = 23$$

Add 1 to both sides $6x - 1 + 1 = 23 + 1$

$$6x = 24$$

Divide both sides by 6 $x = 24 \div 6$

$$x = 4$$

- Finally, write on the board $5x - 4 = 11$. Ask the students to give its mapping diagram.
- Go through how to solve this:

$$5x - 4 = 11$$

Add 4 to both sides $5x - 4 + 4 = 11 + 4$

$$5x = 15$$

Divide both sides by 5 $x = 15 \div 5$

$$x = 3$$

- **The class can now do Exercise 11C from the Pupil Workbook.**

Exercise 11C   Answers

1. a Subtract 3 from both sides, $2x = 4$
   Divide both sides by 2, $x = 2$
   b Subtract 4 from both sides, $3x = 12$
   Divide both sides by 3, $x = 4$
   c Subtract 1 from both sides, $4x = 8$
   Divide both sides by 4, $x = 2$
   d Add 3 to both sides, $2x = 12$
   Divide both sides by 2, $x = 6$
   e Add 5 to both sides, $3x = 18$
   Divide both sides by 3, $x = 6$
   f Add 7 to both sides, $4x = 16$
   Divide both sides by 4, $x = 4$
2. a Subtract 3 from both sides, $2x = 8$; Divide both sides by 2, $x = 4$
   b Subtract 5 from both sides, $3x = 6$; Divide both sides by 3, $x = 2$
   c Add 2 to both sides, $5x = 15$; Divide both sides by 5, $x = 3$
   d Add 1 to both sides, $6x = 12$; Divide both sides by 6, $x = 2$

Plenary

- Remind the class that all of the equations that they have met so far have had whole-number answers.
- Tell them that this is not always the case: for example, $10x + 3 = 11$.
- Go through the mapping and the inverse mapping to solve this equation.
- It will involve division of 8 by 10, which hopefully the class will be able to work out as 0.8. Some may need a calculator to do this.

Key words

- solution
- unknown
- inverse operations

LESSON 11.4

Framework objectives – Real-life graphs

Plot and interpret the graphs of simple linear functions arising from real-life situations, e.g. conversion graphs.

Oral and mental starter

Resources required

OHT 11.3 The Jones family
PCM 11.3 Graphs

- Display OHT 11.3 and explain that this shows the seven members of a family.
- Can they allocate the members of the family to the points on the graph?
- Discuss how they decide.
- A is baby Martin, B is Bill, C is Annie, D is Kim, E is Mum, F is Dad, G is Grandad.

Main lesson activity

- Sketch a grid on the board with the **axes** labelled Temperature (horizontal from 0 to 30°C) and Deckchairs (vertical from 0 to 100).
- Give the class the scene: 'At Whitby (or your local seaside resort), will a deckchair attendant hire out more deckchairs when it is hot or cold?' The response should be 'Hot'.
- Draw a cross on the grid at (30, 100) and ask if this is about right. Be prepared to alter it to a suitable suggestion.
- Now draw a cross on the grid at (5, 0) and ask if this is sensible. Again, alter this in response to a sensible suggestion.
- Draw a straight line between the two and ask if this shows the likely link between the temperature and the number of deckchairs.
- This could prompt a discussion on how the link would not be exactly like this, but that the line probably shows the correct **trend**.
- Explain that sketch graphs like this can be used to illustrate trends. They are not necessarily exactly correct, but are close to reality.
- Ask if anyone could sketch a graph to illustrate how a hot cup of coffee might cool over half an hour.
- A few volunteers should be ready to show this with axes labelled 'Time' and 'Temperature', and a graph showing coffee starting with a high temperature that decreases over time. A straight line is fine for this purpose, but more accurately it would be a curve. Do not discuss this with the class unless they mention it at the time.
- Ask volunteers how they decided which axis to use for time and which for temperature. They may simply be used to putting time on the horizontal axis. Tell the class that when time is involved, it nearly always goes along the horizontal axis.
- **The class can now do PCM 11.3.**
- **The class can now do Exercise 11D from the Pupil Workbook.**

Exercise 11D Answers

1 a £8 **b** £16 **c** 2 miles **d** 5 miles **e** $4\frac{1}{2}$ miles
2 a 9:30 am **b** 6 km **c** From 10 am to 10.30 am **d** 12 noon **e** 12 km
3 a 0°C **b** 8°C **c** 2°C **d** −4°C **e** −6°C **f** 12°C
   g 11th and 13th

Plenary

● Ask if any of the students would like to illustrate their journey to school by sketching a graph on the board. Give them scales of time and distance from school.
● Discuss the following: where to put starting and ending points; how to show time spent waiting; how to show different speeds.

Key words

☐ **axes**
☐ **distance–time graphs**
☐ **trends**
☐ **gradients**

Revision

Framework objectives – Revision of Number 1

Round positive whole numbers to the nearest 10, 100 or 1000 and decimals to the nearest whole number or one decimal place.

Compare and order decimals in different contexts.

Convert terminating decimals to fractions. Recognise the equivalence of fractions and decimals.

Identify equivalent fractions.

Use diagrams to compare two or more simple fractions.

Recognise the equivalence of percentages and fractions.

Understand percentage as the 'number of parts per 100'; calculate simple percentages.

Use ratio notation and simplify ratios.

Oral and mental starter

● The following is a 10-question, National Test-style, mental test on the theme of fractions. Repeat each question twice and allow students 10 seconds to answer.

  1 What percentage is the same as the fraction one quarter?

  2 Which of these fractions is equivalent to $\frac{3}{4}$? [Write the fractions on the board.]

    $\frac{3}{8}$ $\frac{12}{16}$ $\frac{6}{9}$ $\frac{5}{6}$

  3 Which of these decimals is the largest? [Write the decimals on the board.]

    0.23   0.203   0.2   0.3

  4 What is the missing number? [Write the equation on the board.]

    $\frac{2}{7} = \frac{\ldots}{21}$

  5 What is the next number in this sequence, where each number is one half of the previous number?

    Eighty, forty, twenty, ten, …

  6 What fraction of 1 metre is 75 centimetres? [Write 1 m and 75 cm on the board]

  7 One third of a number is 12. What is the number?

  8 Look at these numbers. Which one of them is the decimal equivalent of one-fifth? [Write the decimals on the board.]

    0.5   1.5   0.375   0.125   0.2

  9 What is half of 0.7?

 10 Write seven-tenths as a decimal.

Answers

1 25% **2** $\frac{12}{16}$ **3** 0.3 **4** 6 **5** 5 **6** $\frac{75}{100}$ or equivalent $\frac{3}{4}$ **7** 36
8 0.2 **9** 0.35 **10** 0.7

Main lesson activity

● This is a revision lesson on number, principally covering fractions, decimals and ratios.
● Before letting students start the questions you can go through key points (as suggested below) or discuss some specific questions with the class to remind them of the methods used.

General
○ Equivalence of fractions, percentages and decimals
○ Rounding numbers

Fractions
○ Equivalent fractions
○ Cancelling

Decimals
○ Ordering
○ Change of units for metric measures

Percentages
○ Finding simple percentages

Ratio
○ Cancelling to simplest form

● **The class can now do Exercise 12A from the Pupil Workbook.**

Exercise 12A   Answers

1 a 4.8   **b** 19.1   **c** 0.4
2 1300
3 0.45, 4.03, 4.3, 4.5, 5.4
4 a Musik   **b** CD World
5 a $\frac{1}{4}$, 0.25   **b** $\frac{3}{10}$, 0.3
6 $\frac{1}{2}$, $\frac{50}{100}$, $\frac{5}{10}$ should be circled
7 a $\frac{5}{7}$, $\frac{15}{21}$ is bigger than $\frac{14}{21}$
   b $\frac{2}{3}$, $\frac{16}{24}$ is bigger than $\frac{15}{24}$
8 a <   **b** >   **c** =   **d** >
9 a 90%   **b** 40%   **c** 15%
10 a $\frac{1}{4}$ **b** $\frac{3}{5}$ **c** $\frac{9}{20}$
11 a £8   **b i** £24   **ii** £104
12 28.52
13 a 1 : 4   **b** 3 : 2   **c** 1 : 6   **d** 4 : 1

Plenary

● Go through the answers to the exercise. Discuss and clarify those with
which students had difficulty.

LESSON 12.2

Framework objectives – Revision of Number 2

Multiply and divide integers and decimals by 10, 100, 1000 and explain the effect.

Use efficient written methods to add and subtract whole numbers and decimals with up to two decimal places.

Multiply and divide decimals with one or two places by single-digit whole numbers.

Identify the necessary information to understand or simplify a context or problem.

Represent problems, making correct use of symbols. Use appropriate procedures.

Oral and mental starter

Resources required

OHT 12.1 Diagrams 1

- The following is a 10-question, National Test-style, mental test on the theme of percentages. Repeat each question twice and allow students 10 seconds to answer. The diagrams are on OHT 12.1.

  1 In a group of 60 animals, 30 were rabbits. What percentage were rabbits?
  2 The pie chart shows information about the favourite food of some children. What percentage of the children did not pick burgers?
  3 What percentage is the same as the fraction one-fifth?
  4 What is 10% of £35?
  5 What is 20% of £200?
  6 A survey identified how many people in a village owned dogs. The percentage bar chart shows the results of the survey. Estimate the percentage of the people who do own dogs.

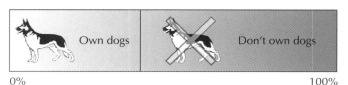

0%   100%

  7 Fifty percent of a number is nine. What is the number?
  8 A CD costing £20 is reduced in a sale by 10%. What is the new price of the CD?
  9 A box of 50 chocolates has 20 that have soft centres. What percentage of the chocolates have soft centres?
 10 Twenty-five percent of a number is six. What is the number?

Answers
1 50%   **2** 65–70%   **3** 20%   **4** £3.50   **5** £40   **6** 35–45%   **7** 18
8 £18   **9** 40%   **10** 24

Main lesson activity

- This is a revision lesson on number, principally covering the four operations.
- Before letting students start the questions you can go through key points (as suggested below) or discuss some specific questions with the class to remind them of the methods used.

General
○ Basic knowledge of tables up to 10 × 10

Four rules
○ Setting out in columns for addition and subtraction
○ Using box method or column methods for long multiplication
○ Using chunking for long division

Power

○ Powers of 10
○ Multiplying and dividing by powers of 10

● **The class can now do Exercise 12B from the Pupil Workbook.**

Exercise 12B **Answers**

1 a 48 **b** 90 **c** 181 **d** 21 **e** 49 **f** 62 **g** 56 **h** 120 **i** 45
2 $1 \times 54, 2 \times 27, 3 \times 18, 6 \times 9$
3 One million 10^6
   10 000 10^4
   Ten 10^1
   One hundred 10^2
   1000 10^3
4 a 1214 **b** 5250 **c** 16.36 **d** 679 **e** 468 **f** 4.66 **g** 4466 **h** 2275
   i 15.56 **j** 73 **k** 119 **l** 0.96
5 a £3.49 + 2 × £2.75 = £8.99 **b** 2 × £4.29 + 4 × £3.20 = £21.38

Plenary

● Go through the answers to the exercise. Discuss and clarify those with
which students had difficulty.

LESSON
12.3

Framework objectives – Revision of Algebra 1

Describe integer sequences; generate terms of a simple sequence, given a rule.

Know the meanings of the word function. Express simple functions in words.

Generate coordinate pairs that satisfy a simple linear rule.

Recognise and use multiples and factors.

Recognise and use highest common factor and lowest common multiple in simple cases.

Recognise and use prime numbers less than 100.

Use squares and positive square roots.

Use cube numbers and cube roots.

Oral and mental starter

- The following is a 20-question, National Test-style, mental test on the theme of the four rules. Repeat each question twice and allow students 10 seconds to answer.
  1 Add the following numbers. [Write 78 and 74 on the board.]
  2 What number do you have to add to 123 to make 200?
  3 Multiply eight by seven.
  4 What number multiplied by nine makes one hundred and eight?
  5 Write the number thirty-four thousand and seventy-nine in figures.
  6 Write down the number that is three less than minus six.
  7 Four boxes of pencils cost £6. How much will seven boxes of pencils cost?
  8 Multiply nought point seven by ten.
  9 A chocolate bar costs one pound and forty pence. I buy four bars. How much change will I get from a ten pound note?
  10 I am thinking of two numbers. When I add them together I get nine. When I multiply them together I get twenty. What are the numbers?
  11 Multiply six by nought point five.
  12 Double sixty-six.
  13 What is the total cost of five video tapes at four pounds ninety-five pence each?
  14 How many seconds are there in 15 minutes?
  15 Work out the value of two squared times three squared.
     [Write $2^2 \times 3^2$ on the board.]
  16 What is three minus nought point two?
  17 How much must be added to this number to make 100? [Write 63.5 on the board.]
  18 Multiply together two, three and five.
  19 I have saved £7 in twenty pence coins. How many coins is that?
  20 Divide thirty by nought point five.

Answers

  1 152   2 77   3 56   4 12   5 34 079   6 –9   7 £10.50   8 7
  9 £4.40   10 4 and 5   11 3   12 132   13 £24.75   14 900   15 36
  16 2.8   17 36.5   18 30   19 35   20 60

Main lesson activity

- This is a revision lesson on algebra.
- Before letting students start the questions you can go through key points (as suggested below) or discuss some specific questions with the class to remind them of the methods used.

Sequences
○ Term-to-term rules

Functions
○ Input values, output values
○ Functions

Multiples, factors and primes
○ Definition of a multiple
○ Definition of a factor
○ Definition of a prime
○ Learning the primes up to 20

Squares, cubes and their roots
○ Definition
○ Powers
○ Notation

- **The class can now do Exercise 12C from the Pupil Workbook.**

Exercise 12C **Answers**

1 **a** 35 and 39 **b** 36 and 21
2 8, 5, 2, –1, –4
3 **a** 12, 7, 10 **b** 14, 17, 30, 33, 4, 8
4 **a** 26 **b** 44
5 $1 \times 18, 2 \times 9, 3 \times 6$
6 1, 2, 4, 8; 1, 3, 5, 15; 1
7 2, 5, 11, 17
8 **a** 9 **b** 16 **c** 49 **d** 100 **e** 27 **f** 8 **g** 125 **h** 81 **i** 1
9 **a** 3 **b** 8 **c** 10 **d** 7 **e** 2 **f** 1 **g** 10 **h** 2 **i** 5

Plenary

- Go through the answers to the exercise. Discuss and clarify those with which students had difficulty.

Framework objectives – Revision of Algebra 2

Know the meanings of the word function. Express simple functions in words.

Generate coordinate pairs that satisfy a simple linear rule.

Use letter symbols to represent unknown numbers. Understand that algebraic operations follow the rules of arithmetic.

Plot the graphs of simple linear functions, where *y* is given explicitly in terms of *x*.

Simplify linear algebraic expressions by collecting like terms. Substitute positive integers into linear expressions.

Use formulae from mathematics and other subjects; substitute integers into simple formulae.

Construct and solve simple linear equations with integer coefficients (unknown on one side only) using an appropriate method (e.g. inverse operation).

Use the order of operations, including brackets.

Oral and mental starter

Resources required

PCM 12.1 Diagrams

- The following is a 10-question, National Test-style, mental test on the theme of reading diagrams. Repeat each question twice and allow students 10 seconds to answer. The diagrams are on PCM 12.1. Distribute this to the class.
  1 What number is the arrow pointing to?
  2 The pie chart shows the number of boys and girls in a youth club. There are 15 girls. How many boys are there?
  3 Estimate the length of this line in centimetres.
  4 The bar chart shows the number of children in some families. How many families are represented?
  5 What is the area of the shaded square?
  6 When the weather gets hotter the sales of ice-cream go up. Which of the diagrams shows this relationship?
  7 Use the timetable to find out how long the journey is from Barnsley to High Green.
  8 What number is the arrow pointing to?
  9 Add one more square to this grid so that it has rotational symmetry of order 2.
  10 Which diagram shows the graph $x + y = 5$?

Answers

1 32   **2** 45   **3** 4.5–5.5 cm   **4** 21   **5** 10 squares   **6** c   **7** 44 minutes   **8** –1.4

9   **10** c

Main lesson activity

- This is a revision lesson on algebra.
- Before letting students start the questions you can go through key points (as suggested below) or discuss some specific questions with the class to remind them of the methods used.

Basic algebra
  ○ Using letters to represent variables
  ○ The difference between a term, an expression and an equation

Manipulative algebra
○ Substituting numbers into expressions
○ Expanding brackets
○ Collecting like terms

Linear equations
○ Rearranging – collecting together variables and numbers on the LHS and RHS respectively
○ Inverse operations (change sides, change signs)
○ Checking answers by substituting into original equation

Graphs
○ Order of coordinates (x followed by y)

BODMAS
○ Order of operations

● **The class can now do exercise 12D from the Pupil Workbook.**

Exercise 12D **Answers**

1 $7a - 4a, 3 \times a, a + a + a$
2 a $6a$ **b** $6a$ **c** $6a$ **d** $11a + 3b$ **e** $3n + 3$ **f** $1 + 8p$
3 a 12 **b** 2 **c** 45 **d** 11
4 $22, 18, 18$
5 a $x = 6$ **b** $b = 11$ **c** $a = 3$ **d** $m = 3$ **e** $a = 4$
6 Zoe has not used BODMAS rules, she should have worked out 24 divided by 4 first.
7 a 23 **b** 20 **c** 15 **d** 2 **e** 20
8 a $-1, 1, 3, 5, 7$
b

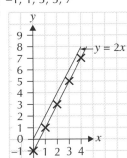

c The lines are parallel, they have the same gradient/slope

Plenary

● Go through the answers to the exercise. Discuss and clarify those with which students had difficulty.

LESSON 12.5

Framework objectives – Revision of Geometry and measures

Know the sum of angles in a triangle. Use angle properties of a quadrilateral.

Know and use the formula for the area of a rectangle; calculate the area of shapes made from rectangles.

Derive and use the formula for the area of a triangle.

Derive and use the formula for the area of a parallelogram.

Understand and use the language and notation associated with reflections. Identify the line symmetry of 2-D shapes.

Understand and use the language and notation associated with rotations. Identify the rotational symmetry of 2-D shapes.

Make and interpret scale drawings.

Generate points in all four quadrants.

Oral and mental starter

Resources required

OHT 12.2 Diagrams 2

- The following is a 10-question, National Test-style, mental test on the theme of Shape, space and measures. Repeat each question twice and allow students 10 seconds to answer. The diagrams are on OHT 12.2.

  1 How many lines of symmetry does a parallelogram have?

  2 A shape is folded in half along its only line of symmetry. After folding it looks like this . What is the name of the original shape?

  3 I face south and turn anticlockwise through 270 degrees. In what direction am I now facing?

  4 What is the sum of the angles in a triangle?

  5 What is the value of angle *a* in this isosceles triangle?

  6 What is the area of this triangle?

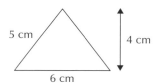

  7 Draw the shape that you get after rotating this shape 90° clockwise.

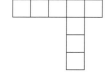

  8 What is the area of a rectangle with a length of 6 cm and a width of 4 cm?

  9 What is the length of a rectangle with an area of 20 cm² and a length of 4 cm?

  10 How many kilometres are equivalent to 5 miles?

  Answers   **1** 0   **2** Isosceles triangle   **3** West   **4** 180°   **5** 70°   **6** 12 cm²   **7**
  8 24 cm²   **9** 5 cm   **10** 8 km

Main lesson activity

- This is a revision lesson on shape, space and measures.
- Before letting students start the questions you can go through key points (as suggested below) or discuss some specific questions with the class to remind them of the methods used.

Symmetry
○ Line symmetry
○ Rotation symmetry

Area
○ Recall of formula for area of square, rectangle, triangle and parallelogram

Angles
○ Definition of acute, obtuse and reflex
○ Angles at a point and on a straight line

Scale drawings
○ Scales
○ Accurate measurements

Measures
○ Conversions between metric units
○ Conversions between metric and imperial units

- **The class can now do Exercise 12E from the Pupil Workbook.**

Exercise 12E **Answers**

1 **b** Isosceles triangle   **c** One line down the centre ($x = 0$)
2 **a** 2, 4, 1   **b** Middle shape should be circled
3 $a = 40°$, $b = 100°$
4 A, C, D
5 **a** $6 \times 5 = 30$ cm^2 **b** $\frac{1}{2}$ of $8 \times 10 = 40$ cm^2 **c** $5 \times 7 = 35$ cm^2
6 **a** 10 miles   **b** 50 miles
7 Sides measure 2 cm and 3 cm so actual size should be 6 cm and 9 cm.

Plenary

- Go through the answers to the exercise. Discuss and clarify those with which students had difficulty.

LESSON 12.6

Framework objectives – Revision of Statistics

Design data collection sheets. Construct frequency tables for gathering discrete data, grouped where appropriate in equal class intervals.

Construct two-way tables for recording discrete data.

Construct diagrams to represent data including bar-line graphs.

Calculate statistics for small sets of discrete data.

Construct simple pie charts.

Interpret diagrams and graphs.

Use vocabulary and ideas of probability, drawing on experience. Understand and use the probability scale from 0 to 1.

Find and justify probabilities based on equally likely outcomes in simple contexts.

Estimate probabilities by collecting data from a simple experiment and recording it in a frequency table.

Compare experimental and theoretical probabilities in simple contexts.

Oral and mental starter

Resources required

OHT 12.3 Diagrams 3

- The following is a 10-question, National Test-style, mental test on the theme of handling data. Repeat each question twice and allow students 10 seconds to answer. The diagrams are on OHT 12.3.

   1 A fair, ordinary, six-sided dice is rolled. What is the probability that the dice shows an odd number?

   2 What is the mean of these numbers? [Write 10, 10 and 25 on the board.]

   3 The pictogram shows the number of trains that go from Barnsley to Leeds and Huddersfield each day. How many more trains go to Leeds than to Huddersfield?

| Leeds | ◇ ◇ ◇ ◇ |
| Huddersfield | ◇ ◇ ◁ |

◇ = 4 trains

   4 What is the range of these numbers? [Write 4, 8, 2, 9, 7, 12, 1, 3, 7, 8, 2 and 3 on the board.]

   5 A letter is picked at random form the word MULTIPLY. What is the probability that it is a vowel?

   M   U   L   T   I   P   L   Y

   6 The table shows the probability that a ball taken at random from a bag is red, blue or green. What is the probability that a ball taken at random is blue or green?

Colour of ball	Red	Blue	Green
Probability	0.3	0.2	0.5

   7 A fair, ordinary, six-sided dice is rolled. What is the probability that the dice shows a score of 7?

   8 A fair, ordinary, six-sided dice is rolled four times and gives a 6 each time. What is the probability that the next throw will be a 6?

   9 What is the median of these numbers? [Write 7, 8, 10, 13, 15 and 20 on the board.]

  10 The table shows the number of pets owned by 10 students. How many pets are owned altogether?

Number of pets	**Frequency**
1	2
2	5
3	3

Answers   **1** $\frac{3}{6}$ or $\frac{1}{2}$ or 0.5   **2** 15   **3** 6   **4** 11   **5** $\frac{2}{8} = \frac{1}{4}$ **6** 0.7   **7** 0   **8** $\frac{1}{6}$ **9** 11.5   **10** 21

Main lesson activity

- This is a revision lesson on handling data.
- Before letting students start the questions you can go through key points (as suggested below) or discuss some specific questions with the class to remind them of the methods used.

Probability
○ Language and definition of probability
○ Writing probabilities as fractions, decimals or percentages

Averages
○ Three averages for discrete data
○ Range of data

Surveys
○ Methods of sampling
○ Unbiased questions with unambiguous response boxes

Collecting and representing data
○ Pie charts, bar charts, pictograms
○ Tally charts, frequency tables

- **The class can now do Exercise 12F from the Pupil Workbook.**

Exercise 12F **Answers**

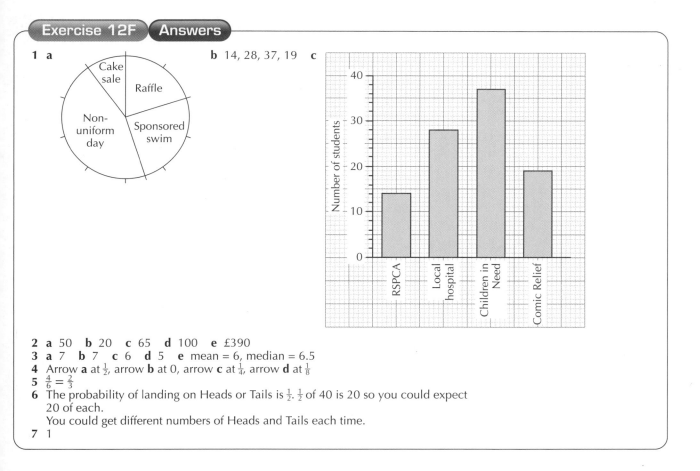

1 a (pie chart: Cake sale, Raffle, Non-uniform day, Sponsored swim)   **b** 14, 28, 37, 19   **c** (bar chart: RSPCA, Local hospital, Children in Need, Comic Relief — Number of students)

2 **a** 50   **b** 20   **c** 65   **d** 100   **e** £390
3 **a** 7   **b** 7   **c** 6   **d** 5   **e** mean = 6, median = 6.5
4 Arrow **a** at $\frac{1}{2}$, arrow **b** at 0, arrow **c** at $\frac{1}{4}$, arrow **d** at $\frac{1}{8}$
5 $\frac{4}{6} = \frac{2}{3}$
6 The probability of landing on Heads or Tails is $\frac{1}{2}$. $\frac{1}{2}$ of 40 is 20 so you could expect 20 of each.
   You could get different numbers of Heads and Tails each time.
7 1

Plenary

- Go through the answers to the exercise. Discuss and clarify those with which students had difficulty.

Statistics **3**

> **Framework objectives** – Statistical surveys
> Plan how to collect and organise small sets of data from surveys and experiments.
> Design data collection sheets or questionnaires to use in a simple survey.

Oral and mental starter

> **Resources required**
>
> PCM 13.1 Surveys

- Write on the board or on an OHT: 'Children eat more junk food than adults.'
- Ask the class how they would investigate this statement to try to establish whether there is any truth in it.
- Encourage them to come up with answers to do with **surveys**, **questionnaires** or even an **experiment** in which they ask people to record what they eat over, for example, one week.
- Write down any key words on the board for them to use later.
- Discuss how, as a class, they could use different approaches to the investigation.

Main lesson activity

- This work could be time-consuming and it is suggested that it should take at least two lessons to complete.
- The results could be used for display or possibly for small groups to make short presentations.
- Show them a problem statement, for example: 'Children eat more junk food than adults.'
- Tell them that you are going to carry out a quick survey amongst the class to try to find out if they think the statement is true.
- Ask them to put up their hands if they eat burgers at least once a week. Record the response on the board.
- Now ask them how many have school lunch, and record how many of those are likely to have, or to have had, chips with their lunch.
- Point out that so far you have been finding out information or data about young people.
- Now ask them the question: 'Do you think that children eat more junk food than adults?'
- Record the results.
- Point out that in surveys some people may not want to answer certain questions because they find them embarrassing or too personal.
- Explain that it is important to keep questions short and simple, and to avoid asking personal questions.

● Explain to the class that they will be looking at statements in the Pupil Workbook and making up questions that they could ask. This work could be undertaken in small groups.

● **The class can now do a survey from PCM 13.1, or begin a problem of their own choice, and/or do Exercise 13A from the Pupil Workbook.**

Exercise 13A   Answers

1 a   i All boys, should ask approximately half girls and boys
     ii Too few
     iii Should not have asked Year 7, only interested in Year 9 views
   b Two reasons from: The sample is big enough. The sample is random. The sample is representative.
2 a Some answers are numbers, some are words, difficult to interpret and group the responses
   b He could have given people answers to choose from, e.g. none, 1–2, 3–4, …
3 a Hand span in cm, height in cm or m
   b About 20, or reasonable answer
   c Ask a mixture of children, adults, male, female

Plenary

● Using PCM 13.1, discuss ways of collecting data for each problem. For example, in the question about old people, teenagers and libraries: design a questionnaire and ask 30 old people and 30 young people.
● The question about girls, boys and clothes: design a questionnaire and ask 30 girls and 30 boys.
● The question about sports teams: look at results of football matches in a Sunday paper. Record at what time goals are scored.

Key words

survey
questionnaire
experiment
statistics
grouped data
class interval
tally
frequency
data-collection sheet
database
sample
primary source
secondary source
data log
two-way table
discrete
continuous

Framework objectives – Grouped frequency tables
Construct frequency tables for gathering discrete data.

Oral and mental starter

Resources required

OHT 13.1 Birthdays
Different sized books or other objects (see Main lesson)

● Write a table on the board, as shown below or use OHT 13.1.

Birthday	Tally	Frequency
Jan – Mar		
Apr – Jun		
Jul – Sep		
Oct – Dec		

● Collect **data** from the students and record it in the tally column. Ask a student to do the recording.
● Ask the students to complete the frequency column.
● Now ask a series of brief questions about the data. For example:

   Which period has the most birthdays?
   How many students are present in the class?
   How many students have birthdays in the first half of the year?

Main lesson activity

● Have a selection of different sized books or other objects set out for this activity.
● Tell the class that part of the task is to measure objects to the nearest centimetre. Remind them when to round up and when to round down.
● Draw a table on the board, or on an OHT, as shown below.

Height of book (h) to nearest centimetre	Tally	Frequency
$22 < h \leqslant 24$		
$25 < h \leqslant 27$		
$28 < h \leqslant 30$		
$31 < h \leqslant 33$		

● You will need to know in advance the size of the books in order to choose sensible groups. The ones shown in the table are examples. Use the notation $22 < h \leqslant 24$ and explain that this means larger than 22 and less than or equal to 24.
● Ask the class to measure, to the nearest centimetre, the height of different books or other objects.
● Ask them to copy the table into their books and record their responses.
● Explain to the class that you want them to measure at least 15 objects and then to complete the **frequency table**.
● Finally, ask them to write down at least two facts about their table.

- Complete the frequency table.
- Draw a line on the board (or on a piece of A4 paper and pass it round the class).
- Record students' estimates of the length of the line.
- Tell students you are going to put the lengths into a grouped table.
- Ask them what needs to be considered when setting up the groups. For example, lowest value, highest value, sensible group widths to give about four or five different groups.
- Decide on the groups and complete the table.
- **The class can now do Exercise 13B from the Pupil Workbook.**

Exercise 13B   Answers

1 Frequencies 4, 4, 5, 7
2 Frequencies 11, 6, 8, 5
3 Answers will vary

Plenary

- Tell the class to copy out another table.

Key words
- [ ] discrete
- [ ] data
- [ ] sample size
- [ ] frequency table

	Tally	Frequency
$0 < n \leqslant 10$		
$11 < n \leqslant 20$		
$21 < n \leqslant 30$		
$31 < n \leqslant 40$		

- Explain that you are going to call out numbers which they will record using five-bar gates.
- Tell the students that when anyone gets 10 in one class, they have to put up a hand.
- When the hands go up, ask those students to total the frequency column.
- Ask them now for the total frequency and the number in the smallest class.

Framework objectives – Which average to use?

Recognise when it is appropriate to use the range, mean, median and mode.

Oral and mental starter

Resources required

PCM 13.2 Averages

- Ask the class to give you three numbers:
    with a mode of 5.
    with a median of 6.
    with a mean of 7.
    with a range of 8.

- Ask the class whether they can make the same three numbers work for more than one statement. For example, 5, 5 and 13 have a mode of 5 and a range of 8.

- Ask the class to give you three numbers and tell you two facts about the numbers. For example, 3, 5 and 10 have a median of 5 and a range of 7.

Main lesson activity

- Write on the board or an OHT a set of data. For example, 3, 3, 3, 3, 3, 3, 3, 3, 3, 100.

- Ask the class to tell you the mode and to explain how they know.

- Now ask for the median. Again, ask them to explain how they know.

- Ask them whether the mean will also be 3. Prompt them to explain that it must be bigger because of the 100, which affects the mean.

- Discuss the disadvantages of using the mean in this case. Explain that the 100 is sometimes called a rogue or **extreme value**.

- Explain that this lesson will look at all types of average and why sometimes one type is better than another.

- Revise the meaning of mode, median, mean and range.

- Give out PCM 13.2 which shows the advantages and disadvantages of each type of average.

- Talk through the examples given in the fourth column.

- Now ask the students to complete the questions on PCM 13.2.

- Explain that the guidelines are not strict rules and that some data requires caution when concluding whether an average is suitable or not.

- **The class can now do Exercise 13C from the Pupil Workbook.**

Exercise 13C Answers

1 **a** 20 **b** 5.5 **c** 4.5 **d** 59 **e** 45
2 **a** Median 1.8 kg, range 1.7 kg, **b** No mode – all different weights
3 **a** Mode £100, mean £200,
   b The mode as it represents most people's wage; there is only one person with a wage greater than the mean and four with less than the mean
4 **a** Mode 0 days, range 5 days **b** Mode 39 g, range 5 g

Plenary

Key words

- ☐ **mode**
- ☐ **mean**
- ☐ **median**
- ☐ **extreme value**
- ☐ **appropriate data**
- ☐ **central value**

- Write down a small set of data on the board. For example, 0, 1, 3, 3, 3, 50.
- Ask the class to write down which average (mode, median or mean) they would not use.
- Now ask them to reveal their answers and give a reason for rejecting the mean.
- Repeat for different data. For example, 6, 6, 6, 6, 8, 9, 10.
- Remind the class of the main advantages and disadvantages of using each average.

Framework objectives – Drawing and using frequency diagrams

Construct frequency diagrams for gathering grouped discrete data.

Oral and mental starter

Resources required

OHT 13.2 Frequency diagrams
OHT 13.3 Time-series graph

● Put the words **frequency**, **table**, **collect**, **tally**, **diagram** and **data** on the board.

● Ask the students to sort the words into an order which they can explain: for example, **collect data**, **tally**, **frequency table**, **diagram**. Now ask them to make the words into a complete sentence. For example: 'I am going to collect some data together in a tally chart, which I will then set out as a frequency table and use the information to draw a frequency diagram.'

● You can add other words such as **compare**, **statistic**, **continuous** and **discrete**.

● This starter can be used to establish a set order of working with statistics, but can also be used as part of the literacy strategy. A further step would be to ask students to spell some of the words before putting them on the board.

Main lesson activity

● Show the class the bar chart on OHT 13.2, 'Favourite pets of class 9Q'.

● Ask the class questions about the chart, for example:

   What is the most popular type of pet?
   How many students are there in the class?
   How many students have pets with four legs?

● Now show the class the frequency diagram on OHT 13.2, 'Heights of class 9P'.

● Ask the class questions about the diagram, for example:

   Can you say how many students there are in the class?
   How many students are between 160 and 170 cm tall?
   How many students are taller than 150 cm?

● Ask the class what the differences are between the two diagrams. They will probably initially point out the gaps in the bar chart. Ask them why there are gaps on a bar chart. Lead them into talking about **discrete data**.

● Refer again to the frequency diagram and point out, if necessary, that this diagram has **continuous data**. Emphasise that there should be no gaps.

● Write down a checklist of what is needed for a good frequency diagram for continuous data:
   ○ title
   ○ suitable class intervals
   ○ axes labelled, with the horizontal axis labelled at the class boundaries
   ○ neat, ruled bars
   ○ no gaps

● You may wish to work through an example from the Pupil Workbook.

- Now show the class OHT 13.3 and ask them to give you a few facts from the graph. Point out that this type of graph can be used to look at trends. It is important that they are familiar with this type of graph and should be able to draw and read from time-series graphs.

- **The class can now do Exercise 13D from the Pupil Workbook.**

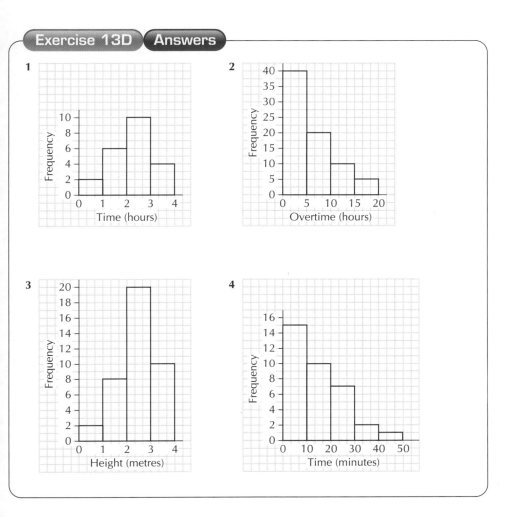

Plenary

- Write four headings on the board: Time, Temperature, Length, Mass. Tell the class that these are the most-used categories for continuous data.
- Ask the class to give you units to put into the four columns. Write them in as they give them to you, for example: seconds, °C, metres, kilograms.
- Summarise the lesson and stress that continuous data has to have a continuous scale on diagrams.

Key words

- bar chart
- line graph
- frequency diagram
- time-series graph
- continuous data
- discrete data

LESSON 13.5

Framework objectives – Stem-and-leaf diagrams
Construct stem-and-leaf diagrams.

Oral and mental starter

Resources required

OHT 13.4 Numbers
OHT 13.5 Stem-and-leaf
diagrams
PCM 13.3 Stem-and-leaf
diagrams

- Using a counting stick, tell the students that, for example,
  the number 6 is at one end and 20 is at the other end.
  Ask them for the range. To vary the task, change the numbers,
  and introduce negatives, fractions and decimals.

- Write the numbers 1, 2, 2, 4, 4, 4, 4 on the board. Ask the class for the
  mode, and how they found it. Repeat this procedure for the median and
  mean. Ask them which average they think best reflects the data.
  Obviously, it depends on what the data is about.
- Change the middle number to 3. Ask the class for the mode and median.
  Ask if the mean will go up, down or stay the same. This could be
  repeated several times, but at this stage keep the numbers in order.
- Now use the same numbers, but change the order. Ask them if changing
  the order makes any difference.
- Ask the class what happens to the mode, median, mean and range if
  each number is increased by one.
- Ask the class what happens to the mode, median, mean and range if the
  numbers are doubled.

Main lesson activity

- Tell the class that they are going to look at larger sets of data and a
  different way to present data sets so that they are easier to analyse.
- Explain that it is quite straightforward to obtain a mode from a list of, for
  example, seven numbers, but as the list becomes longer it is easier to
  make a mistake.
- Display OHT 13.4 or reproduce it on the board. Ask the students to sort
  the numbers into the following groups: 20s, 30s and 40s. Then ask them
  to put these groups into numerical order on three separate lines in their
  books.
- Now, tell them that using a **stem-and-leaf diagram** reduces the amount of
  writing.
- Draw the stem on the board and ask one student to read out their
  numbers in order. Write the numbers on your diagram and let the class
  copy it into their books. Explain that it is important to line up the
  columns of numbers.

```
2 | 6   6   7   8   ...
3 | 0   1   2   2   ...
4 | 0   0   1   1   ...
```

- Explain that to make sense the diagram will need a key. Use the first
  value for the key: for example, 2 | 6 represents 26.
- Ask them to use the diagram to write down the mode and the range.

- Discuss how this is done.
- Ask the students to repeat this exercise for each of the sets of data on PCM 13.3.

- **The class can now do Exercise 13E from the Pupil Workbook.**

Exercise 13E **Answers**

1 a 7, 7, 8, 9; 11, 11, 12, 15, 15, 16; 20, 24, 28
  b 63, 68; 72, 72, 75, 79, 79; 83, 85; 94
  c 18; 24, 24, 27; 30, 35, 36, 38; 42, 43; 50

2 a
3	8			
4	3	5	6	6	9
5	4	6	8	

  b
1	7	8	8		
2	0	1	2	2	7	9
3	4	8	9		

  c
0	4	8	9			
1	0	1	6	7		
2	0	1	1	8	8	9	9
3	0					

  Check for a correct key

3 a
7	5	6	6	9	
8	1	4	6	6	8	9
9	0	4			

  b
4	3	5	5	6	7	8
5	3	4	8		
6	0	1			

  Check for a correct key

4
3	8	8	9
4	0	5	7	8
5	3	7	9

  Check for a correct key

Plenary

- Show the class OHT 13.5. Explain that the two stem-and-leaf diagrams use the same values, but one set is unordered and the other set ordered.
- Ask the students to tell you the difference between the two diagrams.
- Follow up by asking them which they think is better. Prompt them to choose the ordered set of values.
- Tell the class that when creating a stem-and-leaf diagram, it is important to put the data into numerical order, as this will help them if they have to go on and, for example, find the mode or range.
- Reinforce the fact that the diagram needs to be presented neatly with the numbers aligned in columns, so that it is easy to see which is the longest row.

Key words

- range
- median
- mode
- modal class
- mean
- average
- stem-and-leaf diagram

Geometry and measures 4

Framework objectives – Constructing triangles 1
Construct a triangle, given two sides and the included angle (SAS) or two angles and the included side (ASA).

Oral and mental starter

This is a starter activity about geometric acronyms.

- Write on the board, '180 DIAT'. Explain to the class that this is an acronym for 180 degrees in a triangle.
- Ask the class to try to solve the following acronyms. They refer to some of the geometric properties they should know.

> 90 DIARA (90 degrees in a right angle)
> 180 DOASL (180 degrees on a straight line)
> 360 DIACT (360 degrees in a complete turn)
> 3 SIAT (three sides in a triangle)
> 4 SIAQ (four sides in a quadrilateral)

- Ask the class to make up some of their own geometric acronyms.

> **Resources required**
> Rulers
> Protractors

Main lesson activity

- This lesson revises the Year 8 work on constructing triangles. It will also help students to consolidate their line and angle drawing skills.
- Remind the class how to construct a triangle accurately from information given on a sketch as follows.

Constructing a triangle, given two sides and the included angle (SAS)
- Draw a sketch of such a triangle on the board.
- The aim is to construct the triangle so that all the given measurements are exact.
- Remind the class that the angles are measured to the nearest degree and the sides to the nearest millimetre.
- Ask the students to draw the triangle in stages as follows:

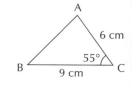

> Draw line BC 9 cm long.
> Draw an angle of 55° at C.
> Draw AC 6 cm long.
> Join AB to complete the triangle.

- Accuracy can be checked by measuring AB. It should be 7.4 cm.

Constructing a triangle when you know two angles and the length of the line between them (ASA)
- Draw a sketch of such a triangle on the board.
- Ask the students to draw the triangle in stages as follows:

> Draw the line AB 8 cm long.
> Draw an angle of 45° at A.

Extend the line.
Draw an angle of 60° at B.
Extend the line to meet the other line.
Label the point C.

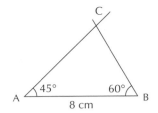

- Accuracy can be checked by measuring angle ACB (it should be 75°) and/or BC (5.9 cm) and/or AC (7.2 cm).

- **The class can now do Exercise 14A from the Pupil Workbook.**

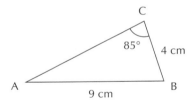

Exercise 14A   **Answers**

1 AC = 5.3 cm
2 DF = 8.2 cm
3 NM = 4.7 cm
4 BC = 4.3 cm
5 XZ = 9.4 cm
6 LN = 6.1 cm

Plenary

Key words

☐ **construct**
☐ **measure**
☐ **protractor**
☐ **ruler**

- Draw the following triangle on the board.

- Ask students to describe how they would construct it.
- Establish the method. For example:

  Draw BC 4 cm long.
  Draw angle of 85° at C.
  Extend the line.
  Use compasses to mark off 9 cm from B to join other line at A.

- If there is time, construct the triangle.

Framework objectives – Constructing triangles 2
Construct a triangle, given three sides (SSS).

Oral and mental starter

Resources required

Compasses
Rulers

- This is a starter to help with spelling and knowledge of mathematical terms.
- Write on the board: Richard Of York Gave Battle In Vain.
- Ask the students if they recognise this mnemonic for the colours of the rainbow: Red, Orange, Yellow, Green, Blue, Indigo, Violet (a mnemonic is an aid to help remember facts).
- Ask the students to write down the names of all of the quadrilaterals that they have met (square, rectangle, parallelogram, rhombus, kite, arrowhead, trapezium).
- Ask the class to work in pairs and, in 5 or 10 minutes, invent a suitable mnemonic for the names of the quadrilaterals.

Main lesson activity

- Remind the class about the two constructions they revised in the last lesson.

    A triangle given two sides and the included angle (SAS):

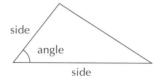

    A triangle given two angles and the included side (ASA):

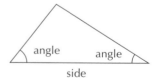

- Explain that this lesson is about how to construct a triangle given three sides (SSS). For this lesson the students will require a ruler and compasses.
- Draw a sketch of such a triangle on the board.

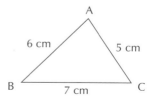

- Ask the students to draw the triangle shown in stages as described below:

    Draw the line BC 7 cm long.
    Set compasses to a radius of 6 cm and, with the centre at B, draw a large arc above BC.

© HarperCollins*Publishers* Ltd 2008

Set compasses to a radius of 5 cm and, with the centre at C, draw a
large arc to intersect the first arc.

The intersection of the arcs is A.

Join AB and AC to complete the triangle.

The **construction lines** should be left on the diagram.

- **The class can now do Exercise 14B from the Pupil Workbook.**

Exercise 14B **Answers**

1 ABC = 56°
2 FED = 109°
3 LNM = 75°
4 PRQ = 127°
5 NLM = 29°
6 ZYX = 37°

Plenary

Key words

☐ **compasses**
☐ **construct**
☐ **construction lines**

- Draw a sketch of this triangle on the board:

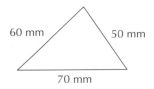

60 mm   50 mm

70 mm

- Ask the class how they would construct the triangle.
- Now draw a sketch of the following triangle on the board:

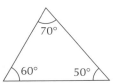

70°

60°   50°

- Ask the class how they would construct this triangle.
- They should say that it is not possible. It could be drawn to any size as you do not know the lengths of any of the sides.
- If time allows, it may be possible to discuss the idea of similar shapes.

LESSON
14.3

Framework objectives – Surface area of cuboids
Calculate the surface area of cubes and cuboids.

Oral and mental starter

Resources required

Empty cereal packets or other cuboidal boxes of different sizes

- Write the number 12 on the board.
- Ask individual students to come up and write three numbers on the board that have a product of 12, allowing repeats. Remind them that 'product' means 'multiply'.
- Examples are: $1 \times 1 \times 12$, $1 \times 2 \times 6$, $1 \times 3 \times 4$, $2 \times 2 \times 3$.
- Repeat the activity using different numbers.

Main lesson activity

- Using an empty cereal packet, ask the class how to find the total **surface area** of the card used to make the packet (ignoring any tabs).
- Open out the packet to show the net.
- The packet is composed of six rectangles. Draw the net on the board to show this.

	3	
5	1	6
	4	
	2	

- Explain that the total surface area is calculated by finding the total of the areas of the six rectangles.
- Stress that this means *adding* the areas of the six rectangles (some students may want to multiply).
- Notice that the six areas go in three pairs: 1 and 2, 3 and 4, 5 and 6.
- Measure and calculate the surface area of the box.
- Show students how to write down the calculation.
- Distribute cereal boxes to small groups.
- Ask the students to measure the length, width and height of the packet to the nearest centimetre to calculate the surface area. Remind them that the unit is one of area.

● Ask students to design a small poster of their calculation. For example:

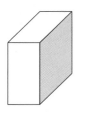 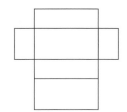

Length = 23 cm
Width = 13 cm
Height = 34 cm

Surface area
= 2 × 23 × 13 + 2 × 23 × 34 + 2 × 13 × 34
= 3046 cm²

● **The class can now do Exercise 14C from the Pupil Workbook.**

Exercise 14C **Answers**

1 2 × 4, 3 × 4, 2 × 3
  2 × 8 + 2 × 12 + 2 × 6 = 16 + 24 + 12 = 52
2 5 × 1, 3 × 1, 5 × 3
  2 × 5 + 2 × 3 + 2 × 15 = 10 + 6 + 30 = 46
3 4 × 6, 2 × 6, 4 × 2
  2 × 24 + 2 × 12 + 2 × 8 = 48 + 24 + 16 = 88
4 3 × 2, 5 × 2, 3 × 5
  2 × 6 + 2 × 10 + 2 × 15 = 12 + 20 + 30 = 62

Plenary

Key words
- [ ] **cube**
- [ ] **cuboid**
- [ ] **surface area**

● Draw a cuboid on the board. Mark the sides *l*, *w* and *h*.
● Ask the class to explain why the formula for the surface area is
  $2lw + 2lh + 2hw$.
● Draw a cube on the board. Mark the side *l*.
● Ask the class to explain why the formula for the surface area is $6l^2$.
● Use the formulae to work out the surface area of some cuboids
  and cubes.

LESSON 14.4

Framework objectives – Volume of a cuboid
Know and use the formula for the volume of a cuboid.

Oral and mental starter

Resources required

PCM 14.1 Volume of cuboids
Cuboid made from
  multi-link cubes
  (4 cm × 3 cm × 2 cm)

- Show the class a **cuboid** made from multi-link cubes, whose length is 4 cm, width is 3 cm and height is 2 cm.
- Remind the class how to find the total surface area of the cuboid by finding the area of its six surfaces and adding them together.
- Draw on the board the cuboid shown below.

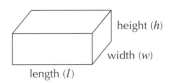

The formula to find the total surface area of any cuboid is:

$A = 2lw + 2lh + 2wh$

So, the surface area of the multi-link cuboid above is:

$$A = (2 \times 4 \times 3) + (2 \times 4 \times 2) + (2 \times 3 \times 2)$$
$$= 24 + 16 + 12$$
$$= 52 \text{ cm}^2$$

Main lesson activity

- Explain to the class that **volume** is the amount of space inside a 3-D shape.
- Show them the multi-link cube and explain that the volume is made from 24 cubes. So, to find the volume of a cuboid, multiply its length by its width by its height. Hence, from the diagram:

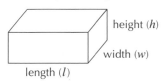

Volume of cuboid = length × width × height

$$V = l \times w \times h = lwh$$

- The metric units of volume in common use are:
  ○ **Cubic millimetre** (mm^3)
  ○ **Cubic centimetre** (cm^3)
  ○ **Cubic metre** (m^3)
  So, the volume of the multi-link cuboid above is $V = 4 \times 3 \times 2 = 24 \text{ cm}^3$

● Draw the following cuboids on the board and work out their volume.

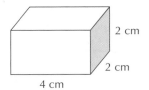

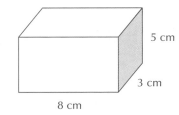

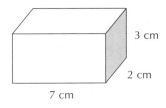

$V = 16$ cm³ $V = 120$ cm³ $V = 42$ cm³

● Explain how to write down the calculations.

● **The class can now do PCM 14.1 followed by Exercise 14D from the Pupil Workbook.**

Exercise 14D   Answers

1 m³, cm³ and mm³ should be circled
2 **a** $2 \times 2 \times 5 = 20$
   b $4 \times 3 \times 2 = 24$
   c $2 \times 2 \times 2 = 8$
3 **a** $2 \times 3 \times 2 = 12$ cm³
   b $2 \times 3 \times 10 = 60$ cm³
   c $4 \times 8 \times 2 = 64$ cm³
   d $4 \times 4 \times 5 = 80$ cm³
   e $5 \times 6 \times 4 = 120$ cm³
   f $4 \times 4 \times 4 = 64$ cm³
4

l	w	h	V
3 m	5 m	4 m	60 m³
12 mm	6 mm	5 mm	360 mm³
30 cm	40 cm	10 cm	12 000 cm³
1 m	5 m	4 m	20 m³
15 cm	20 cm	5 cm	1500 cm³

Plenary

Key words

□ capacity
□ cuboid
□ volume:
  cubic millimetre
  cubic centimetre
  cubic metre

● Draw a cube on the board and mark all lengths, e.g. $3 \times 3 \times 3$.

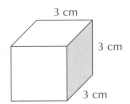

● Ask students to work out the volume using the formula.
● Ask them what special shape this is. They should know the term cube.
● They should also recall cube numbers.
● Link the cube numbers to the volume of cubes of side length 1, 2, 3, 4, and so on.

GCSE Preparation

This is a transition chapter to GCSE and uses textbook format without answer lines.

Framework objectives – BODMAS
Use brackets and the hierarchy of operations.

Oral and mental starter

Resources required

OHT 15.1 BODMAS
 calculations
Student white boards

- Write the following on the board:

  2 4 5 = 30

- Ask students to find a combination of mathematical signs, including brackets, that make the calculation true. For example:

  $(2 + 4) \times 5 = 30$

- Repeat with the following examples:

  3 2 5 = 21 $(3 \times (2 + 5) = 21)$
  12 2 1 = 12 $(12 \times (2 - 1) = 12)$
  12 2 1 = 7 $(12 \div 2 + 1 = 7)$

- Work through more examples with the class if necessary.
- Students could write their answers on mini white boards, if available.

Main lesson activity

- This lesson is a revision of BODMAS.
- From discussion with the students, establish the meaning of BODMAS and its implications.
- Emphasise the important rules, and that addition and subtraction are of equal worth if there are no other operations in the calculation; the same is true for multiplication and division. For these calculations, work from left to right.
- Work through some examples in which you demonstrate the order of operations, such as those given below. OHT 15.1 can also be worked through if further practice is required.

$10 - 2 \times 3 + 1$ Firstly, do the multiplication $10 - 6 + 1$
       Secondly, the subtraction $4 + 1$
       Finally, the addition   5

Point out that because addition and subtraction have equal priority, the order in the last two steps is decided by working from left to right.

$5 \times 3 + 24 \div 6$ Firstly, do the division and the multiplication $15 + 4$
       Then work out the addition   19

$50 \times 3 \div (20 - 5)$ Firstly, work out the bracket $50 \times 3 \div 15$
       Secondly, the multiplication $150 \div 15$
       Finally, the division   10

Point out that because multiplication and division have equal priority, the order in the last two steps is decided by working from left to right.

$(10 - 4) \times 3^2$	Firstly, work out the bracket	6×3^2
	Secondly, the power	6×9
	Finally, the multiplication	54
$60 - 5 \times 3^2$	Firstly, work out the power	$60 - 5 \times 9$
	Secondly, the multiplication	$60 - 45$
	Finally, the subtraction	15

- **The class can now do Exercise 15A from the Pupil Workbook *or* Chapter 1 BODMAS (BIDMAS) (pages 14-15) from Collins GCSE Maths for Edexcel A Workbook and Collins AQA A Workbook; Chapter 5 BODMAS (BIDMAS) (pages 28-29) from Collins AQA B Workbook.**

Exercise 15A   Answers

1 a 6×2, 9 **b** 3×5, 19 **c** $12 \div 2$, 3 **d** $5 \div 2$, 12.5 **e** 6×2, 12 **f** 3^2, 15
2 a 25 **b** 10 **c** 12 **d** 37
3 a 30 **b** 3 **c** 12 **d** 12
4 a 8 **b** 49 **c** 11 **d** 13 **e** 23 **f** 4
5 a $4 \times (3 + 7) = 40$ **b** $10 \div (2 + 3) = 2$ **c** $(5 - 2) \times 4 = 12$ **d** $(20 - 5) \times 2 = 30$
   e $(10 - 2^2) \times 2 = 12$ **f** $24 \div (2^2 + 2) = 4$
6 a 30 **b** 22 **c** 21 **d** 12 **e** 7 **f** 81

Plenary

- Make sure that the students are aware of the order of operations in a problem such as 3×4^2.
- This is a common error when calculating πr^2 for example.
- Explain that $3 \times 4^2 = 3 \times 16 = 48$, and that $(3 \times 4)^2 = 12^2 = 144$ needs a bracket.
- Practise with other examples, such as:
    2×3^2, 4×3^2, $(2 \times 3)^2$, 2×6^2, 3×5^2, $(4 \times 5)^2$, etc …

LESSON 15.2

Framework objectives – Adding and subtracting negative numbers

Add and subtract integers.

Oral and mental starter

Resources required

OHT 15.2 Adding and subtracting negative numbers

- Remind students of the rules for combining two signs when adding and subtracting:

$$-\,- \equiv +,\ -\,+ \equiv -,\ +\,- \equiv -,\ +\,+ \equiv +$$

- Give the students some mental calculations involving these rules, such as:

  5 minus minus 6 (11)
  minus 2 plus minus 3 (–5)
  7 minus plus 6 (1)

- Students should not be allowed to write anything down.
- This activity could be done as a 10-question mental test.

Main lesson activity

- This is a lesson on negative numbers in context.
- Ask students to give you some examples of where negative directed numbers are met in everyday life. Establish that negative numbers are found in temperature, height above and below sea level and money, for example overdrawn bank accounts. Make sure that all the students understand the concept of an overdraft.
- Work through the examples below. OHT 15.2 can also be worked through if further practice is required.

Example 1 What number is missing from the box to make the calculation true?

a $12 + \square = 7$ b $-7 + \square = 12$ c $-10 - \square = 1$

The problems can be solved as equations, or using a number line.

a $\square = 7 - 12 = -5$

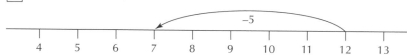

b $\square = 12 + 7 = 19$

c $-\square = 1 + 10 = 11$, so $\square = -11$

Example 2 At midnight the temperature is –3°C. By midday it has risen by 15°. What is the temperature at midday?

Let x be the temperature at midday.
The expression for the temperature at midday is $-3 + 15$.
So, the equation is $x = -3 + 15$.
So, $x = 12$.
Therefore, the answer is 12°C.

- **The class can now do Exercise 15B from the Pupil Workbook *or* Chapter 7 Negative numbers (pages 44-45) from Collins GCSE Maths for Edexcel A Workbook and Collins AQA B Workbook; Chapter 3 Negative numbers (pages 30-31) from Collins AQA A Workbook.**

Exercise 15B Answers

1 a i 65 m **ii** 835 m **iii** 1735 m **b i** 175 m **ii** 695 m **iii** 770 m
  c i +1075 m **ii** –520 m **iii** –595 m
2 a 20°C **b** 82°C **c** 128°C **d** 72°C **e** 108°C **f** 62°C
3 a –£9 **b** –45 m **c** +15 minutes **d** A train moving backwards at 5 mph
4 a 8 **b** –5 **c** 7 **d** –5 **e** 12 **f** –2 **g** –10 **h** 17
5 a –4, –3, –2, –1, 0, 1, 2, 3, 4, 5, 6
  b –2, –1.5, –1, –0.5, 0, 0.5, 1, 1.5, 2, 2.5, 3
6 a –2 **b** 4 **c** –3 **d** –2 **e** –9 **f** 3

Plenary

- Remind students of the rules for multiplying and dividing directed numbers.
- Work through a few examples such as -2×-3 (+6), $-12 \div +3$ (–4).
- Make sure that examples of squaring are covered, i.e. $(-4)^2$ (+16), $+3^2$ (+9).
- Emphasise the fact that all numbers when squared are positive.

Framework objectives – Multiples and factors
Use vocabulary and concepts of factor (divisor), multiple and common factor.

Oral and mental starter

Resources required

OHT 15.3 Multiples, factors
             and prime numbers
Student white boards

- Using a target board such as the one shown, point at a pair of numbers and ask students to identify the LCM (lowest common multiple).
- Students could write their answers on white boards, if available.

2	3	4	5
6	7	8	9
10	12	15	20

Main lesson activity

- This is a revision lesson on multiples, factors and prime numbers.
- Ask students to define the terms and ensure that satisfactory definitions are reached.
- Work through the examples below. OHT 15.3 can also be worked through if further practice is required.

   Example 1 Write down:
       a a multiple of 6
       b a multiple of 5 and 6
       c a multiple of 6 and 9
       d the largest multiple of 7 less than 100
       e the largest multiple of 3 and 8 that is less than 100

       a a multiple of 6 is any number in the six times table: 6, 12, 18, …
       b since 5 and 6 have no common factors, a multiple of 5 and 6 is a multiple of 30 ($5 \times 6 = 30$): 30, 60, 90, …
       c since 6 and 9 share a common factor of 3, any even multiple of 9 will also be a multiple of 6: 18, 36, 54, …
       d think of a multiple of 7 which is near 100: $10 \times 7 = 70$, $11 \times 7 = 77$, $12 \times 7 = 84$, $13 \times 7 = 91$, $14 \times 7 = 98$, $15 \times 7 = 105$, so the largest multiple of 7 less than 100 is 98
       e since 3 and 8 have no common factors, a multiple of 3 and 8 is a multiple of 24. The largest multiple of 24 under 100 is 96: 24, 48, 72, 96, 120, …

Example 2 Find the factors of:
       a 24 (1, 2, 3, 4, 6, 8, 12, 24)
       b 44 (1, 2, 4, 11, 22, 44)
       c 70 (1, 2, 5, 7, 10, 14, 35, 70)
       d 81 (1, 3, 9, 27, 81)
   ○ Recall the ways of finding factors and that, except for square numbers, they come in pairs.

● **The class can now do Exercise 15C from the Pupil Workbook *or* Chapter 8 Multiples and factors (pages 46-47) from Collins GCSE Maths for Edexcel A Workbook and Collins AQA B Workbook; Chapter 4 Multiples and factors (pages 32-33) from Collins AQA A Workbook.**

Exercise 15C **Answers**

1 a 4, 8, 12, 16, 20 **b** 9, 18, 27, 36, 45 **c** 12, 24, 36, 48, 60 **d** 25, 50, 75, 100, 125
2 a 3, 15, 18, 24, 36, 39, 45, 48, 69, 90, 120 **b** 15, 45, 90, 120
  c 8, 24, 36, 48, 64, 120
3 a 48 **b** 48 **c** 49
4 a 48 **d** 45 **c** 42
5 a 1, 2, 3, 4, 6, 8, 12, 16, 24, 48 **b** 1, 2, 3, 4, 5, 6, 10, 12, 15, 20, 30, 60
  c 1, 3, 5, 15, 25, 75 **d** 1, 2, 5, 10, 13, 26, 65, 130
6 a 1, 3 **b** 1, 2, 3, 6 **c** 1, 2, 7, 14

Plenary

● Confirm the definition of prime numbers.
● Ask the students to recall the prime numbers up to 50. They will probably not be able to remember all of them, so be ready to give help.
● Encourage students to write these down. As there is no pattern to the primes, they need to learn them:

2, 3, 5, 7, 11, 13, 17, 19, 23, 29, 31, 37, 41, 43, 47

Framework objectives – Squares, square roots and powers

Use the terms square, positive square root, cube and cube root. Use index notation.

Oral and mental starter

Resources required

OHT 15.4 Powers and roots
Student white boards

- Using a target board, such as the one shown, point at a pair of numbers and ask students to identify the HCF (highest common factor).
- Students could write their answers on white boards, if available.

12	15	8	25
16	21	32	36
10	14	18	27
9	6	42	24

Main lesson activity

- This is a revision lesson on squares, square roots and powers.
- Recall the definition of each of these terms.
- Remind the class that they should know the squares (and corresponding square roots) up to 15 squared and the cubes (and corresponding cube roots) up to 5 cubed. Some mental practice on these might be useful. Ask the class for the value of, for example, 6^2 (36), $\sqrt{81}$ (9), $\sqrt{49}$ (7), 8^2 (64).
- Remind the class about the use of a calculator and the special buttons to calculate squares, square roots and powers.
- Using calculators, work through the examples below. OHT 15.4 can also be worked through if further practice is required.

Example 1 Calculate: **a** 38^2 **b** $\sqrt{2601}$ **c** $\sqrt{1200}$

  a Encourage students to use the square button on their calculator, or just key in $38 \times 38 = 1444$.

  b Make sure students can use the square root button on their calculator to give $\sqrt{2601} = 51$.

  c Using the square root button on their calculator, $\sqrt{1200} = 34.6$ (rounded to 1 decimal place).

Example 2 Calculate: **a** 6^5 **b** 11^3 **c** 30^5

  Make sure that students can use the power button on their calculator.

  a $6^5 = 7776$

  b $11^3 = 1331$

  c $30^5 = 24\,300\,000$

- **The class can now do Exercise 15D from the Pupil Workbook *or* Chapter 8 Square, square root and powers (pages 48-49) from Collins GCSE Maths for Edexcel A Workbook and Collins AQA B Workbook; Chapter 4 Square, square root and powers (pages 34-35) from Collins AQA A Workbook.**

Exercise 15D · Answers

1 a 49 **b** 81 **c** 121 **d** 169 **e** 225
2 a 6 **b** 8 **c** 12
3 a 361 **b** 576 **c** 625 **d** 1024 **e** 2809
4 a 6.32 **b** 8.94 **c** 10.95 **d** 22.36 **e** 30.00
5 a 1024 **b** 1728 **c** 28561 **d** 9261 **e** 46656 **f** 16807 **g** 512 **h** 441
6 a i 1 **ii** 1 **iii** 1 **b i** –1 **ii** 1 **iii** –1
7 a 1 **b** 1 **c** –1 **d** 1

Plenary

- Ask students what $(-3)^2 = -3 \times -3$ is. Hopefully they will say 9.
- Ask students what $\sqrt{9}$ is.
- They will probably say 3 but insist that there is another answer.
- Eventually, make sure they understand that $\sqrt{9} = +3$ or –3.
- Ask for both square roots of 25, 16, etc …

Framework objectives – Decimals in context

Use standard column procedures for the addition, subtraction and multiplication of integers and decimals. Select appropriate operations, methods and strategies to solve number problems.

Oral and mental starter

- Using a target board containing numbers to 1 decimal place, such as the one shown, point at two numbers and ask students to either add or subtract (smallest from largest).
- Students should be encouraged to do this mentally. If they have difficulty, they should be reminded of the mental imagery of the number line, for example:

2.3	1.8	4.2	3.3	1.6
4.1	2.9	3.6	4.9	2.2
3.7	5.2	2.1	1.2	3.1
1.5	5.6	4.5	6.1	3.8

1.8 + 3.4

```
        +1        +1        +1      +0.4
    1.8                          4.8    5.2
```

4.2 – 2.6

```
        –0.6      –1        –1
    1.6    2.2                  4.2
```

Main lesson activity

- This is a revision lesson on adding, subtracting, multiplying and dividing decimals in context.
- Introduce the topic by asking students where they see decimals in daily use. Establish that decimals are found with money, scales, sporting averages and speeds, among others, and illustrate their use in some of these contexts.
- Work through the following problems with the students.

Problem 1

Mr Smith goes out of his house with £16.73 in his pocket. He gets £40 out of the cash machine and then spends £5 on the lottery and buys a scratch card which costs him £1. The scratch card wins him £10. He then pays the paper bill of £7.02, spends £8.95 in the grocery store and buys breakfast in the café which costs him £3.20. He then returns home. How much money does he have left when he gets home?

- Explain that this problem can be set up as a series of additions and subtractions:

    £16.73 + £40 – £5 – £1 + £10 – £7.02 – £8.95 – £3.20

- This can be worked through in stages from left to right, giving:

        £16.73 + £40 – £5 – £1 + £10 – £7.02 – £8.95 – £3.20
    = £56.73 – £5 – £1 + £10 – £7.02 – £8.95 – £3.20
    = £51.73 – £1 + £10 – £7.02 – £8.95 – £3.20
    = £50.73 + £10 – £7.02 – £8.95 – £3.20
    = £60.73 – £7.02 – £8.95 – £3.20
    = £53.71 – £8.95 – £3.20
    = £44.76 – £3.20
    = £41.56

- Alternatively, the positive values can be combined, the negative
  values combined and these totals subtracted, giving:

£16.73	£5.00	£66.73
£40.00	£1.00	− £25.17
+ £10.00	£7.02	£41.56
£66.73	£8.95	
	+ £3.20	
	£25.17	

- Both methods produce the correct answer, i.e. that Mr Smith has
  £41.56 in his pocket when he gets back home. Discuss the advantages
  and disadvantages of both methods.

Problem 2

After an MOT test, Mrs Green needed four new tyres. The total bill
was £312.05. If the MOT test cost £33.25, how much did each tyre cost?

- Discuss the strategy for solving the problem, i.e. deduct
  the cost of the MOT from the total bill and then divide by 4.

$$\begin{array}{r} £312.05 \\ - \ £33.25 \\ \hline £278.80 \end{array} \qquad \begin{array}{r} £69.70 \\ 4\overline{)£278.80} \end{array}$$

Hence, the cost of each tyre is £69.70.

- Present students with another problem:

    It is recommended that a car does not tow a caravan that is
    more than one and a half times its weight. If a car weighs
    1452 kg, what is the maximum weight of a caravan that it can safely tow?

- Discuss strategies to solve this problem.
  It can be solved by straightforward multiplication:

$$\begin{array}{r} 1452 \text{ kg} \\ \times \ 1.5 \\ \hline 726 \text{ kg} \\ 1452 \text{ kg} \\ \hline 2178 \text{ kg} \end{array}$$

Alternatively, it can be solved by dividing 1452 by 2 and adding this to 1452.

Hence, the weight of the caravan should be no more than 2178 kg.

- **The class can now do Exercise 15E from the Pupil Workbook *or* Chapter 5 Addition (pages 20-21),
  Subtraction (pages 22-23) and Multiplication (pages 24-25) from Collins GCSE Maths for Edexcel A
  Workbook and Collins AQA B Workbook; Chapter 1 Addition (pages 6-7), Subtraction (pages 8-9)
  and Multiplication (pages 10-11) from Collins AQA A Workbook.**

Exercise 15E   Answers

1 £4359.33
2 £9.56
3 0.590 kilograms
4 £252.08
5 7.33 cm
6 £9.61
7 £37.35
8 730.8 cm
9 £125.80
10 £69.75

Plenary

- Present students with the following problem:

   A tap can deliver 20 litres of water per minute. The container it is filling has a hole halfway up the side that leaks at a rate of 7.5 litres per minute. The container holds 100 litres. How long will it take to fill the container?

- Discuss the solution:

   The first 50 litres take 50 ÷ 20 = 2.5 minutes.
   After that, the container fills at a rate of 12.5 litres per minute (20 − 7.5), so the second 50 litres take 50 ÷ 12.5 = 4 minutes.
   So, it takes 4 + 2.5 = 6.5 minutes to fill the container.

- The problem can be extended:

   As soon as the container is full, the tap is turned off and a draincock on the bottom of the container is turned on. This drains at 5 litres per minute. How long will it take for the container to empty?

   The first 50 litres drain at 12.5 litres per minute (7.5 + 5)
   = 4 minutes.
   The second 50 litres drain at 5 litres per minute = 10 minutes.
   So, it takes 4 + 10 = 14 minutes to drain the container.

New Maths Frameworking Year 9
National Test Style Questions

CHAPTER 1

Do not use a calculator for these questions.

1 This circle has the numbers 1 to 20 around it.

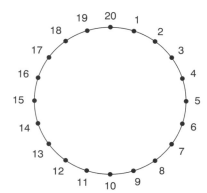

You can make a square by joining up the numbers in the 5 times table.

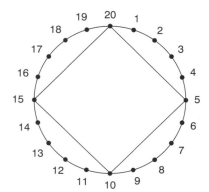

a Join up the numbers in the 4 times table.

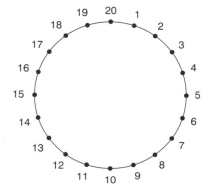

What is the name of the shape you have drawn? _____

b Complete the picture to draw a shape with 10 equal sides.

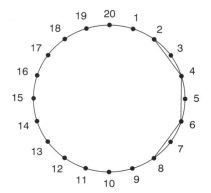

What times table makes this shape? _____

2 Calculate the answers to each of the following.

  a 86 − 39 _____

  b 176 + 58 _____

  c 24 × 5 _____

  d 75 ÷ 5 _____

3 **a** This number line goes from 0 to 100 using five equal steps. Fill in the missing numbers.

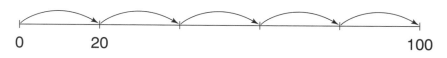

0   20   100

b This number line goes from 0 to 300 using five equal steps. Fill in the missing numbers.

0   300

CHAPTER 2

Do not use a calculator for these questions.

1 Look at these numbers.

$\frac{3}{4}$ 50%   0.15 $\frac{4}{5}$ 80%   0.9

Fill in missing values from the list above to make the following true.

a [............] < [20%]

b [............] > [$\frac{17}{20}$]

c [............] = [............]

d [$\frac{2}{5}$] < [............] < [0.6]

2 Fill in the missing numbers on this number line.

....   12   12.2   12.4   12.6

3 a Fill in the missing number in each of these calculations.

i Half of .... = 15

ii 10% of .... = 15

iii 50% of .... = 15

iv A quarter of .... = 15

b Fill in pairs of numbers to make these calculations true.

i .... × .... = 15

ii .... ÷ .... = 15

4 a i What fraction of this shape is shaded? _____

Write your answer in its simplest form. _____

ii Write this fraction as a percentage. _____

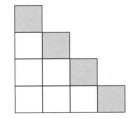

b Put a tick in each row to complete the table. The first one has been done for you.

	Greater than $\frac{1}{2}$	Equal to $\frac{1}{2}$	Less than $\frac{1}{2}$
0.8	✓		
50%			
$\frac{13}{25}$			
0.09			

CHAPTER 3

1 The following formula is used to work out how long clothes take to dry in a tumble dryer.

> Time in minutes (T) = 2 × (100 – temperature setting)

For example, for a temperature setting of 40 degrees, the time taken for clothes to dry would be

$$
\begin{aligned}
T &= 2 \times (100 - 40) \\
&= 2 \times 60 \\
&= 120 \text{ minutes}
\end{aligned}
$$

a How long will the clothes take to dry at 50 degrees?

b If it takes 40 minutes for some clothes to dry, what was the temperature setting on the tumble dryer?

2 Fill in the missing number in each of these calculations.

a 873 − .... = 378   **b** .... − 231 = 612

c 34 × .... = 646   **d** 2128 = ... + 54

e .... ÷ 22 = 484   **f** 899 ÷ .... = 29

3 a Use the pictures of the scales to work out the mass of a cube ,

cone △ and cylinder ⬭ .

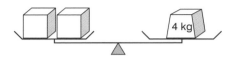 

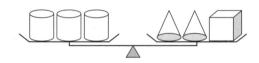

 = ... kg    = ... kg    = ... kg

b Fred has three cubes, one cylinder and one cone.

Put them on the scales so that they balance.

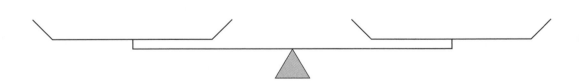

CHAPTER 4

Do not use a calculator for these questions.

1 Magda measures angle a as 130°.

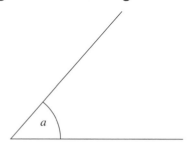

a Explain how you know that Magda is wrong.

_____

_____

_____

b The diagram shows three angles, b, b and 160° around a point P.

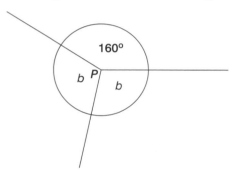

160°

b P b

Work out the value of b.

_____

_____

b = _____ degrees

2 The sketch shows four towns – A, B, C and D.

B is north of C.

D is east of C.

The distance AB = BC.

a Complete the sentences below.

Triangle BCD is a .... triangle.

Triangle ABC is an .... triangle

b Another town, Town E, is north-east of Town C and north of Town D. Mark the position of Town E on the diagram.

CHAPTER 5

Do not use a calculator for these questions.

1 Jake did a survey of left- and right-handedness in his class. His results are shown in the table below.

	Number of boys	Number of girls
Left-handed	2	3
Right-handed	11	14

a How many students are there in Jake's class? _____

b How many students in Jake's class are left-handed? _____

c Two students leave Jake's class. They are both girls. One is left-handed and one is right-handed. Fill in the table for Jake's class now.

	Number of boys	Number of girls
Left-handed		
Right-handed		

2 Hardeep and Natasha carry out a survey on eye colours. Hardeep shows her results in the bar chart below.

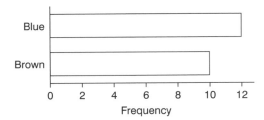

Natasha wants to show the same results on the pictogram below. Complete Natasha's pictogram for her.

Key: ☐ represents 4 people

Blue

Brown

3 These are the number of pens in five students' pencil cases.

   3   7   9   2   4

a What is the range of the number of pens? _____

b What is the median number of pens? _____

c What is the mean number of pens? _____

CHAPTER 6

Do not use a calculator for these questions.

1 **a** What is the area of the triangle on the right? _____

_____

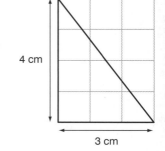

b Four of the triangles are put together to make a quadrilateral.

4 cm

3 cm

i What is the name of this quadrilateral? _____

ii What is the area of this quadrilateral? _____

2 Look at the signpost.

Longtown 16 km

How far is it to Longtown in miles? _____

3 Here are five shapes on a square grid.

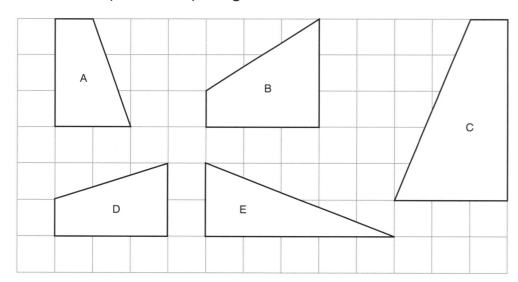

A

B

C

D

E

a **i** Which two shapes fit together to make a square? _____

ii What is the area of the square? _____

b **i** Which two shapes fit together to make a rectangle? _____

ii What is the area of the rectangle? _____

CHAPTER 7

Do not use a calculator for these questions.

1 Here are some number cards.

| 32 | 0.1 | 43 | 0.01 | 4.3 | 3.2 |

   a Use two of the cards to give a correct calculation for this answer.

$$\boxed{} \times \boxed{} = \boxed{4.3}$$

   b Use two of the cards to give a correct calculation for this answer.

$$\boxed{} \div \boxed{} = \boxed{32}$$

   c Which two cards would you multiply together to get the smallest possible answer?

     _____ and _____

   d Which two cards would you multiply together to get the largest possible answer?

     _____ and _____

2 Watermark's bookshop has a '3 for the price of 2' offer.

> **3 for the price of 2**
>
> Buy any three books and the
> cheapest one is free.

   a Ajid buys three books priced at £8.99, £7.50 and £10.20.

     How much does he pay for his three books ? _____

   b **i** Mary wants three books costing £2.50, £6.00 and £8.00.

       How much will she pay for these three books? _____

ii   Mary's friend, Barry, wants three books costing £3.50, £4.00 and £7.00.

How much will he pay for these three books? _____

c   Mary takes the three books costing £6.00, £7.00 and £8.00 to the till and Barry takes the three books costing £2.50, £3.50 and £4.00 to the till.

How much do they pay in total for all six books? _____

CHAPTER 8

1 Here is a flow chart for sorting numbers.
Sort each of the following numbers into the correct box.

25   7   8   16

The first one has been done for you.

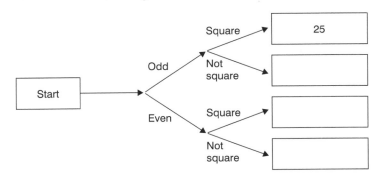

2 The table below shows all the pairs of factors of 24.

$1 \times 24 = 24$

$2 \times 12 = 24$

$3 \times 8 = 24$

$4 \times 6 = 24$

Using the table, or otherwise, write down the factors of

a 12 _____

b 48 _____

3 Find three square numbers that have a product of 36.

_____

4 The 33 times table is given below.

$1 \times 33 = 33$	$2 \times 33 = 66$	$3 \times 33 = 99$	$4 \times 33 = 132$	$5 \times 33 = 165$
$6 \times 33 = 198$	$7 \times 33 = 231$	$8 \times 33 = 264$	$9 \times 33 = 297$	$10 \times 33 = 330$

Use this to write down

a $33 \times 9 =$ ....   **b** $11 \times 33 =$ ....

c $30 \times 33 =$ ....   **d** $17 \times 33 =$ ....

CHAPTER 9

Do not use a calculator for these questions.

1 This tally chart shows the flavours of ice-cream sold with a children's 'Meal Deal' at a restaurant.

Flavour	Boys	Girls
Vanilla	̶H̶̶T̶ ̶H̶̶T̶ ̶H̶̶T̶ ̶H̶̶T̶ II	IIII ̶H̶̶T̶ I
Strawberry	̶H̶̶T̶ ̶H̶̶T̶ III	IIII IIII
Chocolate	̶H̶̶T̶ IIII	IIII ̶H̶̶T̶ ̶H̶̶T̶
Tutti Frutti	̶H̶̶T̶ II	IIII ̶H̶̶T̶ IIII

a How many ice-creams were served with 'Meal Deals' in total? _____

b How many boys chose vanilla ice-cream? _____

c If a child is picked at random, what is the probability of it being a boy that chose

vanilla ice-cream? _____

d If a child is picked at random, what is the probability of it being a child that chose

strawberry ice-cream? _____

2 a Here are two fair spinners, A and B.

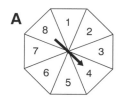
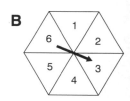

    i Which spinner gives the best chance
    of scoring 1. Tick (✓) the correct answer.

    Spinner A ☐   Spinner B ☐   Doesn't matter ☐

    ii Explain your choice of answer. _____

_____

b A five-sided spinner is spun 200 times. The results are shown in the table below.

Score	1	2	3	4	5
Frequency	35	89	41	17	18

    i Is the spinner fair?   Yes ☐   No ☐

    ii Explain your choice of answer. _____

_____

CHAPTER 10

Do not use a calculator for these questions.

1

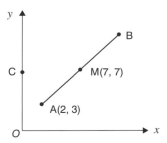

a M is the mid-point of AB.

Write down the coordinates of B. _____

b C is a point on the *y*-axis level with point M.

Write down the coordinates of C. _____

2 a Draw the lines of symmetry on these diagrams.

i

ii

b Write down the order of rotation symmetry of these diagrams.

i

ii

Order _____

Order _____

3 Donald is drawing shapes with a computer program. The drawing tool starts from the position shown, pointing in the direction of the arrow.

He types in the following instructions

FORWARD	3
RIGHT 90°	
FORWARD	2
RIGHT 90°	
FORWARD	3
RIGHT 90°	
FORWARD	2

to get the shape shown.

Write down the instructions he would need to type in to draw a similar shape that is twice the size.

CHAPTER 11

Do not use a calculator for these questions.

1 At Julie's local gym, she can either pay £2.50 each time she goes to the gym, or pay a monthly fee of £10 and only pay £1 each time she goes to the gym.

   a Plot the cost of 10 visits at £2.50 each on the graph below and join up the points with a straight line.

   b Plot the cost of paying a £10 monthly fee and £1 per visit for 10 visits on the same axes.

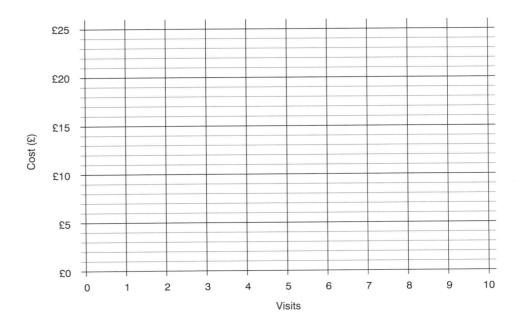

   c If Julie goes to the gym once a week (4 times each month), which method should she use to pay? _____

_____

    Explain your answer. _____

_____

2 Fill in the missing numbers to make these calculations true.

   a ☐ × ☐ − ☐ = 24

   b ☐ ÷ ☐ + ☐ = 24

3 **a** A teacher divides some cards into two piles.
The first pile contains $3n$ cards and the second contains $4n + 1$ cards.

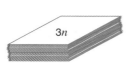 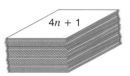

If there are 12 cards in the first pile, how many cards are there in the second pile?

_____

_____

_____

b These two piles contain the same number of cards.

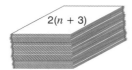 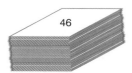

What is the value of n? _____

_____

_____

CHAPTER 12

Do not use a calculator for these questions.

1 Tick the number that is nearest to 1000.

1062	967	1100	897	1080

2 Here are four number cards.

6	3	7	4

Use the cards to make numbers that are as close as possible to the number shown, for example   50   →   47.

a   80   → ☐ ☐   **b**   400   → ☐ ☐

c   7000   → ☐ ☐ ☐ ☐

3 Write down the next three terms in two different sequences, where the first two terms are 1 and 3. Explain the rule that you have used in each case.

a   1,   3, ... , ... , ...

The rule is _____

b   1,   3, ... , ... , ...

The rule is _____

4 Look at these algebraic expressions.

$2n + m$	$n^2 + 2m$	$2n + 3$	$m + 2n$	$2n + 2m$	$3n + m$

a   Which two of these expressions are equivalent? _____

b   Which two expressions have the value 14 when $n = 2$ and $m = 5$?

_____

c   If the expression $2n + 3$ has a value of 13, what is the value of n?

_____

5 **a** Tick the shapes below that have an area of 20 cm².

i

5 cm

4 cm

ii

5 cm

4 cm

iii

4 cm

4 cm

iv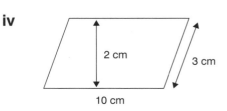

2 cm

3 cm

10 cm

b A square has a perimeter of 20 cm. What is its area? _____

_____

_____

6 Here are some number cards.

| 4 | 5 | 1 | 6 | 4 |

a Write down the mode. _____

b Find the median. _____

c Work out the mean. _____

d Find the range. _____

e A sixth card is added. | 10 |

Work out the new mean _____ and median _____ .

CHAPTER 13

1 The histogram shows the time it takes the students in Class 9A to travel to school. The pie chart shows how long it takes the students in Class 9B to travel to school.

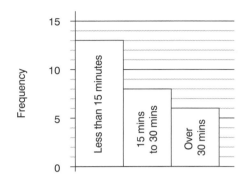

a How many students are in Class 9A? _____

b Explain why you **cannot** tell how many students there are in Class 9B.

_____

_____

c Which class would have the greatest average travelling time? _____

Explain how you can tell. _____

_____

2 This table shows the number of coins that Robyn has in her purse.

Coin	Frequency
1p	3
2p	6
5p	1
10p	5
20p	7
50p	3
£1	4
£2	1

a How many coins does Robyn have in her purse? _____

b What is the total value of the coins in Robyn's purse? _____

c Which value is the modal coin in Robyn's purse? _____

d What is the range of the values of the coins in Robyn's purse? _____

e What is the mean value of the coins in Robyn's purse? _____

CHAPTER 14

Do not use a calculator for these questions.

You will need compasses, a ruler and a protractor for Question **2**.

1 This net is of a cuboid. It is not drawn to scale.

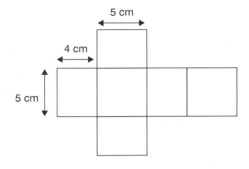

    a   What is the surface area of the cuboid?

_____

_____

_____

_____

    b   What is the volume of the cuboid? Don't forget to include the units.

_____

_____

2 **a**   Use a ruler and compasses to construct an accurate drawing of the triangle shown below.

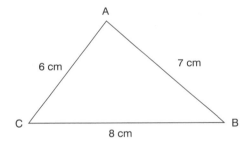

    b   Measure the angle at A. _____ degrees

National Test Answers

Chapter 1

1 a Check that the following numbers are joined: 4, 8, 12, 16 and 20; pentagon
 b Check that the following numbers are joined: 8, 10, 12, 14, 16, 18 and 20; 2 times table
2 a 47 **b** 234 **c** 120 **d** 15
3 a 40, 60, 80 **b** 60, 120, 180, 240

Chapter 2

1 a 0.15 **b** 0.9 **c** $\frac{4}{5}$ = 80% **d** 50%
2 11.6, 11.8
3 a i 30 **ii** 150 **iii** 30 **iv** 60 **b i** 3×5, 1×15, etc **ii** $30 \div 2$, $60 \div 4$, etc.
4 a i $\frac{4}{10}$, $\frac{2}{5}$ **ii** 40% **b**

	Greater than $\frac{1}{2}$	Equal to $\frac{1}{2}$	Less than $\frac{1}{2}$
0.8	✓		
50%		✓	
$\frac{13}{25}$	✓		
0.09			✓

Chapter 3

1 a 100 minutes **b** 80 degrees
2 a 495 **b** 843 **c** 19 **d** 2074 **e** 10 648 **f** 31
3 a Cube = 2 kg; Cone = 8 kg; Cylinder = 6 kg **b**

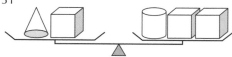

Chapter 4

1 a Possible answers: because *a* is acute/130° is obtuse/misread the scale on protractor/*a* is smaller than 90° **b** 100°
2 a Right-angled, isosceles **b** E forms a rectangle with CDB

Chapter 5

1 a 30 **b** 5 **c**

	Number of boys	Number of girls
Left-handed	2	2
Right-handed	11	13

2 Blue

Brown

3 a 7 **b** 4 **c** 5

Chapter 6

1 a 6 cm² **b i** Trapezium **ii** 24 cm²
2 10 miles
3 a i A and D **ii** 9 cm² **b i** C and E **ii** 15 cm²

Chapter 7

1 a 43×0.1 **b** $3.2 \div 0.1$ **c** 0.01, 0.1 **d** 32, 43
2 a £19.19 **b i** £14 **ii** £11 **c** £22.50

Chapter 8

1

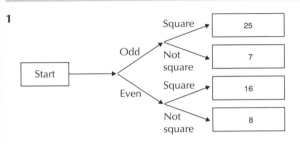

2 a 1, 2, 3, 4, 6, 12 **b** 1, 2, 3, 4, 6, 8, 12, 16, 24, 48
3 1, 1 and 36 or 1, 4 and 9
4 a 297 **b** 363 **c** 990 **d** 561

Chapter 9

1 a 100 **b** 22 **c** $\frac{22}{100}$ or $\frac{11}{50}$ or 0.22 **d** $\frac{22}{100}$ or $\frac{11}{50}$ or 0.22
2 a i Spinner B **ii** Less choice, bigger angle
  b i No **ii** All frequencies should be about 40

Chapter 10

1 a (12, 11) **b** (0, 7)
2 a i   **ii**

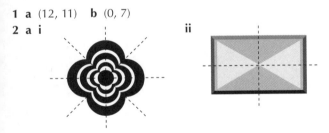

  b i 4 **ii** 2
3 FORWARD   6
   RIGHT 90°
   FORWARD   4
   RIGHT 90°
   FORWARD   6
   RIGHT 90°
   FORWARD   4

Chapter 11

1 a Graph from (0, 0) to (10, 25)
  b Graph from (0, 10) to (10, 20)
  c She should pay £2.50 per visit; this will cost £10 and is cheaper than the monthly membership option which would cost her £14
2 a Any values that work, for example $5 \times 6 - 6$, $2 \times 14 - 4$
  b Any values that work, for example $40 \div 2 + 4$, $12 \div 6 + 22$
3 a 17 **b** $2n + 6 = 46$, $2n = 40$, $n = 20$

Chapter 12

1 967
2 a 76 **b** 376 **c** 6743
3 Any two rules, for example
   Odd numbers / Add 2 each time (5, 7, 9)
   Goes up 1, 2, 3, 4, 5 (6, 10, 15)
4 a $2n + m$ and $m + 2n$ **b** $n^2 + 2m$ and $2n + 2m$ **c** 5
5 a i and iv **b** 25 cm^2
6 a 4 **b** 4 **c** 4 **d** 5 **e** 5, 4.5

Chapter 13

1 a 27
   b A pie chart only shows proportions and not numbers
   c 9B because the largest group has a journey time of more than 30 minutes but the largest group of 9A has a journey time of less than 15 minutes
2 a 30 **b** £9.60 **c** 20p **d** 199p **e** 32p

Chapter 14

1 a 130 cm^2 **b** 100 cm^3
2 a Check that the lengths and angles are accurate **b** $75° \pm 2°$

New Maths Frameworking
Year 9 OHTs

Algebra **1** and **2**

Coordinates

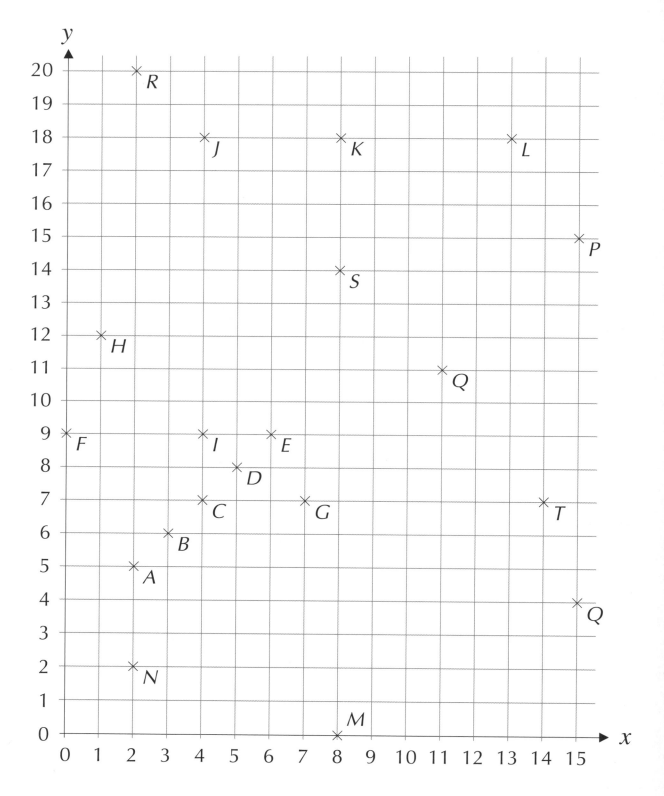

Coordinate grid

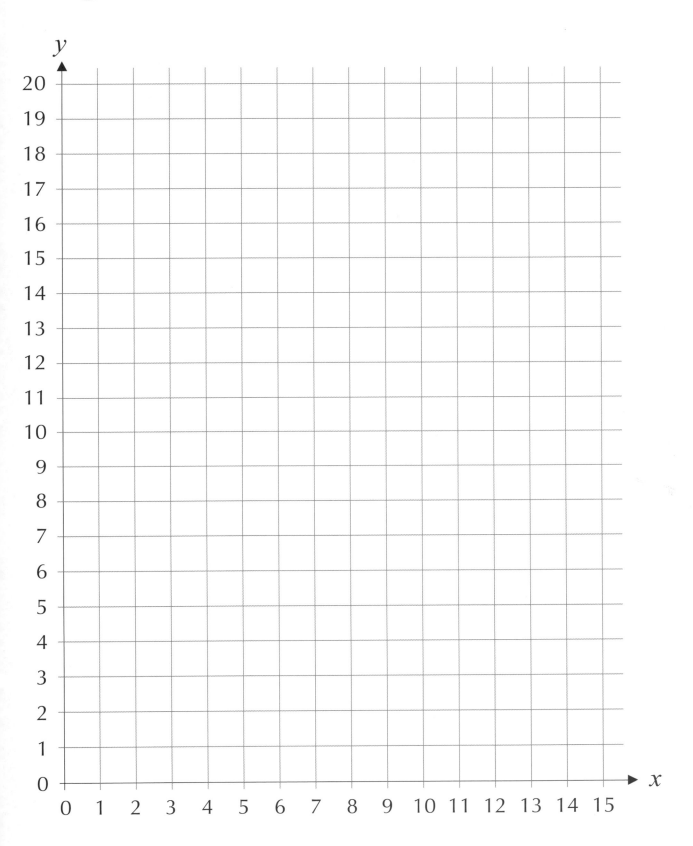

Lines

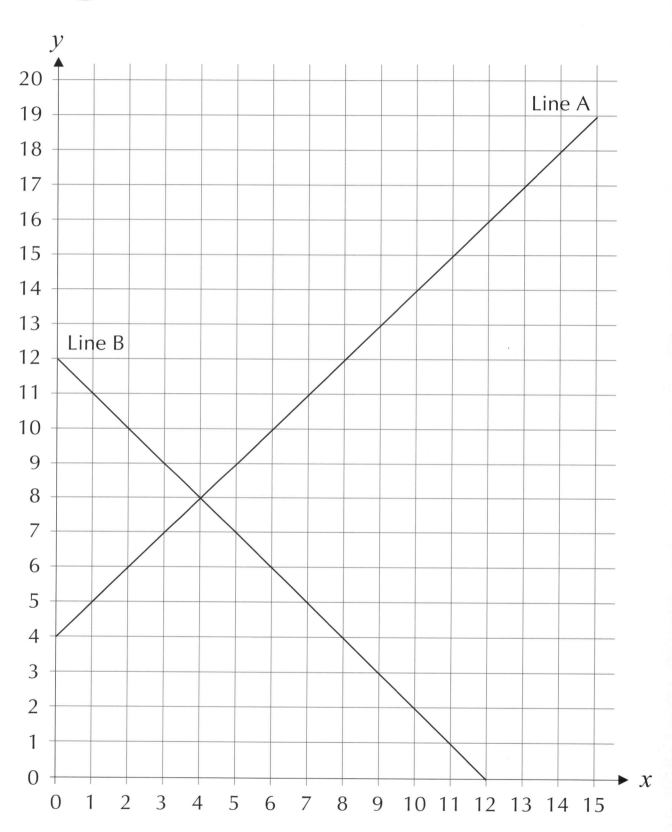

Number **1**

Fraction grid 1

$\frac{1}{4}$			1
		$1\frac{3}{4}$	
	$3\frac{1}{2}$		
			5

Fraction grid 2

$\frac{1}{4}$	$\frac{1}{2}$	$\frac{3}{4}$	1
$1\frac{1}{4}$	$1\frac{1}{2}$	$1\frac{3}{4}$	2
$2\frac{1}{4}$	$2\frac{1}{2}$	$2\frac{3}{4}$	3
$3\frac{1}{4}$	$3\frac{1}{2}$	$3\frac{3}{4}$	4
$4\frac{1}{4}$	$4\frac{1}{2}$	$4\frac{3}{4}$	5

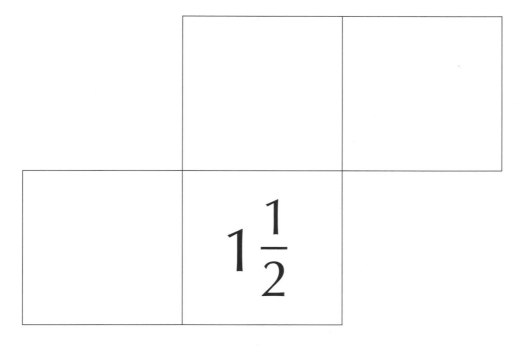

Fraction grid 4

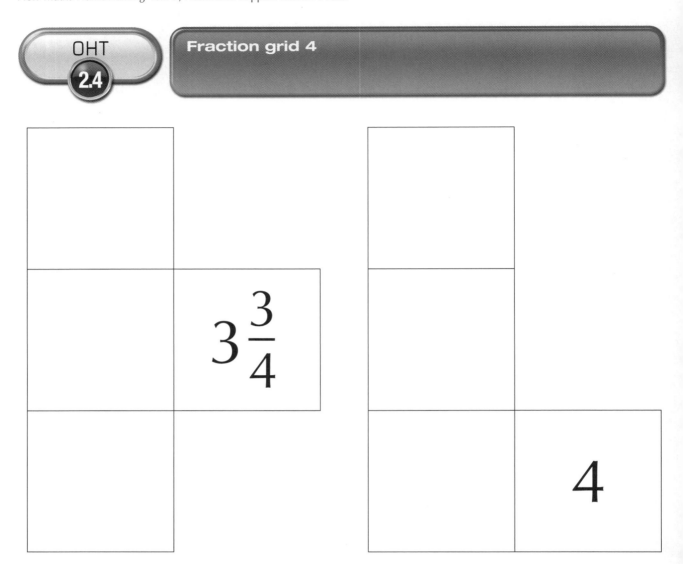

OHT 2.5

Fish

CHAPTER 3

Algebra 3

OHT 3.1

60

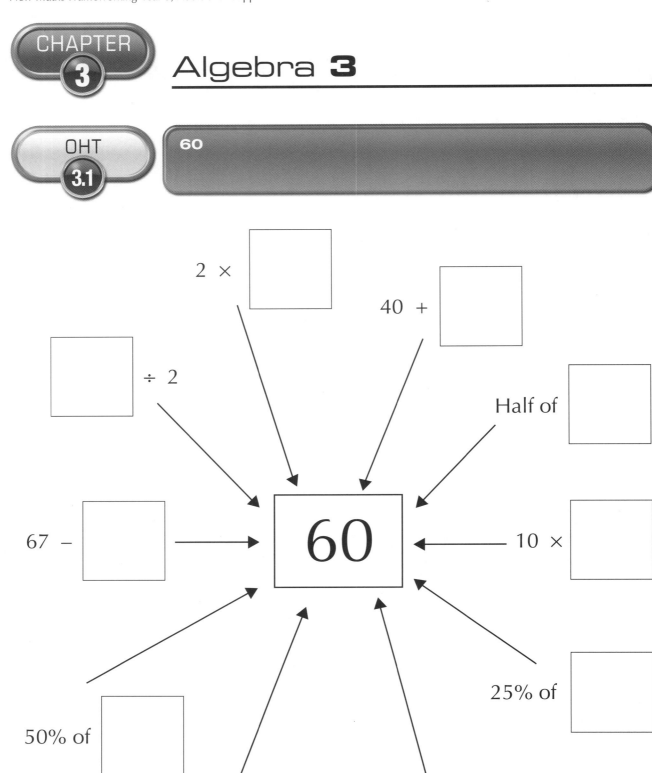

2 ×

40 +

÷ 2

Half of

67 −

60

10 ×

50% of

25% of

$\frac{1}{4}$ of

12 ×

Rules: Boat hire

£6 per hour

2 hours

5 hours

4 hours

6 hours

$1\frac{1}{2}$ hours

$2\frac{1}{4}$ hours

OHT 3.3

Rules: Turkey cooking time

20 minutes per pound plus 20 minutes

5 pounds

10 pounds

8 pounds

6 pounds

$6\frac{1}{2}$ pounds

$7\frac{1}{4}$ pounds

Rules: Car hire

£25 plus £30 per day

2 days

5 days

1 week

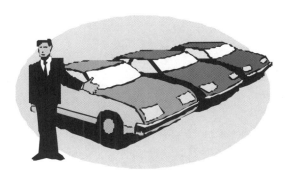

10 days

$4\frac{1}{2}$ days

$2\frac{1}{2}$ days

Reverse rules

Boat hire: £6 per hour

£33

£4.50

Turkey cooking time: 20 minutes per pound plus 20 minutes

3 hours

4 hours
20 minutes

Car hire: £25 plus £30 per day

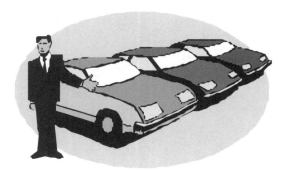

£145

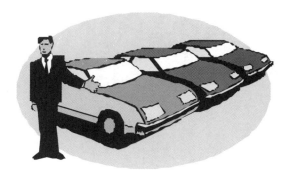

£625

Formulae 1

$$P = 4s$$

6 cm

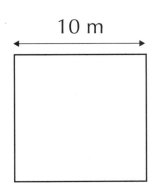

10 m

7 mm

$$P = 2w + 2b$$

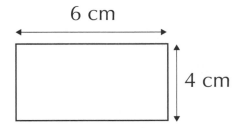

6 cm

4 cm

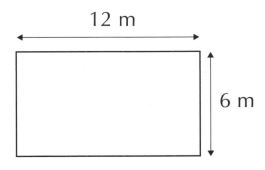

12 m

6 m

9 mm

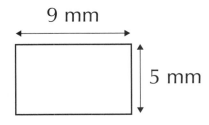

5 mm

Formulae 2

$$C = 50 + 30d$$

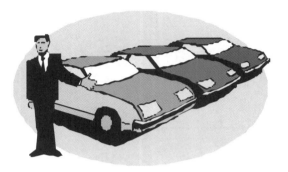

3 days

8 days

2 weeks

10 days

$4\frac{1}{2}$ days

$2\frac{1}{2}$ days

Formulae 3

$P = 4s$

$P = 40$ m

$P = 50$ cm

$P = 2w + 2b$

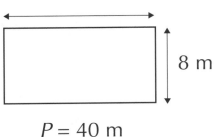

8 m

$P = 40$ m

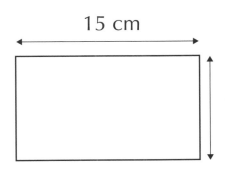

15 cm

$P = 50$ cm

$C = 50 + 30d$

$C = 350$

$C = 95$

Geometry and measures **1**

Triangle pattern

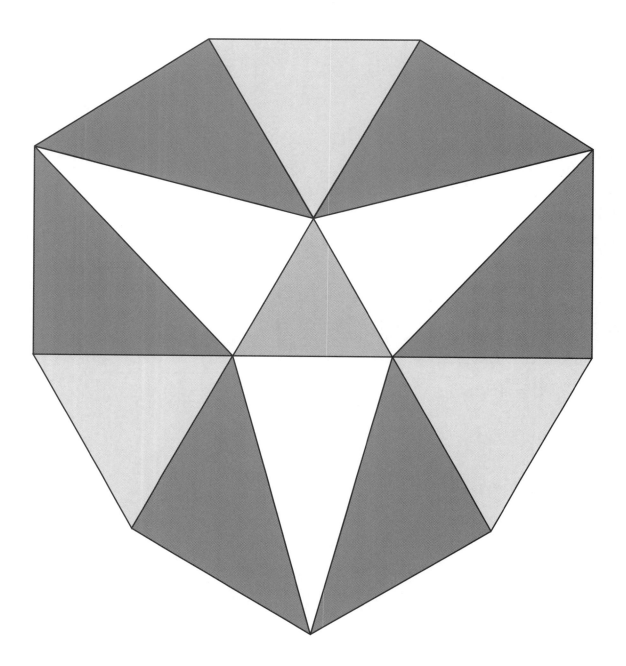

Statistics **1**

Two-way tables

	Brown	Blue	Green
Boys	9	4	1
Girls	7	6	3

Bar charts

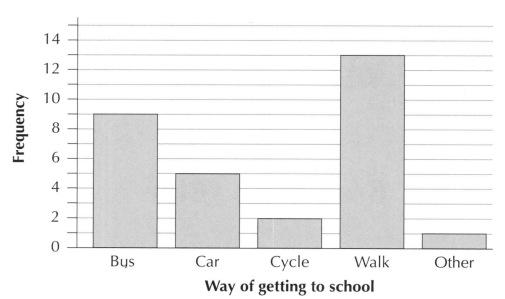

Way of getting to school

It's not too far and it's better than the crowded bus.

It's better than walking and it's quick and easy.

It's too far to walk and it's quicker.

My mum's work is that way and there's no bus.

I wanted to stay at this school even after we moved.

Bar-line graphs

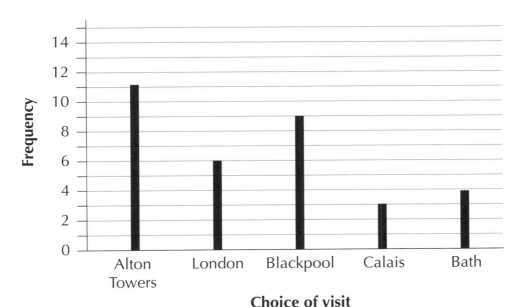

Choice of visit

I like to go and sit on a beach and paddle in the sea.

I like to ride on scary roller coasters.

I like to visit museums and art galleries.

I like to see historic places like Roman baths.

I like to go to foreign countries.

CHAPTER 6

Geometry and measures 2

OHT 6.1 **Rectangles 1**

Work out the area of each of these rectangles.

a

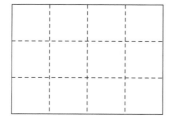

Area = _____ square units

b

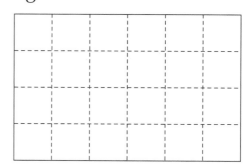

Area = _____ square units

c

7 cm

5 cm

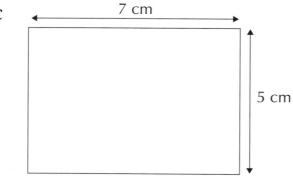

Area = _____ cm²

d

3.5 cm

7 cm

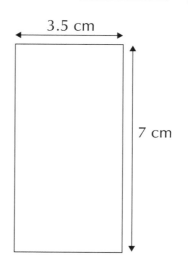

Area = _____ cm²

e

12 mm

7 mm

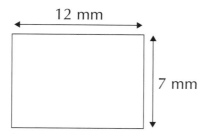

Area = _____ mm²

f

4.5 m

8 m

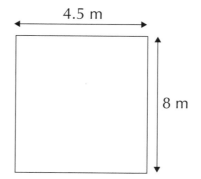

Area = _____ m²

Rectangles 2

Work out the length of each of the sides marked with a letter.

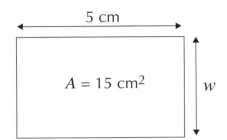

a

5 cm

$A = 15$ cm^2

w

$w =$ _____ cm

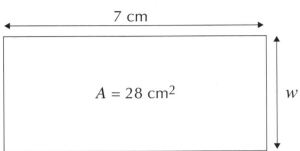

b

7 cm

$A = 28$ cm^2

w

$w =$ _____ cm

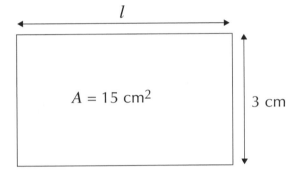

c

l

$A = 15$ cm^2

3 cm

$l =$ _____ cm

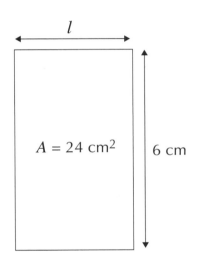

d

l

$A = 24$ cm^2

6 cm

$l =$ _____ cm

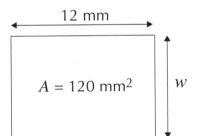

e

12 mm

$A = 120$ mm^2

w

$w =$ _____ mm

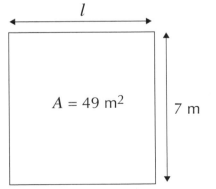

f

l

$A = 49$ m^2

7 m

$l =$ _____ m

Statistics **2**

Complements to 1

0.2   0.4   0.5

0.25

0.35   0.6

0.37

0.45

0.2   0.16

$\frac{1}{2}$ $\frac{1}{3}$ $\frac{3}{10}$ $\frac{1}{5}$

$\frac{3}{4}$

$\frac{7}{12}$

$\frac{7}{8}$ $\frac{1}{6}$ $\frac{5}{7}$ $\frac{4}{9}$

$\frac{5}{9}$ 0.55 $\frac{2}{3}$ $\frac{1}{4}$ 0.92

0.05

0.9   0.8 $\frac{5}{12}$ $\frac{1}{3}$

Geometry and measures 3

OHT 10.1 **Line symmetry**

Alphabet

Coordinates 1

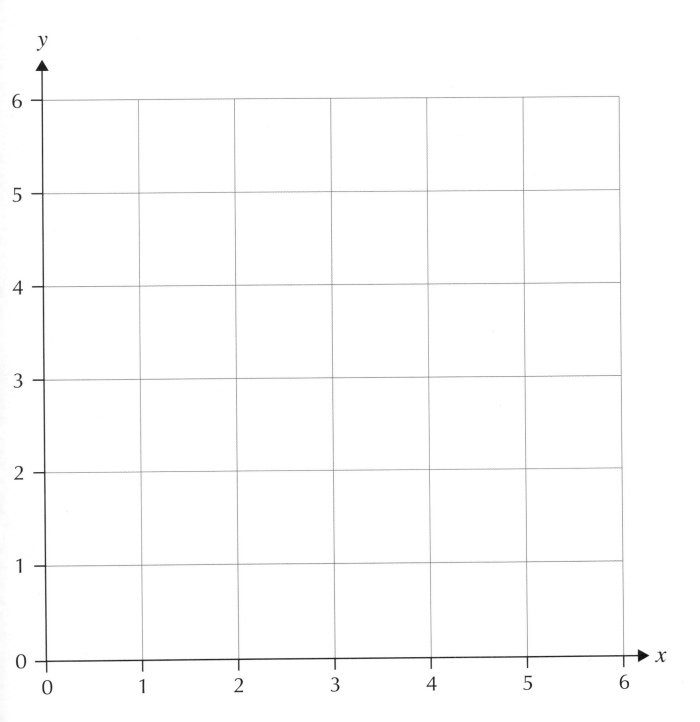

Coordinates 2

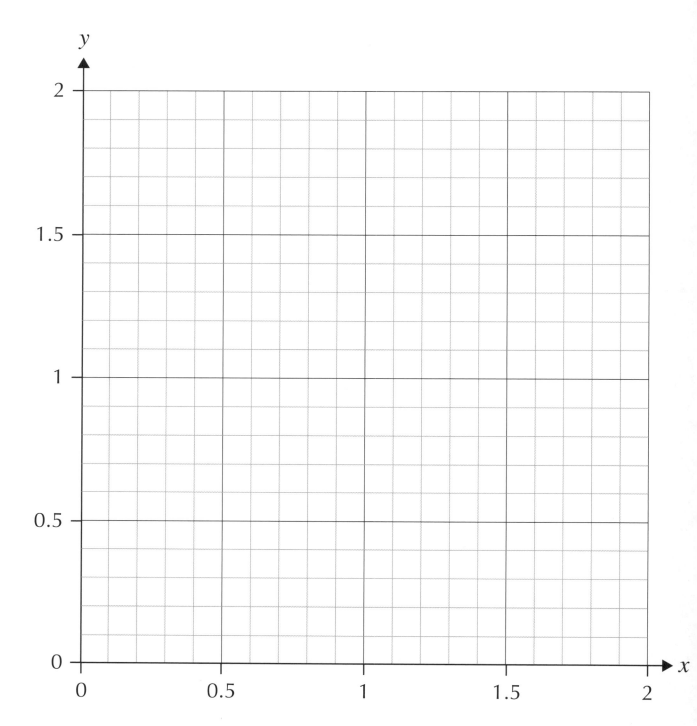

Coordinates 3

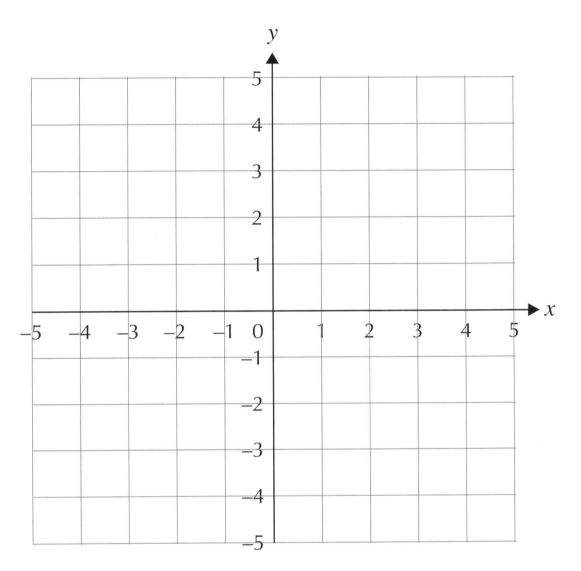

Algebra **5**

$+\,5$

$\times\,2$

$-\,4$

$\div\,2$

Steps

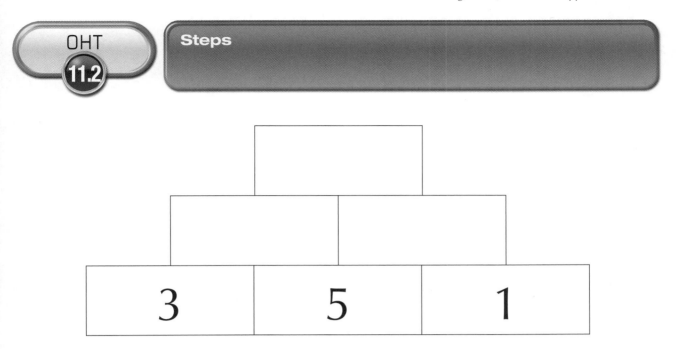

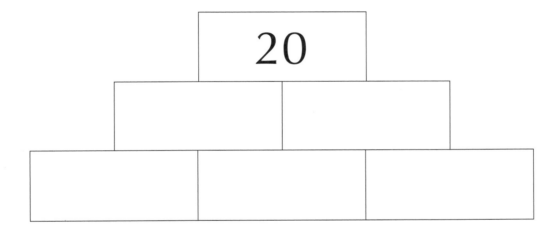

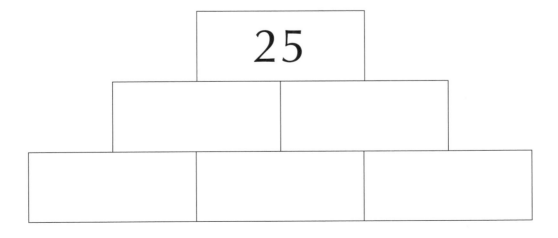

The Jones family

Mum and Dad

Kim and baby Martin

Grandad

Annie

Bill

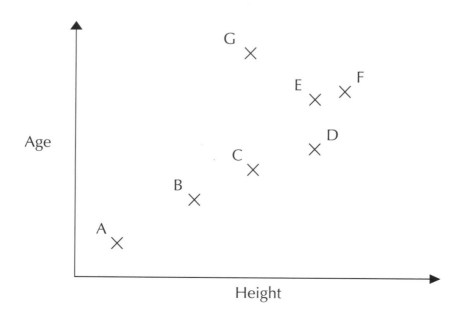

Revision

Diagrams 1

0%   100%

Diagrams 2

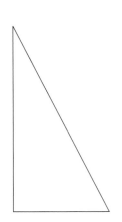

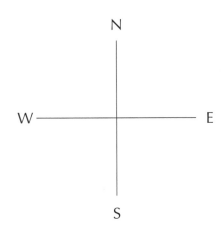

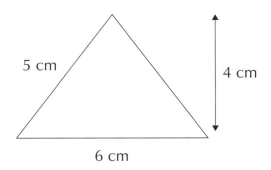

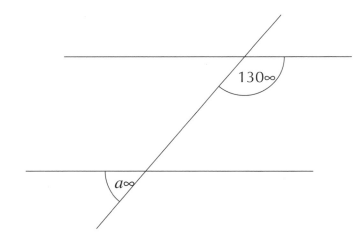

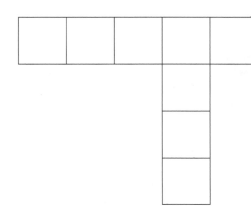

Diagrams 3

Leeds	◇ ◇ ◇ ◇
Huddersfield	◇ ◇ ◁

◇ = 4 trains

M	U	L	T	I	P	L	Y

Colour of ball	Red	Blue	Green
Probability	0.3	0.2	0.5

Number of pets	Frequency
1	2
2	5
3	3

Birthdays

Birthday	Tally	Frequency
Jan – Mar		
Apr – Jun		
Jul – Sep		
Oct – Dec		

Frequency diagrams

Favourite pets of class 9Q

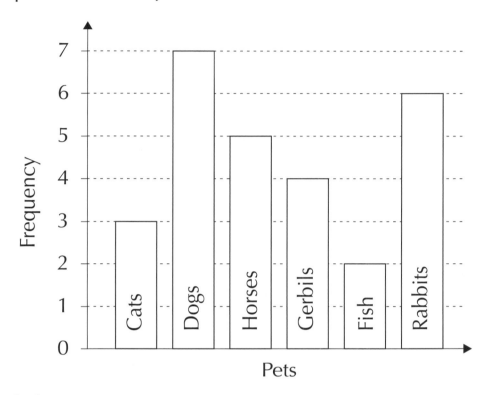

Heights of class 9P

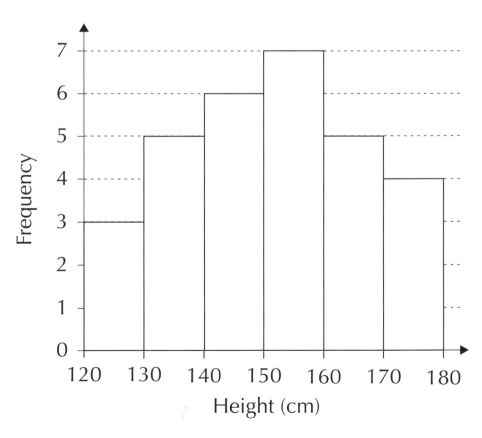

This table shows lawnmower sales at a shop.

Jan	Feb	Mar	Apr	May	Jun	Jul	Aug	Sep	Oct	Nov	Dec
0	25	63	75	92	68	53	32	76	15	0	12

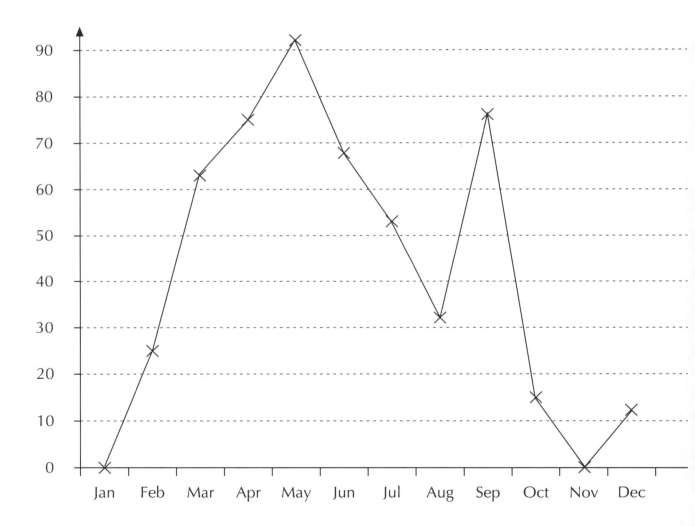

Numbers

34

37

40

36

26

42

42

41

29

32

28

32

37

29

43

42

37

43

41

27

40

42

28

36

38

31

28

33

43

30

26

Stem-and-leaf diagrams

Key   2 | 5 = 25

2	5	6	0	2		
3	7	1	1	9	6	2
4	7	7	6	1	4	

Unordered

2	0	2	5	6		
3	1	1	2	6	7	9
4	1	4	6	7	7	

Ordered

BODMAS calculations

Example

Work out each of the following, using the order of operations given by BODMAS. Show each step of the calculation.

a $10 \div 2 + 3 \times 3$ **b** $10 \div (2 + 3) \times 3$

a Firstly, work out the division and multiplication,
   which gives: $5 + 9$
   Then work out the addition to give: 14

b Firstly, work out the bracket, which gives: $10 \div 5 \times 3$
   There is a choice between division and multiplication,
   so decide on the order by working from left to right:
   Work out the left-hand operation first, which gives: 2×3
   Then work out the remaining operation to give: 6

Example

Work out: **a** $30 - 4 \times 2^2$ **b** $(30 - 4) \times 2^2$

Show each step of the calculation.

a Firstly, work out the power, which gives: $30 - 4 \times 4$
   Secondly, the multiplication, which gives: $30 - 16$
   Finally, the subtraction to give: 14

b Firstly, work out the bracket, which gives: 26×2^2
   Secondly, the power, which gives: 26×4
   Finally, the multiplication to give: 104

Adding and subtracting negative numbers

Example

John is £42.56 overdrawn at the bank. He gets his wages of £189.50 paid in and takes out £30 in cash. How much has he got in the bank now?

An overdrawn amount is negative, so the calculation is:

$$-42.56 + 189.50 - 30$$
$$= 189.50 - 72.56$$
$$= £116.94$$

Example

Find the missing number to make each of these calculations true.

a $10 + \boxed{} = 7$

b $-8 + \boxed{} = 12$

c $-9 - \boxed{} = 6$

You should be able to work out the answers to these using your knowledge of number facts. If you find this difficult, try visualising a number line, or for more difficult questions, rearrange the equation to find the unknown.

a $\boxed{} = 7 - 10 = -3$

b $\boxed{} = 12 + 8 = 20$

c $-\boxed{} = 6 + 9 = 15$, so $\boxed{} = -15$

Multiples, factors and prime numbers

Example

Find the largest number less than 100 that is:
a a multiple of 3
b a multiple of 3 and 5.

a This will be a number in the 3 times table that is close to 100:

$30 \times 3 = 90$
$31 \times 3 = 93$
$32 \times 3 = 96$
$33 \times 3 = 99$
$34 \times 3 = 102$

So, the largest multiple of 3 that is less than 100 is 99.

b Because 3 and 5 have no common factors, multiples common to 3 and 5 are multiples of 15:

15, 30, 45, 60, 75, 90, 105, …

So, the largest number under 100 that is a multiple of both 3 and 5 is 90.

Example

Find the factors of: **a** 35   **b** 180.

a Find all the products that make 35:

$1 \times 35 = 35$ $5 \times 7 = 35$

So, the factors of 35 are {1, 5, 7, 35}.

b $1 \times 180 = 180$ $2 \times 90 = 180$ $3 \times 60 = 180$ $4 \times 45 = 180$
$5 \times 36 = 180$ $6 \times 30 = 180$ $9 \times 20 = 180$ $10 \times 18 = 180$
$12 \times 15 = 180$

So, the factors are {1, 2, 3, 4, 5, 6, 9, 10, 12, 15, 18, 20, 30, 36, 45, 60, 90, 180}.

Remember that factors always come in pairs.

Power and roots

Example

Calculate: **a** 22^2 **b** $\sqrt{289}$ **c** $\sqrt{600}$

a You can either use the square button on your calculator or calculate 22×22.

$$22^2 = 22 \times 22 = 484$$

b Using the square root button on your calculator, $\sqrt{289} = 17$.

c Using the square root button on your calculator, $\sqrt{600} = 24.5$ (rounded to 1 decimal place).

Example

Calculate 7^4.

Using the power button on your calculator, $7^4 = 2401$.

Remember $7^4 = 7 \times 7 \times 7 \times 7$.

New Maths Frameworking Year 9
Homework

Algebra **1** and **2**

Name: _____

Form: _____

Do not use a calculator for this exercise.

1 Work out each of the following additions.

    a 14 + 28_____

    b 43 + 70 _____

    c 38 + 75 _____

    d 52 + 95_____

    e 240 + 630 _____

    f 148 + 121_____

2 Work out each of the following subtractions.

    a 27 − 9 _____

    b 50 − 27 _____

    c 85 − 28 _____

    d 67 − 23_____

    e 145 − 52 _____

    f 307 − 123 _____

3 Write in the missing numbers in each of the following calculations.

    a ☐ + 8 = 29

    b 45 − ☐ = 21

    c 19 + ☐ = 52

    d ☐ − 13 = 19

    e 48 − ☐ = 8

    f 28 + ☐ = 55

4 Find a volunteer, such as a parent, brother, sister or friend.

Ask them the following ten questions. Repeat the question if necessary. Ask the person to work out the answer mentally. Write down their answer. When you have asked all ten questions, mark the test and ask the person to sign to say that they have done it.

    1 8 + 10 _____

    2 19 + 30 _____

    3 52 + 37 _____

    4 123 + 59_____

    5 88 + 55 _____

    6 20 − 7 _____

    7 68 − 32 _____

    8 62 − 19 _____

    9 128 − 59_____

    10 82 − 37 _____

Total: _____ out of 10. Signature: _____

HOMEWORK
1.2

Name: _____

Form: _____

Do not use a calculator for this exercise.

1 Work out the following multiplications.

a 3×6 _____   **b** 8×6 _____   **c** 7×9 _____

d 8×9 _____   **e** $5 \times 2 \times 9$ _____   **f** $9 \times 5 \times 3$ _____

g 70×6 _____   **h** 7×60 _____

2 Complete the following multiplication tables.

a

×	7	8	9
4			
6			54
10			

b

×	2	6	8
5			
7	14		
8			

3 Work out the following multiplications mentally. You may make jottings on rough paper if needed.

a 27×3 _____   **b** 4×18 _____   **c** 2×54 _____

d 39×2 _____   **e** 15×3 _____   **f** 3×34 _____

4 Find a volunteer, such as a parent, brother, sister or friend.

Ask them the following ten questions. Repeat the question if necessary. Ask the person to work out the answer mentally. Write down their answer. When you have asked all ten questions, mark the test and ask the person to sign to say that they have done it.

1 8×10 _____

2 7×8 _____

3 2×18 _____

4 21×3 _____

5 18×5 _____

6 20×7 _____

7 68×2 _____

8 4×19 _____

9 28×5 _____

10 82×3 _____

Total: _____ out of 10. Signature: _____

Name: _____

Form: _____

HOMEWORK 1.3

1   The first term in a sequence is given. Use the rule to work out the next five terms in each sequence.

a    The rule is add 3

26 | | | | |

b   The rule is subtract 5

61 | | | | |

c   The rule is add 4

–16 | | | | |

d   The rule is multiply by 2

5 | | | | |

e   The rule is multiply by 3 then add 1

1 | | | | |

2   Work out the rule that has been used to generate each of the following sequences.

a 17, 21, 25, 29, 33, ...   The rule is _____

b 87, 78, 69, 60, 51, ...   The rule is _____

c 7, 2, –3, –8, –13, ...   The rule is _____

d 5, 15, 45, 135, 405, ...   The rule is _____

e 200, 100, 50, 25, 12.5, ...   The rule is _____

3   Work out the missing terms in each sequence.

a | | 6 | 10 | 14 | | 22

b | 40 | 33 | 26 | | 12 |

Name: _____

Form: _____

1 Fill in the outputs of each function machine.

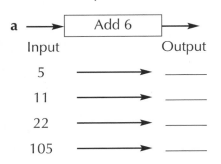

a ⟶ | Add 6 | ⟶

Input   Output

5 ⟶ _____

11 ⟶ _____

22 ⟶ _____

105 ⟶ _____

b ⟶ | Subtract 5 | ⟶

Input   Output

20 ⟶ _____

42 ⟶ _____

9 ⟶ _____

99 ⟶ _____

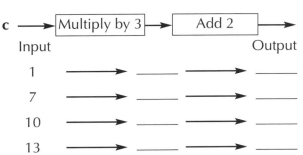

c ⟶ | Multiply by 3 | ⟶ | Add 2 | ⟶

Input   Output

1 ⟶ _____ ⟶ _____

7 ⟶ _____ ⟶ _____

10 ⟶ _____ ⟶ _____

13 ⟶ _____ ⟶ _____

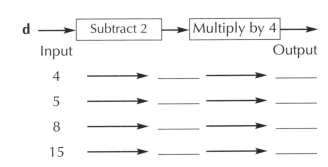

d ⟶ | Subtract 2 | ⟶ | Multiply by 4 | ⟶

Input   Output

4 ⟶ _____ ⟶ _____

5 ⟶ _____ ⟶ _____

8 ⟶ _____ ⟶ _____

15 ⟶ _____ ⟶ _____

2 Fill in the inputs of these function machines.

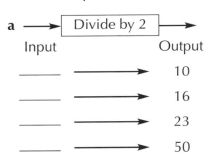

a ⟶ | Divide by 2 | ⟶

Input   Output

_____ ⟶ 10

_____ ⟶ 16

_____ ⟶ 23

_____ ⟶ 50

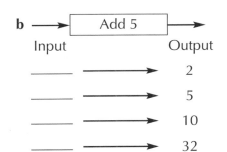

b ⟶ | Add 5 | ⟶

Input   Output

_____ ⟶ 2

_____ ⟶ 5

_____ ⟶ 10

_____ ⟶ 32

3 Fill in the missing function of these function machines.

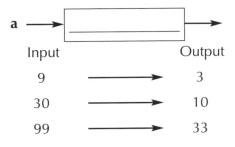

a ⟶ | _____ | ⟶

Input   Output

9 ⟶ 3

30 ⟶ 10

99 ⟶ 33

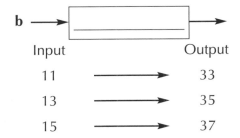

b ⟶ | _____ | ⟶

Input   Output

11 ⟶ 33

13 ⟶ 35

15 ⟶ 37

Name: _____

Form: _____

1 Match each of the word statements to an expression. The letter n stands for 'a number'. The first one has been done for you.

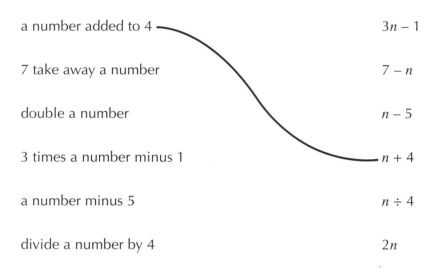

a number added to 4 $3n - 1$

7 take away a number $7 - n$

double a number $n - 5$

3 times a number minus 1 $n + 4$

a number minus 5 $n \div 4$

divide a number by 4 $2n$

2 In this question the letters a, b and c represent three numbers.

Write down the value of each expression for the values of a, b and c given below.

$a = 4$ $b = 5$ $c = 6$

a $a + 5$ _____   **b** $10 - c$ _____   **c** $b + 3$ _____

d $b - 1$ _____   **e** $2b$ _____   **f** $3a$ _____

3 Fill in the missing outputs for each function machine.

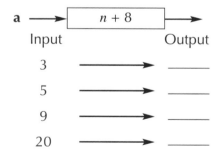

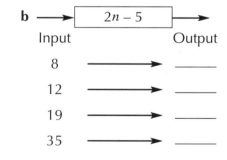

HOMEWORK
1.6

Name: _____

Form: _____

For each equation you should:

a complete the table of values by working out the value of *y* for each value of *x*;

b complete the coordinates of the points for the graph;

c plot the points and draw a straight line through them.

1 The equation is $y = x + 5$

a

x	0	2	3	5
y				

b (0, _____)

(2, _____)

(3, _____)

(5, _____)

c

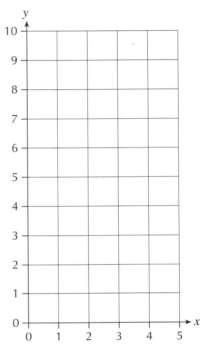

2 The equation is $y = 6 - x$

a

x	0	2	3	6
y				

b (0, _____)

(2, _____)

(3, _____)

(6, _____)

c

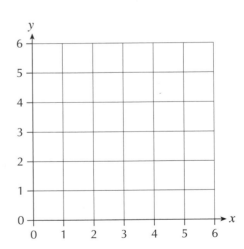

continued...

Name: _____

Form: _____

3 The equation is $y = 4x$

a

x	0	1	2	3
y				

b (0, _____)

(1, _____)

(2, _____)

(3, _____)

c

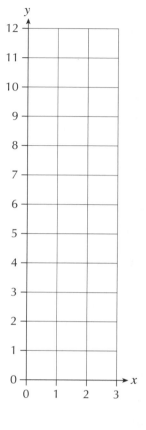

4 The equation is $y = 3x - 1$

a

x	0	1	2	3	4
y					

b (0, _____)

(1, _____)

(2, _____)

(3, _____)

(4, _____)

c

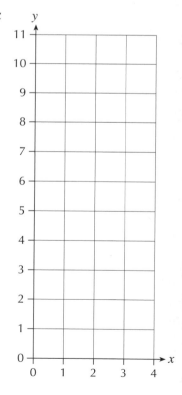

Number **1**

Name: _____

Form: _____

1 Round each number to the nearest 10.

   a 51 _____   **b** 68 _____   **c** 55 _____

   d 207 _____   **e** 312 _____   **f** 465 _____

2 Round each number to the nearest 100.

   a 293 _____   **b** 620 _____   **c** 250 _____

   d 2791 _____   **e** 6132 _____   **f** 2250 _____

3 Round each car price to the nearest £1000.

   a   **b**   **c**

      £_____   £_____   £_____

4 Round each number to the nearest whole number.

   a 2.8 _____   **b** 7.1 _____   **c** 13.5 _____

   d 9.82 _____   **e** 5.32 _____   **f** 18.76 _____

5 Round each number to one decimal place.

   a 7.82 _____   **b** 8.37 _____   **c** 0.65 _____

   d 12.63 _____   **e** 18.79 _____   **f** 10.52 _____

6 Round each number to one decimal place.

   a 7.821 _____   **b** 6.378 _____   **c** 12.053 _____

   d 11.609 _____   **e** 0.073 _____   **f** 8.998 _____

Name: _____

Form: _____

1   Write down the numbers that the arrows are pointing to on the number line.

2   Circle the larger number in each pair of decimal numbers below.

    a 0.8   0.9   **b** 3.2   3.6   **c** 11.3   11.2

    d 9.9   10.0   **e** 4.3   3.4   **f** 6.5   8.5

    g 10.25   10.4   **h** 4.15   4.2   **i** 5.13   5.03

3   Put these numbers in order of size, starting with the smallest.

    a 2.3, 3.7, 7.3, 3.2   _____ , _____ , _____ , _____

    b 0.7, 3.7, 1.7, 0.5   _____ , _____ , _____ , _____

    c 20.3, 16.2, 11.5, 12.6 _____ , _____ , _____ , _____

    d 73.5, 41.2, 14.3, 35.7 _____ , _____ , _____ , _____

4   Put these amounts of money in order of size, starting with the smallest.

    a £1.09, £1.90, £0.99, £9.91 _____ , _____ , _____ , _____

    b £4.31, £4.13, £3.14, £3.41 _____ , _____ , _____ , _____

HOMEWORK
2.3

Name: _____

Form: _____

1 Write down how much of each shape is shaded as a fraction and a decimal.

  a

  fraction _____

  decimal _____

  b

  fraction _____

  decimal _____

  c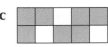

  fraction _____

  decimal _____

2 Write each fraction as a decimal.

  a $\frac{1}{10}$ _____

  b $\frac{7}{10}$ _____

  c $\frac{9}{10}$ _____

  d $\frac{1}{100}$ _____

  e $\frac{13}{100}$ _____

  f $\frac{31}{100}$ _____

3 Write each decimal as a fraction.

  a 0.2 _____

  b 0.9 _____

  c 0.09 _____

  d 0.11 _____

  e 0.27 _____

  f 0.35 _____

4 Fill in the missing numbers to complete the equivalences below.

  a $0.3 = \frac{}{10} = \frac{}{100}$

  b $0.45 = \frac{}{100}$

  c $0.8 = \frac{}{5} = \frac{}{10} = \frac{}{100}$

Name: _____

Form: _____

1 Fill in the missing values to make the fractions equivalent.

a $\dfrac{2}{7} = \dfrac{4}{\rule{0.5cm}{0.4pt}} = \dfrac{6}{\rule{0.5cm}{0.4pt}} = \dfrac{}{28}$

b $\dfrac{3}{8} = \dfrac{6}{\rule{0.5cm}{0.4pt}} = \dfrac{9}{\rule{0.5cm}{0.4pt}} = \dfrac{}{32}$

c $\dfrac{1}{9} = \dfrac{2}{\rule{0.5cm}{0.4pt}} = \dfrac{3}{\rule{0.5cm}{0.4pt}} = \dfrac{}{36}$

d $\dfrac{3}{5} = \dfrac{6}{\rule{0.5cm}{0.4pt}} = \dfrac{9}{\rule{0.5cm}{0.4pt}} = \dfrac{}{20}$

2 Fill in the missing values to make the fractions equivalent.

a $\dfrac{4}{5} = \dfrac{16}{\rule{0.5cm}{0.4pt}}$

b $\dfrac{3}{7} = \dfrac{9}{\rule{0.5cm}{0.4pt}}$

c $\dfrac{2}{3} = \dfrac{12}{\rule{0.5cm}{0.4pt}}$

d $\dfrac{5}{6} = \dfrac{25}{\rule{0.5cm}{0.4pt}}$

3 Fill in the missing values to make the fractions equivalent.

a $\dfrac{1}{6} = \dfrac{}{24}$

b $\dfrac{5}{8} = \dfrac{}{32}$

c $\dfrac{2}{5} = \dfrac{}{25}$

d $\dfrac{4}{9} = \dfrac{}{27}$

4 Circle the fractions that are equivalent to $\frac{3}{4}$.

$\dfrac{6}{8}$ $\dfrac{5}{6}$ $\dfrac{3}{40}$ $\dfrac{12}{16}$ $\dfrac{33}{44}$

5 Circle the fractions that are equivalent to $\frac{3}{8}$.

$\dfrac{15}{40}$ $\dfrac{5}{10}$ $\dfrac{2}{5}$ $\dfrac{6}{16}$ $\dfrac{33}{44}$

Name: _____

Form: _____

1 Circle the fraction in each pair that is the larger. Use the diagram below to help you.

	Halves
	Thirds
	Quarters
	Fifths
	Sixths
	Eighths

a $\frac{2}{3}$ $\frac{7}{8}$ **b** $\frac{1}{4}$ $\frac{2}{9}$ **c** $\frac{1}{3}$ $\frac{2}{5}$ **d** $\frac{5}{6}$ $\frac{4}{5}$ **e** $\frac{7}{8}$ $\frac{8}{9}$

f $\frac{1}{5}$ $\frac{2}{9}$ **g** $\frac{3}{4}$ $\frac{4}{5}$ **h** $\frac{3}{5}$ $\frac{5}{8}$ **i** $\frac{1}{6}$ $\frac{1}{8}$ **j** $\frac{3}{8}$ $\frac{4}{9}$

2 Use the diagram in question 1 to put the signs < (less than), > (greater than) or = (equals) between the pairs of fractions below.

a $\frac{1}{3}$ — $\frac{1}{4}$ **b** $\frac{2}{5}$ — $\frac{3}{8}$ **c** $\frac{2}{3}$ — $\frac{6}{9}$ **d** $\frac{2}{4}$ — $\frac{4}{8}$ **e** $\frac{2}{6}$ — $\frac{3}{9}$

f $\frac{3}{5}$ — $\frac{5}{9}$ **g** $\frac{5}{6}$ — $\frac{7}{8}$ **h** $\frac{3}{4}$ — $\frac{6}{8}$ **i** $\frac{2}{8}$ — $\frac{1}{4}$ **j** $\frac{1}{6}$ — $\frac{2}{9}$

Name: _____

Form: _____

1 Write down how much of each shape is shaded as a fraction in its simplest form and a percentage.

a

b

c

fraction _____   fraction _____   fraction _____

percentage _____   percentage _____   percentage _____

2 Write down each of these fractions as a percentage. The first one has been done for you.

a $\frac{1}{20}$ = ___5%___   **b** $\frac{3}{10}$ = _____   **c** $\frac{1}{4}$ = _____

d $\frac{2}{5}$ = _____   **e** $\frac{1}{2}$ = _____   **f** $\frac{9}{20}$ = _____

g $\frac{4}{5}$ = _____   **h** $\frac{99}{100}$ = _____   **i** $\frac{4}{25}$ = _____

3 Write each of these percentages as a fraction in its simplest form. The first one has been done for you.

a 10% = $\frac{1}{10}$ _____   **b** 20% = _____   **c** 95% = _____

d 80% = _____   **e** 64% = _____   **f** 15% = _____

g 25% = _____   **h** 6% = _____   **i** 75% = _____

4 By converting the percentage to a fraction or the fraction to a percentage, put the sign < (less than), > (greater than) or equals (=) between each pair of numbers.

a $\frac{3}{5}$ ____ 65%   **b** $\frac{7}{10}$ ____ 75%   **c** 40% ____ $\frac{2}{5}$

d $\frac{3}{4}$ ____ 75%   **e** 35% ____ $\frac{8}{25}$

Name: _____

Form: _____

1 Write these percentages as fractions (hundredths).

a 13% = $\dfrac{}{100}$

b 24% = $\dfrac{}{100}$

c 73% = $\dfrac{}{100}$

d 6% = $\dfrac{}{100}$

e 30% = $\dfrac{}{100}$

f 9% = $\dfrac{}{100}$

2 Calculate each of the percentages below by first finding 1% of the quantity and then multiplying. You may use a calculator to help you.

a 1% of £400 = $\dfrac{1}{100}$ × £400 = £400 ÷ 100 = **£4**

Find **i** 2% of £400 = 2 × £4 = £_____

ii 9% of £400 = _____ × _____ = £_____

iii 20% of £400 = _____ × _____ = £_____

b 1% of 600 kg = $\dfrac{1}{100}$ × 600 = 600 ÷ 100 = _____ kg

Find **i** 3% of 600 kg = 3 × _____ kg = _____ kg

ii 12% of 600 kg = _____ × _____ kg = _____ kg

iii 35% of 600 kg = _____ × _____ kg = _____ kg

c 1% of 3000 m = $\dfrac{1}{100}$ × 3000 = _____ = _____ m

Find **i** 4% of 3000 m = 4 × _____ m = _____ m

ii 18% of 3000 m = _____ × _____ m = _____ m

iii 40% of 3000 m = _____ × _____ m = _____ m

3 Use a calculator to work out each of the following quantities.

a 33% of 90 = 33 ÷ 100 × 90 = _____

b 12% of 160 = 12 ÷ 100 × 160 = _____

c 48% of 250 = _____ = _____

d 3% of 265 = _____ = _____

Name: _____

Form: _____

1 Match the equivalent ratios.

a    1 : 4

b    4 : 3

c 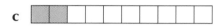   3 : 1

d    2 : 1

2 Reduce each ratio to its simplest form.

   a 5 : 10   **b** 12 : 2   **c** 6 : 18   **d** 9 : 18

   _____ : _____   _____ : _____   _____ : _____   _____ : _____

   e 20 : 15   **f** 16 : 20   **g** 12 : 28   **h** 9 : 27

   _____ : _____   _____ : _____   _____ : _____   _____ : _____

3 There are 9 red and 15 white counters in a bag.
Write the ratio of **red to white counters** then rewrite the ratio in its simplest form. _____ : _____

_____ : _____

4 There are 32 cars in the car-park. A quarter of them are British. The rest are foreign.
Write the ratio of **British cars to foreign cars** then rewrite the ratio in its simplest form. _____ : _____

_____ : _____

5 There are 80 pupils taking Maths GCSE.
25 of them are taking the Higher paper. The rest are taking the Foundation paper.
Write the ratio of **Higher to Foundation** then rewrite the ratio in its simplest form. _____ : _____

_____ : _____

Algebra **3**

Name: _____

Form: _____

1 Fill in the boxes to make each addition or subtraction correct.

a $9 + \boxed{} = 12$ **b** $10 + \boxed{} = 32$ **c** $11 - \boxed{} = 8$

d $\boxed{} + 22 = 41$ **e** $\boxed{} - 9 = 15$ **f** $\boxed{} - 15 = 10$

2 Fill in the boxes to make each multiplication or division correct.

a $\boxed{} \times 8 = 40$ **b** $\boxed{} \times 6 = 36$ **c** $7 \times \boxed{} = 49$

d $24 \div \boxed{} = 8$ **e** $25 \div \boxed{} = 5$ **f** $\boxed{} \div 6 = 3$

3 Write down two pairs of numbers that could go in the empty boxes to make each calculation correct.

a $\boxed{} + \boxed{} = 23$ $\boxed{} + \boxed{} = 23$

b $\boxed{} - \boxed{} = 12$ $\boxed{} - \boxed{} = 12$

c $\boxed{} \times \boxed{} = 32$ $\boxed{} \times \boxed{} = 32$

d $\boxed{} \div \boxed{} = 4$ $\boxed{} \div \boxed{} = 4$

4 Fill in the boxes to make each calculation correct.

a $2 \times \boxed{} = 23 - 7$ **b** $\boxed{} \times 5 = 34 - 14$

c $\boxed{} \times 4 + 8 = 36$ **d** $3 \times \boxed{} - 1 = 29$

e $3 \times \boxed{} + 1 = 28$ **f** $\boxed{} \times 9 + 3 = 21$

g $\boxed{} \times 4 - 6 = 22$ **h** $6 \times \boxed{} - 24 = 0$

Name: _____

Form: _____

1 The rule for the perimeter of a square is:

   Perimeter = length of side × 4

   a What is the perimeter of a square with a side of

   i 10 cm?_____

   ii 12 m? _____

   iii 6 cm? _____

   d A square has a perimeter of 60 cm. What is the length of one side of the square?

   _____

2 A garden centre uses this rule for the cost of a plant:

   Cost = £1 × number of leaves + £4

   a How much will it cost for a plant with

   i 8 leaves? _____

   ii 14 leaves? _____

   iii 32 leaves? _____

   b A plant is sold for £14. How many leaves does it have? _____

3 A DIY shop uses the following rule for the cost of bags of sand:

   Total cost = number of bags × cost of a bag + £8

   to work out how much to charge a customer for delivery.

   a How much would it cost to deliver

   i 6 bags of building sand costing £2.50 a bag?   _____

   ii 10 bags of grit sand costing £1.75 a bag?   _____

   iii 8 bags of building sand and 20 bags of grit sand?   _____

   b A customer was charged £28 in total for a delivery of building sand. How many bags were delivered?

   _____

HOMEWORK
3.3

Name: _____

Form: _____

1 Simplify each of these expressions.

a $g + g + g + g$ _____

b $k + k + k + k - k$ _____

c $5a + 4a$ _____

d $6c + 7c$ _____

e $10m - 7m$ _____

f $9d - 4d$ _____

g $8q + 3q$ _____

h $7a + 5a - 3a$ _____

2 Draw lines to match equivalent expressions or terms. One has been done for you.

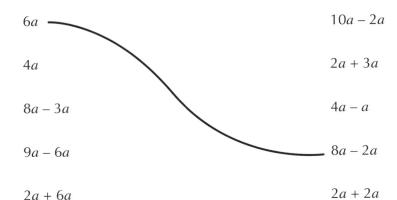

$6a$	$10a - 2a$
$4a$	$2a + 3a$
$8a - 3a$	$4a - a$
$9a - 6a$	$8a - 2a$
$2a + 6a$	$2a + 2a$

3 Simplify each expression to give another expression which has only two terms.

a $c + c + c + c + d + d + d$ _____

b $p + p + q - p + q + q + q - q$ _____

c $j + j - j + k + k + k + k - k$ _____

d $s + s - s - s + t + t - t$ _____

e $a + a + a + b + b + a + a + b$ _____

4 Simplify each algebraic expression.

a $8a + 5a + 9b + 7b$ _____

b $9m + 2m + 5n + 2n$ _____

c $8a - 2a + 4n + 6n$ _____

d $6p - p + q + 6q$ _____

e $7c + 3c + 6d - d$ _____

Name: _____

Form: _____

1 The average distance travelled on a motorway can be worked out by the formula:

$$D = 50H \qquad \text{where} \qquad D = \text{distance travelled, in miles}$$
$$H = \text{driving time in hours}$$

Use the formula to work out the distance travelled if the driving time is

a 6 hours. _____

b 4 hours. _____

c $3\frac{1}{2}$ hours. _____

2 Mr Smith uses this rule for the pocket money he gives his children:

$$P = A + 6 \qquad \text{where} \qquad P = \text{pocket money, in pounds}$$
$$A = \text{child's age}$$

Use the formula to work out what pocket money the children get.

a Denise, who is 12 years old. _____

b Paul, who is 8 years old. _____

c Annie, who is 4 years old. _____

3 To warm milk in the microwave Mr. Wilson uses this formula:

$$T = 2m + 30 \qquad \text{where} \qquad T = \text{time, seconds}$$
$$m = \text{centilitres of milk}$$

Use the formula to work out how long the following amounts of milk should be warmed for.

a 10 centilitres _____

b 70 centilitres _____

c 1 litre _____

4 Work out the value of **Y** where **X** = 9 using the formula:

$$Y = 3X - 2 \qquad Y = 3 \times \underline{\hspace{2cm}} - 2$$
$$Y = \underline{\hspace{2cm}} - 2$$
$$Y = \underline{\hspace{2cm}}$$

5 Work out the value of **P** where *X* = 12 using the formula:

$$P = 5X + 7 \qquad P = 5 \times \underline{\hspace{2cm}} + 7$$
$$P = \underline{\hspace{2cm}} + 7$$
$$P = \underline{\hspace{2cm}}$$

Name: _____

Form: _____

1 Fill in the spaces to solve each equation.

a $x + 5 = 11$

Subtract _____ from both sides

$x + 5$ _____ $= 11$ _____

$x =$ _____

b $x + 7 = 19$

_____

_____

$x =$ _____

c $x - 8 = 13$

Add _____ to both sides

$x - 8$ _____ $= 13$ _____

$x =$ _____

d $x - 6 = 24$

_____

_____

$x =$ _____

e $x - 10 = 20$

_____

_____

_____

f $x + 14 = 28$

_____

_____

_____

2 Fill in the spaces to solve each equation.

a $5x = 35$

Divide both sides by _____

$5x \div$ _____ $= 35 \div$ _____

$x =$ _____

b $7x = 21$

Divide both sides by _____

$7x \div$ _____ $= 21 \div$ _____

$x =$ _____

c $2x = 24$

_____

_____

$x =$ _____

d $8x = 32$

_____

_____

$x =$ _____

e $2x = 9$

_____

_____

f $8x = 64$

_____

_____

Geometry and measures 1

Name: _____

Form: _____

1 Match the triangle to the appropriate statement and the statement to the name of the triangle. The first one is done for you.

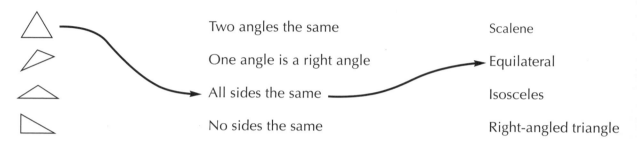

2 Draw lines of symmetry on those triangles which have reflective symmetry.

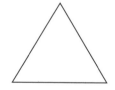

3 Draw an isosceles triangle, a right-angled triangle and a scalene triangle on the three grids below.

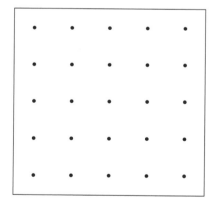
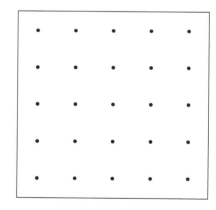

Name: _____

Form: _____

1 Find the missing angles.

a

105°

$a =$ _____ °

b

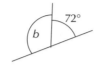

72°

$b =$ _____ °

c

135°

$c =$ _____ °

2 Find the missing angles.

a

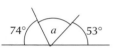

74° a 53°

$a =$ _____ °

b

b 32°

$b =$ _____ °

c

39°
82°
c

$c =$ _____ °

d

d 35°

$d =$ _____ °

e

53°   52° e

$e =$ _____ °

f

81°   38°
f

$f =$ _____ °

3 Find all the missing angles.

a

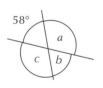

58° a c b

$a =$ _____ °

$b =$ _____ °

$c =$ _____ °

b

142° d f e

$d =$ _____ °

$e =$ _____ °

$f =$ _____ °

c

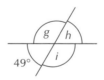

g h i 49°

$g =$ _____ °

$h =$ _____ °

$i =$ _____ °

Name: _____

Form: _____

1 Find the missing angles.

a

b

c

$a =$ _____ ° $b =$ _____ ° $c =$ _____ °

2 Find the missing angles.

a

b

c

$a =$ _____ ° $b =$ _____ ° $c =$ _____ °

d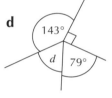

e

f

$d =$ _____ ° $e =$ _____ ° $f =$ _____ °

3 Find all the missing angles.

a

b

c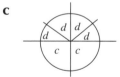

$a =$ _____ ° $b =$ _____ ° $c =$ _____ °

$d =$ _____ °

HOMEWORK
4.4

Name: _____

Form: _____

1 Find the size of the angle marked by a letter in each scalene triangle.

a

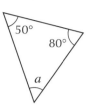

b

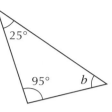

c

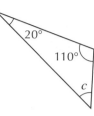

_____
_____
_____

_____
_____
_____

_____
_____
_____

d

e

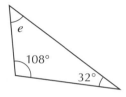

f

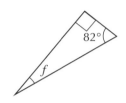

_____
_____
_____

_____
_____
_____

_____
_____
_____

2 Find the size of the unknown angle(s) in each isosceles triangle.

a

b

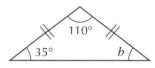

c

_____
_____
_____

_____
_____
_____

_____
_____
_____

3 Find the size of the angle marked by a letter in each quadrilateral.

a

b

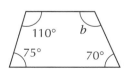

c

_____
_____
_____

_____
_____
_____

_____
_____
_____

Statistics **1**

Name: _____

Form: _____

1 Donald has been carrying out a survey to find out what students eat at lunchtime.
   He collected data from 30 students in a Year 7 class.

   chips, pizza, soup, soup, soup, pizza, chips, pizza, sandwiches, pizza, soup, soup, soup, chips, chips,
   pizza, pizza, pizza, soup, soup, soup, pizza, soup, pizza, sandwiches, chips, pizza, chips, soup, soup

   a Design a suitable tally chart and complete it using the data.

   b Explain why Donald's method of collecting data may not give a true picture of the whole school.

   _____

   _____

2 Alex did a survey of how many hours students spent watching TV each week. She asked
   25 Year 11 students.

2	5	6	0	15	13	18	7	3	8
2	1	3	7	2	9	17	10	13	7
9	6	3	2	4					

   a Use the data to complete her observation sheet.

Number of hours watching TV	Tally	Frequency
0–4		
5–9		
10–14		
15–19		

   b Explain why Alex's method of collecting data may not give a true picture of the whole school.

HOMEWORK
5.2

Name: _____

Form: _____

1   The table shows the favourite drinks of some Year 9 boys and girls.

	Tea	Milk	Cola	Water	Totals
Boys	2	4	10	4	
Girls	4	6	4	6	
Totals					

a Fill in the totals in the table.

b Which was the most popular drink for boys and girls combined? _____

c What fraction of the pupils who chose tea were boys? _____

d What percentage of the pupils who chose milk were girls? _____

e What percentage of the boys chose cola? _____

2   The table shows the opening times for a hairdressers'.

	Opening time a.m.	Closing time p.m.
Monday	9.00	5.00
Tuesday	9.00	5.00
Wednesday	8.00	1.00
Thursday	10.00	5.00
Friday	9.00	7.00
Saturday	9.00	12.30

a How many hours is the hairdressers' open on Thursday? _____

b Which day has the earliest opening time? _____

c On which day is the hairdressers' open the longest? _____

d Josie works at the hairdressers' after school. She starts at 3.30p.m. How many hours does
     she work each week? _____

e Kath has a Saturday job at the hairdressers'. She is paid £5.50 per hour. How much does
     she earn? _____

Name: _____

Form: _____

1 a Students in a class were asked how many hours sleep they had the previous night, to the nearest half hour or hour. Their answers were:

8, $7\frac{1}{2}$, 8, 7, $7\frac{1}{2}$, 8, $9\frac{1}{2}$, $8\frac{1}{2}$, 7, $7\frac{1}{2}$, 7, 9, 8, 7, 8, $7\frac{1}{2}$, 7, $8\frac{1}{2}$, $9\frac{1}{2}$, 9, $8\frac{1}{2}$, $7\frac{1}{2}$, $6\frac{1}{2}$, 8, 9, $8\frac{1}{2}$, 8, $7\frac{1}{2}$, $6\frac{1}{2}$, 8

Complete the tally chart and frequency columns.

Hours sleep	Tally	Frequency
$6\frac{1}{2}$		
7		
$7\frac{1}{2}$		
8		
$8\frac{1}{2}$		
9		
$9\frac{1}{2}$		

b Draw a bar-line graph to show the number of hours of sleep.

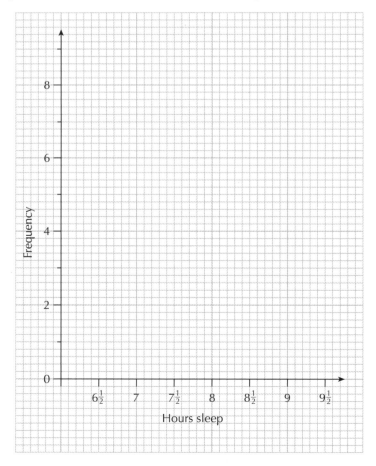

continued…

HOMEWORK
5.3

Name: _____

Form: _____

2 This table shows the favourite colours of students in one class.

Colour	Frequency
Blue	7
Red	5
Green	3
Black	9
Purple	6

Draw a bar chart to show
the data.

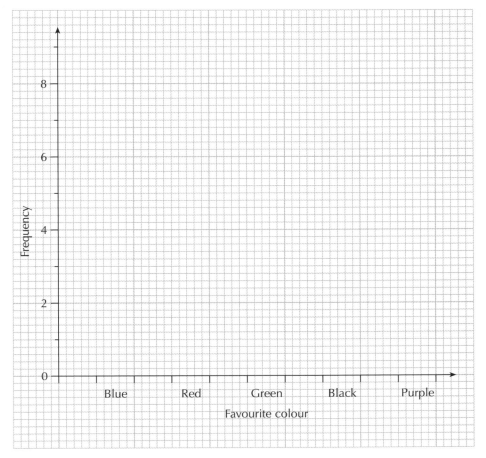

Name: _____

Form: _____

1 For each set of numbers find the mode.

   a £4, £5, £9, £9, £4, £4, £7, £8   Mode _____

   b 60, 62, 64, 62, 60, 61, 62, 62, 66   Mode _____

   c 5.6, 5.7, 5.6, 5.7, 5.4, 5.6, 5.7, 5.4, 5.7, 5.7   Mode _____

2 Find the median of each set of numbers. Remember to first write the numbers in order, starting with the smallest.

   a 5, 9, 12, 2, 8   _____   Median _____

   b 3, 4, 5, 5, 6, 8   _____   Median _____

   c 26, 27, 23, 33, 36, 34, 28   _____   Median _____

3 Find the mean and range of each set of numbers. Remember, to find the mean you add up all of the numbers then divide this total by the number of values in the list. You may use a calculator.

   a 5, 7, 8, 12, 10, 12

      Mean _____   Range _____

   b 9, 12, 6, 8, 13

      Mean _____   Range _____

   c 0.4, 0.6, 0.8, 0.9, 0.3

      Mean _____   Range _____

4 Here are the number of chips served by two dinner ladies over a week.

      Mavis 21, 24, 18, 20, 17
      Doris   29, 18, 16, 23, 24

   a Work out the mean number of chips for each dinner lady.

      Mean for Mavis _____

      Mean for Doris _____

   b Which dinner lady should you go to in order to get most chips, and why?

   _____

   _____

Name: _____

Form: _____

Draw pie charts for the following data. Don't forget to label them.

1 This table shows goals scored in 20 ice hockey matches.

Goals	Frequency
0	2
1	4
2	6
3	5
4	3
Total	20

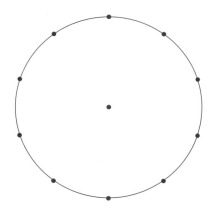

2 This table shows the favourite console game of 180 teenagers.

$360 \div 180 =$ _____ °

Game	Frequency	Angle
Action	42	
Adventure	27	
Racing	75	
Fighting	36	
Total	180	

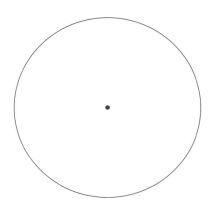

3 This table shows the favourite shops of 45 young people.

$360 \div 45 =$ _____ °

Shop	Frequency	Angle
Sweet	15	
Computing	8	
Book	10	
Cosmetic	5	
Other	7	
Total	45	

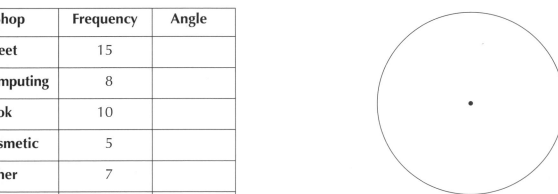

HOMEWORK 5.6

Name: _____

Form: _____

This paragraph is from the Sun newspaper.

> Robert Pires came to Arsenal's rescue after blundering Jens Lehmann had threatened their Champions League dream. Pires headed home an Ashley Cole cross on 59 minutes to bag the Gunners a priceless equaliser in this all English quarter final. And he spared the blushes of German keeper Lehmann, whose failure to clear his lines had allowed Chelsea striker Eidur Gudjohnsen to pounce six minutes earlier.

This paragraph is from the Guardian newspaper.

> Chelsea were much improved against their habitual tormentors, yet still not quite good enough. Arsenal, behind when Jens Lehmann's error let Eidur Gudjohnsen score, recovered with a handsome Robert Pires goal and will expect to advance from the second leg of this Champions League quarter final on April 6th. Their cause is aided by the suspension of Marcel Desailly.

Count how many letters there are in each word. Do not count names or numbers (underlined).
Then draw a bar-line graph of the data.

SUN

Number of letters	Tally	Total
1		
2		
3		
4		
5		
6		
7		
8		
9		
10		

GUARDIAN

Number of letters	Tally	Total
1		
2		
3		
4		
5		
6		
7		
8		
9		
10		

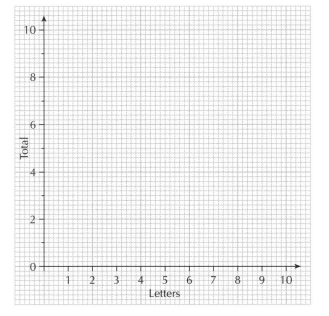

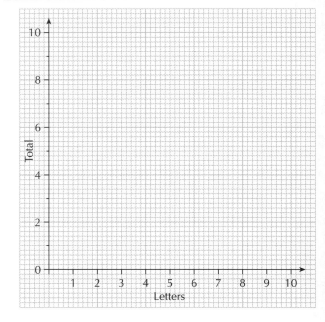

CHAPTER
6

Geometry and measures 2

HOMEWORK
6.1

Name: _____

Form: _____

1 What metric unit would you use to measure the following?

a Width of a magazine _____

b The amount in a can of pop _____

c The area of the front of this workbook _____

d The mass of 50p coin _____

2 Change each of the following imperial units into the approximate metric equivalent given in brackets.

a 6 inches (cm)   **b** 12 ft (m)   **c** 15 miles (km)

_____   _____   _____

d 4 lb (kg)   **e** 2 gallons (litres)

_____   _____

3 Sam goes on a diet and loses 16 lb. Approximately how many kilograms is this? _____

4 A cask holds 10 gallons of wine. Approximately how many litre bottles of wine can be filled from the cask? _____

5 Here is a recipe for pancakes. Rewrite the recipe using metric units. Remember that 1 ounce (oz) is about 30 grams and 1 pint is about 600 millilitres.

Pancakes	
Egg	1 egg
Flour	3 oz
Milk	$\frac{1}{4}$ pint

Pancakes		
Egg	1 egg	
Flour	_____	g
Milk	_____	ml

6 Winston is buying a car. He has a brochure showing speed, weight and petrol tank capacity of the car from a British dealer. Rewrite these using metric units.

Top speed	120 mph
Weight	2000 lb
Petrol tank	8 gallons

Top speed	_____	kmph
Weight	_____	kg
Petrol tank	_____	litres

Name: _____

Form: _____

1 Work out the area of each rectangle using the formula $A = l \times w$.

a

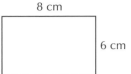

8 cm

6 cm

Area = _____

= _____ cm^2

b

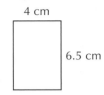

4 cm

6.5 cm

Area = _____

= _____ cm^2

c

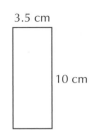

3.5 cm

10 cm

Area = _____

= _____ cm^2

2 Complete the table using the formula $A = l \times w$. Give the correct units for each area. You may use a calculator.

l	w	A
10 cm	12 cm	
6 m	9 m	
10 cm	8.5 cm	
12 km	6 km	

3 Divide each shape into rectangles. Work out the area of each rectangle then find the total area of the shape.

a

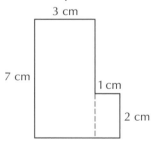

3 cm

7 cm

1 cm

2 cm

A = _____ + _____

A = _____ + _____

A = _____ cm^2

b

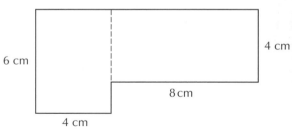

6 cm

4 cm

8 cm

4 cm

A = _____ + _____

A = _____ + _____

A = _____ cm^2

continued…

Name: _____

Form: _____

c

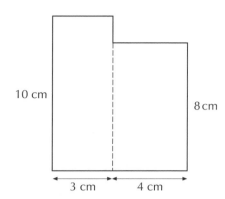

d

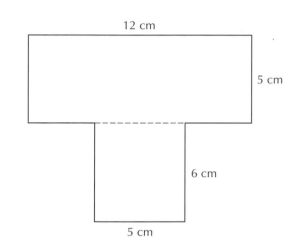

A = _____ + _____

A = _____ + _____

A = _____ cm²

A = _____ + _____

A = _____ + _____

A = _____ cm²

4 Find the unknown length or width for each rectangle.

a

? cm

40 cm² | 10 cm

_____ cm

b

? cm

35 cm² | 5 cm

_____ cm

c

9 cm

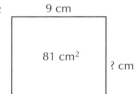

81 cm² | ? cm

_____ cm

d

8 cm

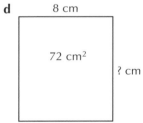

72 cm² | ? cm

_____ cm

Name: _____

Form: _____

1 Work out the area of each triangle by counting squares.

a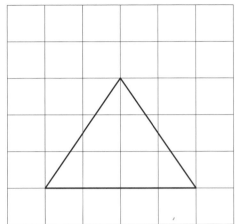

b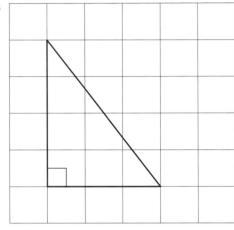

Area = _____ cm²   Area = _____ cm²

2 Work out the area of each triangle by first finding the area of the rectangle that encloses it.

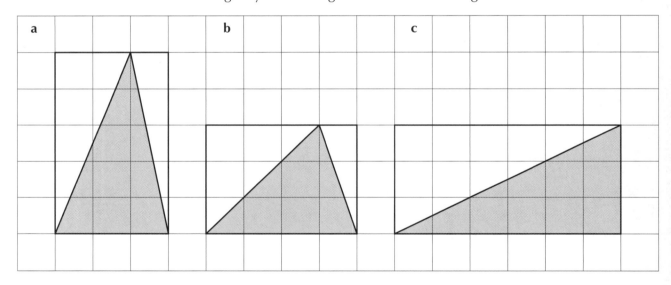

_____   _____   _____

Area = _____ cm²   Area = _____ cm²   Area = _____ cm²

continued…

Name: _____

Form: _____

3 Use the formula to work out the area of each right-angled triangle.

Area $= \frac{1}{2} \times b \times h$

a

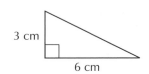

3 cm
6 cm

_____

b

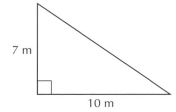

7 m
10 m

_____

c

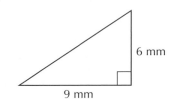

6 mm
9 mm

_____

4 Use the formula to work out the area of each triangle.

Area $= \frac{1}{2} \times b \times h$

a

5 cm
6 cm

_____

b

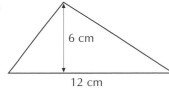

6 cm
12 cm

_____

c

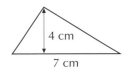

4 cm
7 cm

_____

HOMEWORK 6.4

Name: _____

Form: _____

1 Work out the area of the parallelogram.

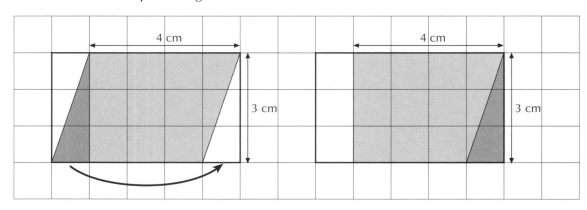

Area = _____ cm × _____ cm

Area = _____ cm^2

2 Use the formula $A = b \times h$ to work out the area of each parallelogram.

a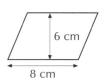

6 cm

8 cm

b

10 cm

6 cm

c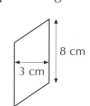

8 cm

3 cm

d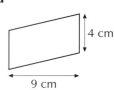

4 cm

9 cm

$A = $ _____

$A = $ _____

$A = $ _____

$A = $ _____

3 On the grid draw **three** different parallelograms which have an area of 12 square units.

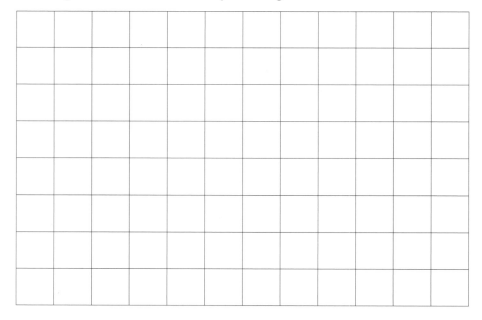

Number **2**

Name: _____

Form: _____

1 Complete these statements.

$10 \times 10 \times 10 = 10^3 = 1000$

$10 \times 10 \times 10 \times 10 \times 10 =$ _____ $=$ _____

$10 \times 10 \times 10 \times 10 \times 10 \times 10 \times 10 =$ _____ $=$ _____

2 Complete the following.

a Write 1 million in figures. _____

b Write 1 million as a power of 10. _____

c Write ten thousand in figures. _____

d Write ten thousand as a power of 10. _____

3 Work out each of these multiplications. Do not use a calculator.

a $7 \times 10^3 = 7 \times 1000 =$ _____

b $8 \times 10^5 = 8 \times 100\,000 =$ _____

c $3 \times 10^2 = 3 \times$ _____ $=$ _____

d $12 \times 10^3 =$ _____ $=$ _____

e $18 \times 10^6 =$ _____ $=$ _____

4 Work out each of these multiplications. Do not use a calculator.

a $6.5 \times 10^2 = 6.5 \times 100 =$ _____

b $3.7 \times 10^3 = 3.7 \times 1000 =$ _____

c $7.7 \times 10^4 = 7.7 \times$ _____ $=$ _____

d $4.3 \times 10^5 =$ _____ $\times$ _____ $=$ _____

Name: _____

Form: _____

✖ **Do not use a calculator for this exercise.**

1 Work out the answer to each addition. Remember to set out the question in columns first.

a 437 + 86

b 652 + 339

c 778 + 616

2 Work out the answer to each addition. Remember to set out the question in columns first.

a 6.56 + 4.97

b 3.46 + 5.19

c 16.38 + 21.23

d 6 + 0.8 + 2.5

e 4.2 + 2.36 + 8

f 8.8 + 13.2 + 0.08

3 Work out the perimeter of each of the following rectangles.

a

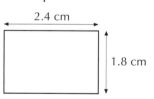

b

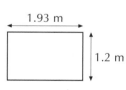

Perimeter = 2.4 + 1.8 + 2.4 + 1.8

= _____

Perimeter = _____

= _____

Name: _____

Form: _____

Do not use a calculator for this exercise.

1 Work out the answers to each subtraction. Remember to set out the question in columns first.

  a 437 – 86

  b 652 – 339

  c 778 – 616

2 Work out the answer to each subtraction. Remember to set out the question in columns first.

  a 6.56 – 4.97

  b 8.46 – 5.19

  c 26.38 – 11.23

  d 6 – 0.8

  e 4.2 – 2.36

  f 88.32 – 13.7

3 A beaker containing water weighs 1.34 kg.
The beaker alone weighs 0.18 kg.
How much does the water weigh?

Answer _____ kg

4 A computer disc holds 1.44 MB of information.
If the disc already has 0.78 MB on it, will there
be enough space for a file of length 0.65 MB?
Show your working.

Yes ☐   No ☐

Name: _____

Form: _____

Do not use a calculator for this exercise.

1 Work out the answer to each multiplication.

  a   46
     × 6

  b   348
     × 7

  c   7.68
     × 3

  d   4.36
     × 5

2 Work out the answer to each multiplication. Remember to set out the question in columns first.

  a 63×6

  b 6.9×8

  c 3.14×8

  d 9×25.6

  e 1.074×5

  f 8×62.07

3 Find the area of each of these rectangles.

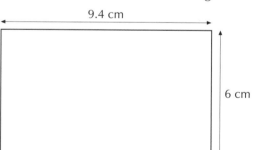

  a 9.4 cm, 6 cm

Area = 6×9.4 = _____ cm²

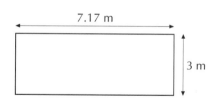

  b 7.17 m, 3 m

Area = 3×7.17 = _____ m²

Name: _____

Form: _____

Do not use a calculator for this exercise.

1 Work out the answer to each division.

a 6⟌7 8   **b** 5⟌8 5   **c** 4⟌8 4

d 6⟌9 . 6   **e** 4⟌1 . 5 2   **f** 7⟌1 5 . 4

2 Work out the answer to each division. Remember to set out the question in columns first.

a 306 ÷ 9   **b** 34.4 ÷ 8   **c** 8.22 ÷ 6

3 Work out each division. Each answer has a remainder.

a 5⟌9 6   **b** 6⟌8 7   **c** 7⟌1 0 8

d 6⟌9 . 2   **e** 8⟌10 . 6   **f** 9⟌2 3 . 7

4 Find the missing lengths for each of these rectangles.

a

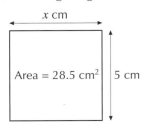

$x = 28.5 ÷ 5 =$ _____ cm

b

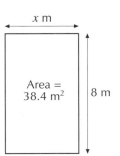

$x =$ _____ ÷ _____

$=$ _____ m

HOMEWORK 7.6

Name: _____

Form: _____

Do not use a calculator for this exercise.

For each question show your working. Set out your calculations using column methods.

1 What is the difference between 82.6 and 37.8?

2 What is the sum of 16.4 and 3.65?

3 There are 60 minutes in 1 hour.
How many minutes are there in
7 hours?

4 There are 7 days in a week.
How many days are there in
14 weeks?

5 John has a bag of sugar
containing 1.5 kg. He uses
0.67 kg to make some biscuits.
How much sugar is left?

6 Five friends spend £23.45 on a
meal. They share the bill
equally. How much will each
person pay?

continued…

HOMEWORK 7.6

Name: _____

Form: _____

7 Mia and Marlene are shopping for clothes.

a Mia buys a hat, jacket and trousers. How much does she pay altogether?

PRICES	
Jackets	£27.50
Trousers	£22.35
T-shirts	£12.99
Hats	£7.25
Skirts	£19.50

b Marlene wants a jacket, skirt and a T-shirt. She has £60 to spend.
Does she have enough money? You must show your working.

Yes ☐   No ☐

Algebra **4**

Name: _____

Form: _____

1 Write down the first **five** multiples of these numbers.

    a 4 _____   **b** 9 _____

    c 12 _____   **d** 18 _____

    e 45 _____

2 Write the next **two** multiples of 5 after 45.   _____ , _____

3 Write the next **two** multiples of 11 after 77.   _____ , _____

4 Write the next **two** multiples of 14 after 42.   _____ , _____

5 Write the next **two** multiples of 22 after 44.   _____ , _____

6 Write the next **two** multiples of 60 after 420.   _____ , _____

7 Circle the number which is **not** a multiple of 5.

    5   15   20   32   45

8 Circle the number which is **not** a multiple of 8.

    16   24   20   48   72

9 Circle the number which is **not** a multiple of 25.

    300   125   150   200   90

10 Shade in the squares containing numbers that are multiples of 3.

    Which letter have you shaded? _____

21	63	36	10
17	18	23	80
7	9	17	43
44	12	40	61
37	99	20	14

Name: _____

Form: _____

1 Write each number as different pairs of factors.

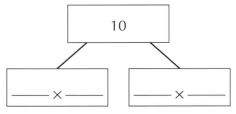

a

10

____ × ____   ____ × ____

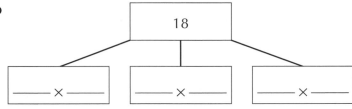

b

18

____ × ____   ____ × ____   ____ × ____

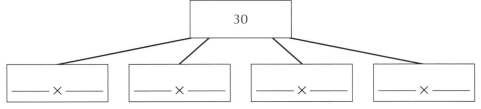

c

30

____ × ____   ____ × ____   ____ × ____   ____ × ____

d

15

____ × ____   ____ × ____

2 Write down all of the factors for each of these numbers.

a 28 _____   **b** 50 _____   **c** 56 _____

3 Circle the number which is **not** a factor of 32.

   1   2   4   12   16   32

4 Circle the number which is **not** a factor of 40.

   1   2   4   8   12   20

5 Circle the number which is **not** a factor of 42.

   1   4   6   14   21

6 Circle the number which is **not** a factor of 48.

   2   3   6   8   24   28

7 Shade the factors of 48.

   Shade the factors of 30.

   Shade the factors of 18.

   Which letter do the shaded squares make? _____

1	9	5	48	7
24	37	14	32	41
10	6	15	11	55
2	19	80	13	25
8	3	16	30	31

Name: _____

Form: _____

1 a List all of the factors of 12. _____

   b List all of the factors of 8. _____

   c Circle the factors which appear in both lists. Complete the following sentences.

     The common factors of 8 and 12 are _____ , _____ and _____ .

     The **highest common factor** of 8 and 12 is _____ .

2 a List all of the factors of 15. _____

   b List all of the factors of 25. _____

   c Circle the factors which appear in both lists. Complete the following sentences.

     The common factors of 15 and 25 are _____ and _____ .

     The **highest common factor** of 15 and 25 is _____ .

3 a List all of the factors of 27. _____

   b List all of the factors of 45. _____

   c The common factors of 27 and 45 are _____ .

     The **highest common factor** of 27 and 45 is _____ .

4 a List the first **ten** multiples of 5. _____

   b List the first **ten** multiples of 6. _____

   c Circle the multiple which appears in both lists. Complete this sentence.

     The **lowest common multiple** of 5 and 6 is _____ .

5 a List the first **ten** multiples of 3. _____

   b List the first **ten** multiples of 6. _____

   c Circle the multiples which appear in both lists. Complete the following sentences.

     Some common multiples of 3 and 6 are _____ .

     The **lowest common multiple** of 3 and 6 is _____ .

Name: _____

Form: _____

1 Circle the numbers which are **not** prime.

     2   6   7   10   13   15   17   21   23

2 Put these numbers into the Venn diagram.

     1   3   5   7   8   9   11   13   17   19

prime   less than 10

3 Write each of these non-prime numbers as a product of two or more prime numbers.

   a 34 = _____ × _____   **b** 39 = _____ × _____

   c 51 = _____ × _____   **d** 95 = _____ × _____

   e 45 = _____ × _____ × _____   **f** 42 = _____ × _____ × _____

   g 50 = _____ × _____ × _____

Name: _____

Form: _____

 1 Complete each of the following.

$3^2 = 3 \times 3 = $ _____

$5^2 = 5 \times 5 = $ _____

$7^2 = $ _____ $\times$ _____ $= $ _____

$9^2 = $ _____ $= $ _____

$11^2 = $ _____ $= $ _____

2 Complete these sentences.

a The eighth square number is _____.

b The _____ square number is 144.

c The tenth square number is _____.

3 Continue the number patterns.

1	=	1	=	1^2
1 + 3	=	4	=	2^2
1 + 3 + 5	=	_____	=	_____
_____	=	_____	=	_____
_____	=	_____	=	_____
_____	=	_____	=	_____

 4 Continue the pattern of square numbers.

a $10^2 = 100$ **b** $20^2 = 400$ **c** $30^2 = $ _____

d $40^2 = $ _____   **e** $50^2 = $ _____   **f** $60^2 = $ _____

g $70^2 = $ _____   **h** $80^2 = $ _____   **i** $90^2 = $ _____

5 Draw the next two patterns and complete the numbers.

1   4   9

_____   _____

Name: _____

Form: _____

1 Complete the following.

The square of 2 is 2 × 2 = 4.   The square root of 4 is 2.

The square of 4 is _____ × _____ = _____ .   The square root of _____ is 4.

The square of 6 is _____ × _____ = _____ .   The square root of _____ is _____ .

The square of 8 is _____ × _____ = _____ .   The square root of _____ is _____ .

The square of 10 is _____ × _____ = _____ .   The square root of _____ is _____ .

The square of 12 is _____ × _____ = _____ .   The square root of _____ is _____ .

2 Find the square roots of each of the following.

   a $\sqrt{49}$ = _____   **b** $\sqrt{25}$ = _____   **c** $\sqrt{121}$ = _____

   d $\sqrt{81}$ = _____   **e** $\sqrt{1}$ = _____   **f** $\sqrt{64}$ = _____

   g $\sqrt{100}$ = _____   **h** $\sqrt{4}$ = _____   **i** $\sqrt{9}$ = _____

3 Draw lines to match each square root with its answer. Use a calculator.

   $\sqrt{441}$ 19

   $\sqrt{1225}$ 21

   $\sqrt{256}$ 27

   $\sqrt{361}$ 35

   $\sqrt{676}$ 16

   $\sqrt{729}$ 26

4 Use a calculator to help you find these square roots.

   a $\sqrt{1156}$ = _____   **b** $\sqrt{961}$ = _____   **c** $\sqrt{2025}$ = _____

   d $\sqrt{1296}$ = _____   **e** $\sqrt{2500}$ = _____   **f** $\sqrt{1024}$ = _____

Name: _____

Form: _____

 1 Complete the following.

$1^3 = 1 \times 1 \times 1 = 1$

$3^3 =$ _____ $\times$ _____ $\times$ _____ $=$ _____

$5^3 =$ _____ $=$ _____

$7^3 =$ _____ $=$ _____

$9^3 =$ _____ $=$ _____

 2 Work out the answers to the following.

a $11^3 =$ _____   **b** $12^3 =$ _____   **c** $13^3 =$ _____

d $14^3 =$ _____   **e** $15^3 =$ _____   **f** $16^3 =$ _____

3 Complete these sentences.

a _____ is the fourth cube number.

b The sixth cube number is _____.

c 512 is the _____ cube number.

d The next cube number after 27 is _____.

 4 Use a calculator to work out each of the following.

a $26^3 =$ _____   **b** $22^3 =$ _____   **c** $19^3 =$ _____

d $30^3 =$ _____   **e** $31^3 =$ _____   **f** $27^3 =$ _____

Name: _____

Form: _____

1 Complete the following.

The cube of 1 is 1 × 1 × 1 = 1.   The cube root of 1 is 1.

The cube of 3 is _____ × _____ × _____ = _____ .   The cube root of _____ is 3.

The cube of 5 is _____ × _____ × _____ = _____ .   The cube root of _____ is _____ .

The cube of 7 is _____ × _____ × _____ = _____ .   The cube root of _____ is _____ .

The cube of 9 is _____ × _____ × _____ = _____ .   The cube root of _____ is _____ .

2 Without using a calculator, work out these cube roots.

a $\sqrt[3]{27}$ = _____

b $\sqrt[3]{125}$ = _____

c $\sqrt[3]{1000}$ = _____

d $\sqrt[3]{8}$ = _____

e $\sqrt[3]{216}$ = _____

f $\sqrt[3]{64}$ = _____

3 Complete these sentences.

a The cube root of 729 is _____ .

b The number that must be cubed to give 512 is _____ .

c _____ is the cube root of 216.

d _____ cubed is equal to 125.

4 Use a calculator to work out these cube roots.

a $\sqrt[3]{5832}$ = _____

b $\sqrt[3]{3.375}$ = _____

c $\sqrt[3]{0.125}$ = _____

d $\sqrt[3]{4913}$ = _____

e $\sqrt[3]{2744}$ = _____

f $\sqrt[3]{10648}$ = _____

Statistics 2

Name: _____

Form: _____

1 Draw arrows on the probability scale to indicate the likelihood of each of these events.

Impossible   Very unlikely   Unlikely   Even   Likely   Very likely   Certain

  a Father Christmas will come down the chimney on Christmas Eve.
  b You will get some homework today.
  c Rolling a dice and getting a score of 1.
  d A coin will land on Heads when thrown.
  e It will rain this week.

2 Work out the probability of each event, giving your answer as a fraction. Draw an arrow to show its position on the probability scale.

```
|----------------|----------------|----------------|
0                              1/2                  1
```

  a Probability of a tossed coin landing on Tails = _____

  b Probability of choosing the white ball from this bag = _____

  c Probability of choosing a black ball from this bag = _____

3 Ken is rolling a 1–6 dice. Work out the probability of each event, giving your answer as a fraction. Cancel down your answers if possible. Draw an arrow to show its position on the probability scale.

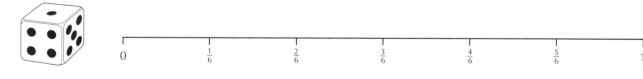

```
0      1/6     2/6     3/6     4/6     5/6      1
```

  a Probability of throwing a 6 = _____

  b Probability of throwing an even number = _____

  c Probability of throwing a number less than 7 = _____

  d Probability of throwing a number more than 7 = _____

  e Probability of throwing a 2 or 3 = _____ = _____

Name: _____

Form: _____

1 A bag contains four white balls and five black balls.

The probability of picking a black ball = $\frac{5}{9}$

The probability of picking a white ball = _____

2 The spinner can land on 1, 2 or 3.

The probability of landing on 1 = _____

The probability of landing on 2 = _____

The probability of landing on 3 = _____

3 A bag contains three white, two grey and five black counters.

The probability of picking a white counter = _____

The probability of picking a grey counter = _____

The probability of picking a black counter = _____

The probability of picking a white or grey counter = _____

The probability of picking a white or black counter = _____

The probability of picking a white, grey or black counter = _____

The probability of picking a red counter = _____

4 The probability of getting an even number on a normal dice = _____

The probability that the dice will land on an odd number = _____

5 The following cards are in a bag.

A card is taken at random from the bag.

What is the probability that it is the letter M? _____

What is the probability that it is a letter from the word CAT? _____

What is the probability that it is a vowel? _____

What is the probability it is a consonant? _____

What is the probability it is a letter from the word FOUR? _____

6 I have 12 tickets out of 200 tickets in a raffle and my friend has 8 tickets.

What is the probability that I will win the raffle? _____

What is the probability that my friend will win the raffle? _____

What is the probability that either my friend or I will win the raffle? _____

Name: _____

Form: _____

1 a A bag of counters contains 10 counters, which are either red or blue.
After taking out a counter and putting it back 100 times the results are:

Write down the number of red counters in the bag. _____

Write down the number of blue counters in the bag. _____

Colour	Frequency
Red	78
Blue	22

b If a counter was taken out and replaced 1000 times fill in the table for the
number of each colour you would expect to get.

Colour	Frequency
Red	
Blue	

2 a A dice is thrown 600 times. The results are:

Score	1	2	3	4	5	6
Frequency	95	110	92	108	89	106

Explain how you can tell that the dice is fair. _____

_____

b Another dice is thrown 600 times. The results are:

Score	1	2	3	4	5	6
Frequency	105	156	96	89	52	102

Explain how you can tell that the dice is biased. _____

_____

c Fill in the table to show how many of each number you would get if you threw a **fair** dice
1200 times.

Score	1	2	3	4	5	6
Frequency						

HOMEWORK 9.4

Name: _____

Form: _____

1 a A drawing pin is dropped 10 times. The results are:

	Frequency
Point up	7
Point down	3

Using your results, what is the probability of the pin landing point up?

Give your answer as a fraction. _____

b The same drawing pin is dropped 50 times. The results are:

	Frequency
Point up	32
Point down	18

Using your results, what is the probability of the pin landing point up?

Give your answer as a fraction. _____

c You have worked out two values for the probability that a pin lands point up.

Which do you think is more accurate? _____

2 a A coin is flipped 20 times. The results are:

	Frequency
Heads	8
Tails	12

Using your results, what is the probability of the coin landing on Tails? Give your answer as a fraction and as a decimal.

Fraction _____   Decimal _____

Based on these results is the coin fair? _____

b The same coin is flipped 200 times. The results are:

	Frequency
Heads	68
Tails	132

Using your results, what is the probability of the coin landing on Tails? Give your answer as a fraction and as a decimal.

Fraction _____   Decimal _____

Based on these results is the coin fair? _____

Explain your answer. _____

_____

Geometry and measures 3

Name: _____

Form: _____

1 All of these shapes have line symmetry. Draw the lines of symmetry on each shape.

a 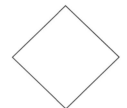   b 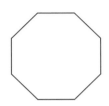   c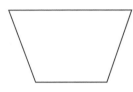

d 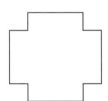   e    f

g 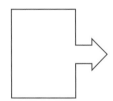   h    i

2 Add one more square to this shape to give it a line of symmetry. Draw the line of symmetry on. Each answer should be different.

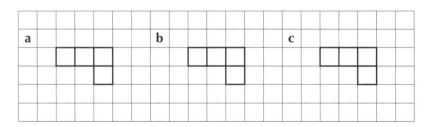

Name: _____

Form: _____

1 All of these shapes have rotational symmetry about the centre shown. Use tracing paper to find the order of rotational symmetry.

a

Order _____

b

Order _____

c
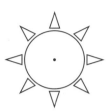
Order _____

d

Order _____

e

Order _____

f
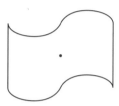
Order _____

g
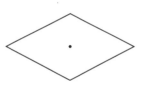
Order _____

h
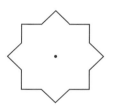
Order _____

i

Order _____

2 Add one more square to these shapes to give them rotational symmetry of the order shown.

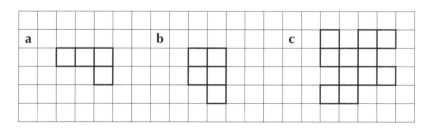

Order 2   Order 2   Order 4

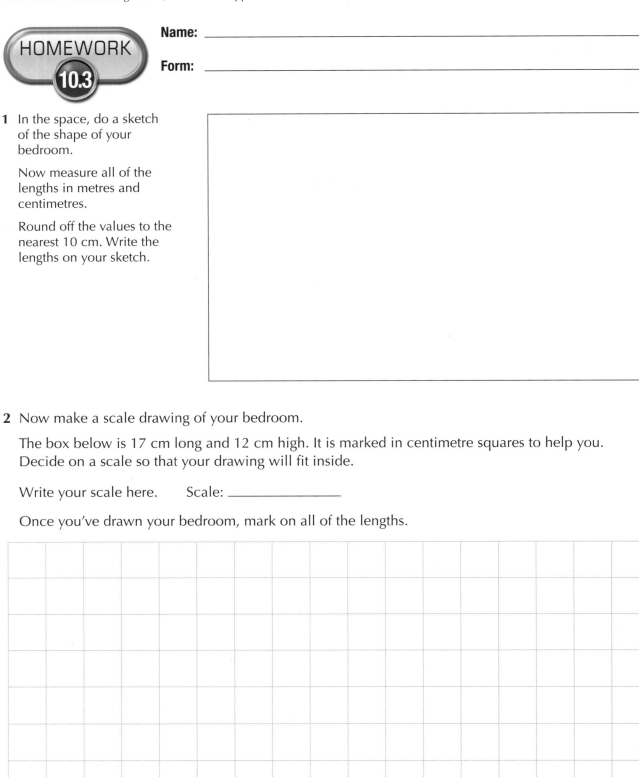

HOMEWORK 10.3

Name: _____

Form: _____

1   In the space, do a sketch of the shape of your bedroom.

Now measure all of the lengths in metres and centimetres.

Round off the values to the nearest 10 cm. Write the lengths on your sketch.

2   Now make a scale drawing of your bedroom.

The box below is 17 cm long and 12 cm high. It is marked in centimetre squares to help you. Decide on a scale so that your drawing will fit inside.

Write your scale here.   Scale: _____

Once you've drawn your bedroom, mark on all of the lengths.

HOMEWORK
10.4

Name: _____

Form: _____

1 Match these coordinates to the points marked on the grid with letters.

a (–3, 5) _____

b (–2, 0) _____

c (1, –3) _____

d (–4, –2) _____

e (0, 4) _____

f (4, –4) _____

g (5, 2) _____

h (–3, –5) _____

i (–5, 2) _____

j (3, 4) _____

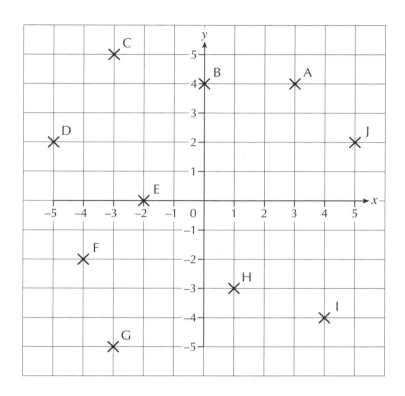

2 a The coordinates below give three of the four corners of a rectangle.

Plot the points, join them with a ruler and complete the rectangle. Write down the coordinates of the fourth corner.

(–4, 5) (2, 5) (2, –3) _____

b The coordinates below give three of the four corners of a square.

Plot the points, join them with a ruler and complete the square. Write down the coordinates of the fourth corner.

(1, 0) (4, –1) (3, –4) _____

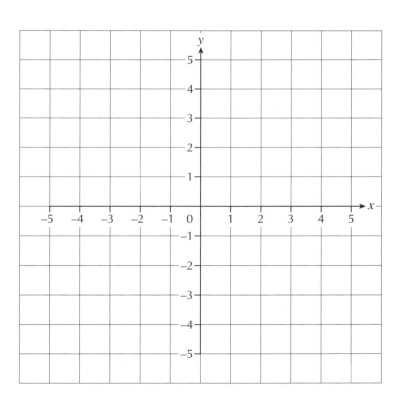

continued...

Name: _____

Form: _____

3 a Plot the points below on the grid.

Join the points with a ruler as you plot them.
(0.6, 3.8) (2.2, 3.8) (0.6, 2.2) (2.2, 2.2)

Name the letter you have drawn _____

b Plot these points on the grid.
Join the points with a ruler as you plot them.
(0.8, 1.6) (1.4, 0) (2, 0.8) (2.6, 0) (3.2, 1.6)

Name the letter you have drawn _____

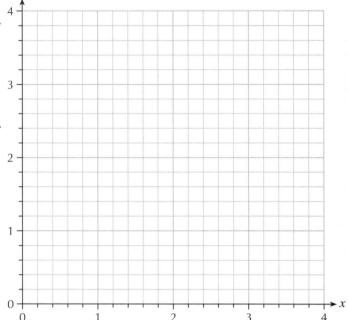

4 a The coordinates below give three of the
four corners of a parallelogram.

Plot the points, join them with a ruler and
complete the parallelogram. Write down
the coordinates of the fourth corner.

(−0.6, 0.8) (0.3, 0.8) (−0.1, −0.3) _____

b The coordinates below give three of the
four corners of a kite.

Plot the points, join them with a ruler and
complete the kite. Write down the
coordinates of the fourth corner.

(0.5, −0.9) (0.9, −0.2) (0.5, 0.2) _____

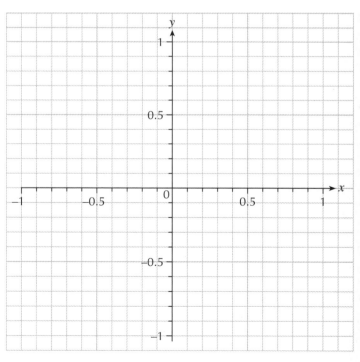

Algebra 5

Name: _____

Form: _____

Do not use a calculator for this exercise.

1 Complete each of the following calculations.

   a $8 + 2 \times 6 =$ _____ + _____ = _____

   b $32 + 18 - 5 =$ _____ − _____ = _____

   c $4^2 - 2 \times 5 =$ _____ − _____ = _____

   d $40 - 8 \times 4 =$ _____ − _____ = _____

   e $18 - 12 \div 4 =$ _____ = _____

2 Complete each of the following calculations.

   a $4 \times 6 + 3 \times 5 =$ _____ + _____ = _____

   b $6^2 - 8 \times 4 =$ _____ − _____ = _____

   c $9 \times 6 - 24 \div 2 =$ _____ − _____ = _____

   d $7 \times 7 - 6 \times 6 =$ _____ − _____ = _____

   e $48 \div 8 + 6 \times 3 =$ _____ = _____

3 Complete each calculation – remember, brackets first!

   a $32 \div (5 + 3) =$ _____ ÷ _____ = _____

   b $5 \times (8 - 2) =$ _____ × _____ = _____

   c $(28 - 8) \times 7 =$ _____ × _____ = _____

   d $(7 - 2) \times (7 + 2) =$ _____ × _____ = _____

   e $3^2 \times (9 - 3) =$ _____ = _____

4 Complete each of the following calculations.

   a $8 + 4 \times 3 + 3^2 =$ _____ + _____ + _____ = _____

   b $5 \times 4 - 5 + 9 \div 3 =$ _____ − _____ + _____ = _____

   c $(8 - 2) \times 5 + 7 =$ _____ × _____ + _____ = _____ + _____ = _____

   d $29 + (7 - 2) \times 4 =$ _____ + _____ × _____ = _____ + _____ = _____

Name: _____

Form: _____

1 Expand each of the following brackets.

   a $5(6 + 3) = 5 \times 6 + 5 \times 3 =$ _____ + _____ = _____

   b $7(2 + 7) = 7 \times 2 + 7 \times 7 =$ _____ + _____ = _____

   c $3(8 - 3) = 3 \times 8 - 3 \times 3 =$ _____ − _____ = _____

   d $5(2 + 9) =$ _____ × _____ + _____ × _____ = _____ + _____ = _____

   e $6(6 - 3) =$ _____ × _____ − _____ × _____ = _____ − _____ = _____

   f $2(6 + 9) =$ _____ × _____ + _____ × _____ = _____ + _____ = _____

2 Simplify each of the following.

   a $3 \times a =$ _____

   b $8 \times b =$ _____

   c $10 \times c =$ _____

   d $7 \times m =$ _____

3 Expand each of the following brackets.

   a $6(a + 2) = 6a + 6 \times 2 =$ _____ + _____

   b $4(b - 3) = 4b - 4 \times 3 =$ _____ − _____

   c $9(c - 6) =$ _____ − _____ = _____ − _____

   d $4(d + 5) =$ _____ + _____ = _____ + _____

   e $8(e - 3) =$ _____ − _____ = _____ − _____

   f $5(f - 3) =$ _____ − _____ = _____ − _____

Name: _____

Form: _____

1 Fill in the spaces to solve each of the following equations.

a $3x + 5 = 20$

Subtract _____ from both sides

$3x + 5$ _____ $= 20$ _____

$3x =$ _____

Divide both sides by _____

$x =$ _____ $\div$ _____

$x =$ _____

b $4x + 7 = 11$

Subtract _____ from both sides

$4x + 7$ _____ $= 11$ _____

$4x =$ _____

Divide both sides by _____

$x =$ _____ $\div$ _____

$x =$ _____

c $5x + 7 = 22$

Subtract _____ from both sides

$5x + 7$ _____ $= 22$ _____

$5x =$ _____

Divide both sides by _____

$x =$ _____ $\div$ _____

$x =$ _____

d $4x - 7 = 25$

Add _____ to both sides

$4x - 7$ _____ $= 25$ _____

$4x =$ _____

Divide both sides by _____

$x =$ _____ $\div$ _____

$x =$ _____

e $6x - 5 = 25$

Add _____ to both sides

$6x - 5$ _____ $= 25$ _____

$6x =$ _____

Divide both sides by _____

$x =$ _____ $\div$ _____

$x =$ _____

f $2x - 11 = 13$

Add _____ to both sides

$2x - 11$ _____ $= 13$ _____

$2x =$ _____

Divide both sides by _____

$x =$ _____ $\div$ _____

$x =$ _____

2 Solve each of the following equations.

a $5x + 7 = 32$

_____ both sides

_____ $=$ _____

_____ $=$ _____

Divide both sides by _____

$x =$ _____

$x =$ _____

b $6x - 7 = 11$

_____ both sides

_____ $=$ _____

_____ $=$ _____

Divide both sides by _____

$x =$ _____

$x =$ _____

HOMEWORK 11.4

Name: _____

Form: _____

1 The distance–time graph shows the journey of a jogger on a 5-mile run. At one point she ran up a steep hill and at another point she stopped to admire the view.

  a How many minutes into the run was the start of the hill?

  _____

  b For how long did she stop to admire the view?

  _____

2 In some houses the hot water tank refills with cold water whenever hot water is taken out. The heating system then heats the water to a pre-set temperature.

  The graph shows the temperature of the water in a hot water tank in a house from 7.00 am to 9.00 am.

  Dad always takes a shower in the morning. Mum always has a bath and the two children get up so late that they only have time to wash their face and hands.

  a At what time did Dad take a shower? _____

  b At what time did Mum take a bath? _____

  c At what time did the first child wash? _____

  d Gran likes to take as hot a bath as possible when everyone is out of the house.

   Estimate when the water will be back to its maximum temperature _____

3 A graph shows a car park's charges.

  a How much are the charges for each of these stays?

   i 30 minutes _____

   ii Less than 1 hour _____

   iii 2 hours _____

   iv 2 hours 59 minutes _____

   v 3 hours 30 minutes _____

   vi 6 hours _____

  b For how long can a person park for each of these amounts?

   i £1 _____   **ii** £2 _____   **iii** £5 _____

  c This type of graph is called a step graph. Explain why it is given this name. _____

_____

Revision

Name: _____

Form: _____

Do not use a calculator for this exercise.

1 How much of each shape is shaded? Tick the correct box.

a

More than a half ☐

Half ☐

Less than a half ☐

b

More than a third ☐

Third ☐

Less than a third ☐

c

More than a quarter ☐

Quarter ☐

Less than a quarter ☐

2 a About 33% of this rectangle is dotted.

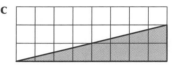

What percentage is **i** striped _____

ii plain _____

b About $\frac{1}{10}$ of this rectangle is grey.

What percentage is **i** black _____

ii white _____

3 Identify which **four** of the following are equivalent.
Circle the equivalent values.

    0.06   60%   0.60 $\frac{60}{100}$ $\frac{3}{5}$ 6% $\frac{6}{10}$

4 If $\frac{5}{12}$ of the members of a youth club are girls, what fraction are boys? _____

5 This is the sign at the Airport Long Stay car park.

How much would it cost to park for 9 days? _____

> **FLYPARK**
> £6.50 per day or
> £42.50 for a full week

6 a Add 356 to half of 422.

_____

_____

_____

b Take a quarter of 156 from 200.

_____

_____

_____

HOMEWORK
12.2

Name: _____

Form: _____

✗ **Do not use a calculator for this exercise.**

1 a Add together 143 and 328.

b Subtract 183 from 562.

c Multiply 66 by 4.

d Divide 132 by 6.

2 Write a number at the end of each equation to make it correct.

a $27 + 53 = 17 +$ _____

b $76 - 28 = 66 -$ _____

c $50 \times 17 = 5 \times$ _____

d $400 \div 10 = 4000 \div$ _____

3 Use $+$, $-$, $\times$ or $\div$ to make each calculation correct.

For example: $3 + 7 = 2 \times 5$

a 9 _____ $6 = 20$ _____ 5

b 15 _____ $3 = 4$ _____ 3

c 5 _____ $2 = 15$ _____ 5

d 8 _____ $4 = 4$ _____ 2

4 A teacher decides to buy each of her 32 students a Christmas gift of a pen costing 98p. How much will it cost her altogether?

5 Litter bins cost £29 each. A school has a budget of £500 to spend on bins. How many can they buy?

6 Alf and Bert are paid £48 for doing a job. They decide to share the money in the ratio 3 : 5. How much does Alf get?

7 Work out:

a 2×0.6 _____

b $20 \div 0.1$ _____

c 0.1×60 _____

d 20×30 _____

Name: _____

Form: _____

1 This advert shows how much a plumber charges.

  a How much would Ivor charge for a job that

  lasted 2 hours? _____

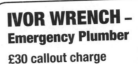

IVOR WRENCH –
Emergency Plumber
£30 callout charge
plus £20 per hour

  b If Ivor charged £110 for a job, how long did it last ?

_____

2 a What is the next coordinate in this list?

    (2, 1), (4, 3), (6, 5), (8, 7), (_____ , _____)

  b Explain why the coordinate (29, 28) could not be in this sequence.

_____

3 From the box choose a number that is

14	24
49	15
12	11
21	2

  a A multiple of 4. _____

  b A factor of 45. _____

  c A square number. _____

  d A prime number. _____

4 Write down the answer for each of the following.

  a $6^2 =$ _____

  b $9^2 =$ _____

  c $2^3 =$ _____

  d $5^3 =$ _____

  e $\sqrt{16} =$ _____

  f $\sqrt{64} =$ _____

  g $\sqrt[3]{64} =$ _____

  h $\sqrt[3]{27} =$ _____

5 The diagrams show some patterns made with black and white squares.

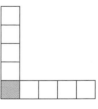

    Pattern 1   Pattern 2   Pattern 3   Pattern 4

  a How many white squares will there be in Pattern 5? _____

  b How many black squares will there be in Pattern 5? _____

  c How many white squares will there be in Pattern 10? _____

  d How many black squares will there be in Pattern 10? _____

Name: _____

Form: _____

1 The graph shows a rectangle ABCD.

  a The equation of the line AB is $x = 1$, as it passes through 1 on the *x-axis*.

    What is the equation of the line CB?

    _____

  b Write down the equations of the two lines of symmetry of the rectangle? .

    _____ and _____

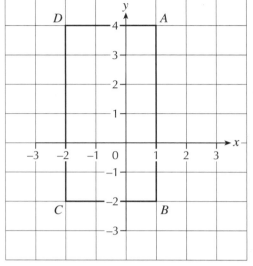

2 A box of pencils contains x pencils. A box of pencils costs £y.

  a Write a term for the number of pencils in six boxes. _____

  b Write a term for the cost of five boxes. _____

  c Which expression represents the cost of x boxes of pencils?

    Circle the answer.   £$(x + y)$ £xy

3 Solve the following equations.

  a $x + 5 = 7$ **b** $3x = 12$ **c** $x - 6 = 10$

  _____   _____   _____

  _____   _____   _____

  _____   _____   _____

4 Look at the following algebraic expressions.

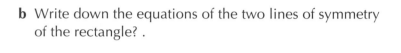

    $2 \times n$ $n^3 \div n$ $n + n$ $0.5n$ $n \div 2$ $n \times n$ $3n - n$ $n \times 2$ $6n \div 3$

  a Which two expressions will always give the same answer as $\frac{n}{2}$?

    _____ and _____

  b Four of the expressions above are the same as $2n$. Write down another expression that is the same as $2n$.

    _____

Name: _____

Form: _____

1 These shapes have both line and rotational symmetry.

   i Draw on the lines of symmetry.   **ii** State the order of rotational symmetry.

a   **b**   **c**

Order _____   Order _____   Order _____

2 In parts **a** to **c,** write down the name of the triangle being described.

  a It has no equal angles. It has no lines of symmetry. _____

  b It has one pair of equal angles. It has one line of symmetry. _____

  c It has three lines of symmetry. It has rotational symmetry of order 3. _____

  d The picture shows a rhombus.

    State whether the following statements are true or false.

    i It has 4 equal sides. _____

    ii It has 4 lines of symmetry. _____   **iii** It has rotational symmetry of order 4 _____ .

3 a Write down the coordinates of:

    A(____ , ____) B(____ , ____)

    C(____ , ____) D(____ , ____)

  b EFG are three vertices of a square.

    Write down the coordinates of the other

    vertex. (____ , ____)

  c Write down the coordinates of the

    mid-point of IH. (____ , ____)

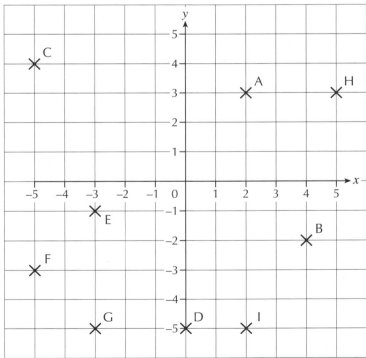

continued…

Name: _____

Form: _____

4 Calculate the area of each of the following shapes.

a

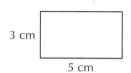

3 cm

5 cm

Area = _____ cm²

b

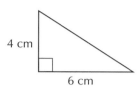

4 cm

6 cm

Area = _____ cm²

c

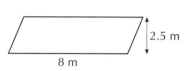

2.5 m

8 m

Area = _____ m²

Name: _____

Form: _____

1 This bar chart shows the favourite pets of 80 students.

a How many students chose a rabbit as their favourite pet? _____

b How many more students preferred a cat than a horse? _____

c What is the difference between the number of students that chose the most and least popular pets? _____

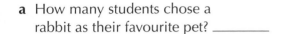

2 This table shows the types and colours of vehicles passing school between 9.00 am and 10.00 am.

	Red	Black	White	Blue
Lorries	2	6	0	3
Vans	3	1	7	2
Cars	6	5	9	8

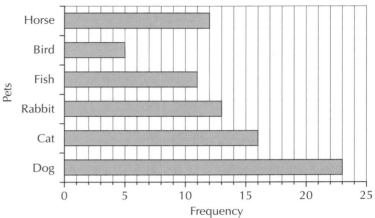

a How many white vans passed the school? _____

b How many lorries passed the school altogether? _____

c How many more blue vehicles than red vehicles passed the school? _____

3 This is the calendar for the first 2 months of 2008.

January					
M		7	14	21	28
Tu	1	8	15	22	29
W	2	9	16	23	30
Th	3	10	17	24	31
F	4	11	18	25	
Sa	5	12	19	26	
Su	6	13	20	27	

February					
M		4	11	18	25
Tu		5	12	19	26
W		6	13	20	27
Th		7	14	21	28
F	1	8	15	22	29
Sa	2	9	16	23	
Su	3	10	17	24	

a The Disney marathon in Florida was on the second Sunday in January.

What date was this? _____

b There are 5 days the same (Fridays) in February. This only happens every 4 years. Explain why.

_____

c Mr Henry went to Florida for a holiday. He arrived on the 22nd of January and left on the 11th of February. For how many **nights** was he in Florida? _____

CHAPTER 13

Statistics 3

HOMEWORK 13.1

Name: _____

Form: _____

---

1 The questions below are taken from some questionnaires that have been carried out. Criticise each question.

    a 'Old people use libraries more than teenagers.'

        How old are you?   Under 10 ☐   10 to 59 ☐   Over 60 ☐

    _____

    b 'Girls spend more on clothes than boys.'

        Girls own more clothes than boys.   Agree ☐   Disagree ☐

    _____

    c 'More men wear glasses than women.'

        Do you have bad eyesight?   Yes ☐   No ☐

    _____

    d 'Students who enjoy playing sports eat healthier foods.'

        Healthy food may be good for you but most of it doesn't taste very good does it? Yes ☐ No ☐

    _____

2 For each of the statements below, criticise the method used to collect the data.

    a 'Taller people have longer fingers.'

        Standing in the street with a metre rule and asking people if you can measure their height and finger length.

    _____

    b 'Sports teams tend to score more towards the end of matches as the opponents become tired.'

        Going to Sunday morning football matches and recording the times of the goals.

    _____

    c 'When people holiday abroad one year, they stay in Britain the following year.'

        Surveying people at a weekly meeting of pensioners.

    _____

    d 'Families eat out more than they used to.'

        Standing outside MacDonald's and doing a survey.

    _____

Name: _____

Form: _____

1 John asked 20 people to estimate the size of an angle. Put these angles into the grouped frequency table.

24   32   35   33   32   25   28   22   38   35
30   32   36   24   29   37   38   39   30   36

Angle estimate (a) in degrees	Tally	Frequency
$20 < a \leq 25$		
$25 < a \leq 30$		
$30 < a \leq 35$		
$35 < a \leq 40$		

2 The heights of 30 people are listed below. Put these heights into the grouped frequency table.

1.4   1.9   1.8   1.6   1.8   1.3   1.9   1.3   1.1   1.7
1.6   1.2   1.1   1.7   1.7   1.6   1.9   1.1   1.9   1.8
1.5   1.3   1.7   1.6   1.5   1.8   1.6   1.2   1.1   1.1

Height (h) in metres	Tally	Frequency
$1.0 < h \leq 1.2$		
$1.2 < h \leq 1.4$		
$1.4 < h \leq 1.6$		
$1.6 < h \leq 1.8$		
$1.8 < h \leq 2.0$		

3 The temperature of 16 towns in Britain is recorded on 1 day. Put these temperatures into the grouped frequency table.

12   10   9   13   12   14   17   16
18   10   12   11   15   15   12   13

Temperature (°C)	Tally	Frequency
8–10		
11–13		
14–16		
17–19		

Name: _____

Form: _____

1 Work out the **median** of each set of numbers and say if it is a suitable average. If it isn't, explain why.

Suitable

a 2, 4, 8, 9, 30, 42   Median = _____   Y ☐   N ☐

   If No, give a reason. _____

b 23, 23, 24, 25, 25, 26, 27, 28, 28, 28   Median = _____   Y ☐   N ☐

   If No, give a reason. _____

c 2, 28, 29, 30, 31, 32, 98   Median = _____   Y ☐   N ☐

   If No, give a reason. _____

2 Work out the **mode** of each set of numbers and say if it is a suitable average. If it isn't, explain why.

Suitable

a 2, 4, 8, 8, 8, 12, 14   Mode = _____   Y ☐   N ☐

   If No, give a reason. _____

b 23, 23, 24, 25, 25, 26, 27, 28, 28, 28   Mode = _____   Y ☐   N ☐

   If No, give a reason. _____

c 2, 3, 4, 4, 5, 7, 7, 9, 10   Mode = _____   Y ☐   N ☐

   If No, give a reason. _____

3 Work out the **mean** of each set of numbers and say if it is a suitable average. If it isn't, explain why.

Suitable

a 2, 5, 6, 7, 20   Mean = _____   Y ☐   N ☐

   If No, give a reason. _____

b 1, 2, 3, 3, 4, 5, 5, 6, 7   Mean = _____   Y ☐   N ☐

   If No, give a reason. _____

c 2, 30, 40, 50, 128   Mean = _____   Y ☐   N ☐

   If No, give a reason. _____

continued…

Name: _____

Form: _____

4 Here are the weights of eight parcels.

   2.4 kg   2.4 kg   1.2 kg   1.8 kg   2.0 kg   2.4 kg   1.4 kg   2.4 kg

Find the **mean**, **median** and **range** of the weights.

Mean _____ kg   Median _____ kg   Range _____ kg

Why would you not use the mode as a measure of the average weight of the eight parcels?

_____

Which is the best average, the mean or the median? _____

Give a reason for your choice. _____

_____

Name: _____

Form: _____

1 The table shows the amount of time added on at the end of 44 football matches. Display the data in a frequency diagram.

Time (*t*) in minutes	Frequency
$0 < t \leq 1$	3
$1 < t \leq 2$	7
$2 < t \leq 3$	15
$3 < t \leq 4$	12
$4 < t \leq 5$	5
$5 < t \leq 6$	2

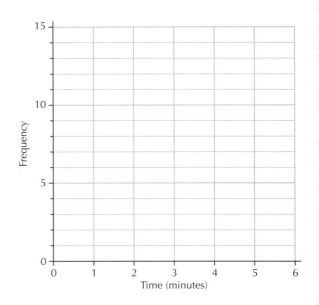

2 The table shows the wages of workers at a factory. Display the data in a frequency diagram.

Wages (*w*) in £	Frequency
$0 < w \leq 5$	38
$5 < w \leq 10$	20
$10 < w \leq 15$	12
$15 < w \leq 20$	4

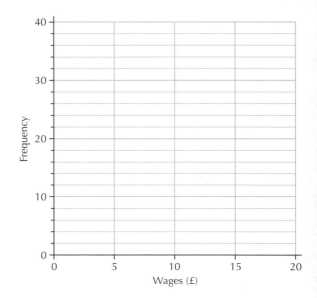

3 The table shows the maximum temperature each day in February. Display the data in a frequency diagram.

Temperature (*t*) in °C	Frequency
$0 < t \leq 2$	4
$2 < t \leq 4$	8
$4 < t \leq 6$	12
$6 < t \leq 8$	4

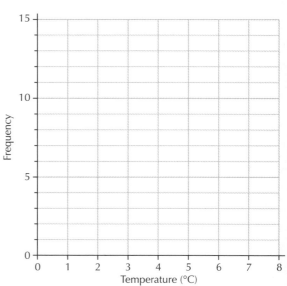

Name: _____

Form: _____

1 Write down the numbers used in each stem-and-leaf diagram.

a
1	3 3 5 9
2	0 2 3 3 8 9
3	3 6 8

_____

_____

_____

| **Key** 1 | 3 represents 13 |

b
5	2 5
6	1 3 6 6 8
7	4 8
8	0

_____

_____

_____

_____

| **Key** 5 | 2 represents 52 |

2 Put the numbers into a stem-and-leaf diagram. The stem is already given in each question. Remember to include a key.

a 42, 43, 43, 47, 48, 51, 52, 52, 56, 61, 62

4	
5	
6	

1	
2	
3	

b 10, 12, 15, 21, 24, 24, 26, 32, 38

3 Put the numbers into a stem-and-leaf diagram. Work out the numbers you need to use for the stem. Remember to include a key.

a 42, 45, 46, 47, 52, 54, 56, 58, 60, 62, 63, 65, 65

b 2, 3, 3, 5, 7, 8, 10, 11, 12, 15, 16, 20, 23, 23, 26

4 Draw a stem-and-leaf diagram to show these temperatures. Remember to include a key.

16°C, 18°C, 20°C, 22°C, 26°C, 26°C, 28°C, 32°C, 33°C, 34°C

Geometry and measures **4**

Name: _____

Form: _____

By following steps 1 to 6 you will construct this triangle accurately.

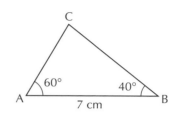

1 Use your ruler to draw the line AB 7 cm long. Mark the ends A and B. Label the line '7 cm'.

2 Put your protractor on the end marked A and measure an angle of 60° round from the line AB. Mark with a dot.

3 Draw a straight line from A, through the dot and beyond. You should now have drawn a 60° angle. Label it.

4 Now put your protractor on the end marked B and measure an angle of 40° round from the line AB. Mark with a dot.

5 Draw a straight line from B, through the dot and beyond. You should now have drawn a 40° angle. Label it.

6 You should notice that your lines cross. Mark this point C. You have constructed the triangle ABC.

What is the size of angle C? _____°.

Measure the lengths of sides AC and BC.

Length of AC _____ cm.

Length of BC _____ cm.

Name: _____

Form: _____

By following steps 1 to 7 you will construct this triangle accurately.

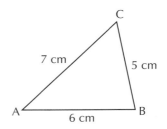

1 Use your ruler to draw the line AB 6 cm long. Mark the ends A and B. Label the line '6 cm'.

2 Set your compasses to a width of 7 cm.

3 Put the point of the compasses onto point A and draw an arc.

4 Set your compasses to a width of 5 cm.

5 Put the point of the compasses onto point B and draw an arc making sure that it crosses your first arc.

6 Mark the point where the arcs cross as C.

7 Draw a line from A to C and label it '7 cm' and draw a line from B to C and label it '5 cm'.
You have constructed the triangle ABC.

What type of triangle is this?

_____

HOMEWORK
14.3

Name: _____

Form: _____

1 This is the net of a cuboid.

   a Write down the following:

     Width _____

     Length_____

     Height_____

   b Work out the surface area of the cuboid.

     _____

     _____

     _____

     _____ cm²

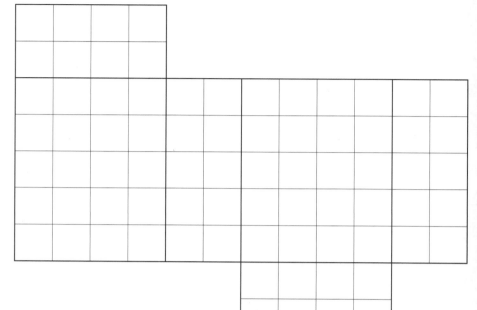

2 a For the cuboid on the right, write down the following:

     Width _____

     Length_____

     Height_____

   b Work out the surface area of the cuboid.

     _____

     _____ cm²

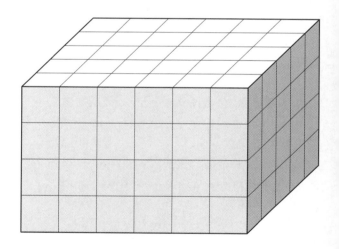

3 Work out the surface area of each of these cuboids.

   a _____

     _____

     _____ cm²

   b _____

     _____

     _____ m²

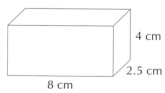

310

HOMEWORK
14.4

Name: _____

Form: _____

1 This is the net of a cuboid.

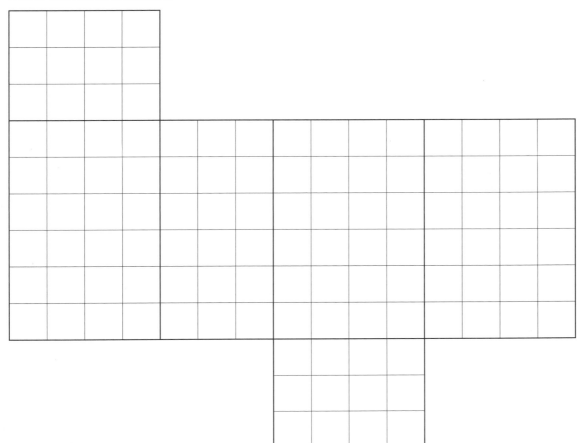

a Write down the following:

Width _____   Length _____   Height _____

b Work out the volume of the cuboid.

_____

_____cm³

2 The picture shows a cuboid.
   a Write down the following:

Width _____

Length _____

Height _____

b Work out the volume of the cuboid.

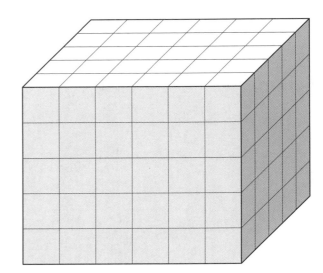

_____

_____ cm³

Name: _____

Form: _____

continued...

3 Work out the volume of each of these cuboids.

a _____

_____

_____ cm^3

b _____

_____

_____ m^3

GCSE Preparation

Name: _____

Form: _____

Do not use a calculator for this exercise.

1 Use BODMAS to work out each of the following.

   a $2 \times 7 - 8 = $ _____

   c $4 \times 6 \div 2 = $ _____

   b $20 \div 5 + 5 = $ _____

   d $4^2 \times 2 - 6 = $ _____

2 Use BODMAS to work out each of the following. Remember to work out the brackets first.

   a $(9 + 4) - 4 = $ _____

   c $25 \div (6 - 1) = $ _____

   b $6 \times (9 - 2) = $ _____

   d $10 - (5 - 2)^2 = $ _____

3 Use BODMAS to work out each of the following.

   a $20 - 3 \times 2^2 = $ _____

   c $32 \div 2^2 + 8 = $ _____

   e $35 \div (8 - 1) = $ _____

   g $(18 - 6) \div 4 = $ _____

   i $12 + 4 \times 5 = $ _____

   k $4^2 \times (4 - 1) = $ _____

   b $8 \times (7 - 3) = $ _____

   d $(20 - 2) \div 3 = $ _____

   f $16 + 4 \times 3 = $ _____

   h $15 \div (4 + 1) = $ _____

   j $(3^2 + 1) \times 5 = $ _____

   l $(6 - 1)^2 - 5 = $ _____

4 Put in brackets to make each of these calculations true.

   a $2 \times 5 + 7 = 24$

   d $18 \div 3 + 3 = 3$

   b $20 \div 2 + 2 = 5$

   e $5 \times 12 - 8 = 20$

   c $28 \div 4 + 3 = 4$

   f $10 - 2^2 \times 2 = 128$

Name: _____

Form: _____

1 Complete the balance column in the statement table below.

Transaction	Amount paid in	Amount paid out	Balance
			£64.37
Standing order		£53.20	£11.17
Cheque	£32.00		
Direct debit		£65.50	
Cash	£20.00		
Wages	£124.80		
Loan		£169.38	

2 Calculate each of the following.

a −4 − 3 − 6 = _____

b −1 + 3 + 6 = _____

c −2 + (−4) = _____

d +5 − (+7) = _____

e −6 + −6 + +3 = _____

f −8 − −8 + −1 = _____

g +7 − −6 + −1 = _____

h −6 − 5 + −5 = _____

3 Fill in the numbers on these number lines.

a
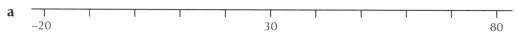

b

4 Fill in the missing numbers from each of the boxes below to make each calculation true.

a −4 + −3 = ☐

b 8 + ☐ = 6

c −2 + ☐ = 2

d ☐ − −8 = 9

e −3 − ☐ = 2

f +1 − ☐ = 5

HOMEWORK
15.3

Name: _____

Form: _____

Do not use a calculator for this exercise.

1 Write down the first 5 multiples of each of the following.

a 11, _____, _____, _____, _____

b 15, _____, _____, _____, _____

c 20, _____, _____, _____, _____

2 From the numbers in the box, write down those that are:

3	7	8	13	14	15	18	24
36	39	48	49	64	69	90	120

a multiples of 2. _____

b multiples of 7. _____

c multiples of 9. _____

3 Find the largest number less than 50 that is:

a a multiple of 6. _____

b a multiple of 3 and 5. _____

4 Write down all of the factors of each of the following.

a 34 _____

b 52 _____

c 80 _____

d 100 _____

e 180 _____

5 Find the common factors of 15 and 25. Remember to list all of the factors of 15 and 25 first.

_____

_____

_____

Name: _____

Form: _____

1 Write down the value of each of the following.

   a 6^2 _____

   b 8^2 _____

   c 12^2 _____

   d $\sqrt{49}$ _____

   e $\sqrt{81}$ _____

   f $\sqrt{100}$ _____

2 Calculate the value of each of the following.

   a 22^2 _____

   b 26^2 _____

   c 31^2 _____

   d $\sqrt{1089}$ _____

   e $\sqrt{1225}$ _____

   f $\sqrt{1764}$ _____

3 Calculate the value of each of the following.

   a 5^4 _____

   b 9^3 _____

   c 15^4 _____

   d 18^3 _____

   e 3^9 _____

   f 5^7 _____

HOMEWORK
15.5

Name: _____

Form: _____

1 Mr Rashid is going to change the oil in his car. It needs 4 litres of clean oil. He has 1.85 litres of clean oil.

   a How much more oil will he need?

   b He buys a 3 litre bottle of oil. How much will he have left after he has changed his oil?

2 A camper takes a tent weighing 2.8 kg, a sleeping bag weighing 1.9 kg, a sleeping mat weighing 0.75 kg, a stove weighing 1.32 kg and food weighing 4.65 kg on a camping trip.

   a What is the total weight of this basic equipment?

   b The equipment is to be packed into a rucksack that weighs 2.2 kg. If the total weight that the camper carries is not to exceed 20 kg, what weight of clothes can he carry?

continued...

Name: _____

Form: _____

3 Lara goes on holiday. Her case weighs 22.3 kg. The airline has a luggage allowance
   of 18 kg. Excess weight is charged at £10.30 per kilogram. How much will Lara be
   charged for her case?

4 John is walking in the Lake District. To work out how long a walk will take he uses the
   following rules:

   For every 5 km allow 1 hour.
   For every 100 m of height climbed allow 10 minutes.

   Approximately how long will it take John to do a route that is 17 km long, which climbs 1450 m?

New Maths Frameworking
Year 9 Homework Answers

Homework Answers

Chapter 1   Algebra 1 and 2

Homework 1.1
1 a 42   **b** 113   **c** 113   **d** 147   **e** 870   **f** 269
2 a 18   **b** 23   **c** 57   **d** 44   **e** 93   **f** 184
3 a 21   **b** 24   **c** 33   **d** 32   **e** 40   **f** 27
4 Check test has been done and marked correctly

Homework 1.2
1 a 18   **b** 48   **c** 63   **d** 72   **e** 90   **f** 135   **g** 420   **h** 420
2 a 28, 32, 36, 42, 48, 54, 70, 80, 90
   b 10, 30, 40, 14, 42, 56, 16, 48, 64
3 a 81   **b** 72   **c** 108   **d** 78   **e** 45   **f** 102
4 Check test has been done and marked correctly

Homework 1.3
1 a 26, 29, 32, 35, 38, 41   **b** 61, 56, 51, 46, 41, 36   **c** −16, −12, −8, −4, 0, 4
   d 5, 10, 20, 40, 80, 160   **e** 1, 4, 13, 40, 121, 364
2 a Add 4   **b** Subtract 9   **c** Subtract 5   **d** Multiply by 3   **e** Divide by 2
3 a −2, 2, 18   **b** 47, 19, 5

Homework 1.4
1 a 11, 17, 28, 111   **b** 15, 37, 4, 94   **c** 3, 5, 21, 23, 30, 32, 39, 41   **d** 2, 8, 3, 12, 6, 24, 13, 52
2 a 20, 32, 46, 100   **b** −3, 0, 5, 27
3 a Divide by 3   **b** Add 22

Homework 1.5
1 $7 - n, 2n, 3n - 1, n - 5, n \div 4$
2 a 9   **b** 4   **c** 8   **d** 4   **e** 10   **f** 12
3 a 11, 13, 17, 28   **b** 11, 19, 33, 65

Homework 1.6
1 a 5, 7, 8, 10   **b** 5, 7, 8, 10
2 a 6, 4, 3, 0   **b** 6, 4, 3, 0
3 a 0, 4, 8, 12   **b** 0, 4, 8, 12
4 a −1, 2, 5, 8, 11   **b** −1, 2, 5, 8, 11
Check graphs are plotted correctly

Chapter 2   Number 1

Homework 2.1
1 a 50   **b** 70   **c** 60   **d** 210   **e** 310   **f** 470
2 a 300   **b** 600   **c** 300   **d** 2800   **e** 6100   **f** 2300
3 a £7000   **b** £12 000   **c** £7000
4 a 3   **b** 7   **c** 14   **d** 10   **e** 5   **f** 19

5 a 7.8   **b** 8.4   **c** 0.7   **d** 12.6   **e** 18.8   **f** 10.5
6 a 7.8   **b** 6.4   **c** 12.1   **d** 11.6   **e** 0.1   **f** 9.0

Homework 2.2

1

2 a 0.9   **b** 3.6   **c** 11.3   **d** 10.0   **e** 4.3   **f** 8.5   **g** 10.4   **h** 4.2   **i** 5.13
3 a 2.3, 3.2, 3.7, 7.3   **b** 0.5, 0.7, 1.7, 3.7   **c** 11.5, 12.6, 16.2, 20.3   **d** 14.3, 35.7, 41.2, 73.5
4 a £0.99, £1.09, £1.90, £9.91   **b** £3.14, £3.41, £4.13, £4.31

Homework 2.3

1 a $\frac{3}{4}$, 0.75   **b** $\frac{2}{5}$, 0.4   **c** $\frac{7}{10}$, 0.7
2 a 0.1   **b** 0.7   **c** 0.9   **d** 0.01   **e** 0.13   **f** 0.31
3 a $\frac{1}{5}$ **b** $\frac{9}{10}$ **c** $\frac{9}{100}$ **d** $\frac{11}{100}$ **e** $\frac{27}{100}$ **f** $\frac{35}{100} = \frac{7}{20}$
4 a $\frac{3}{10} = \frac{30}{100}$ **b** $\frac{45}{100}$ **c** $\frac{4}{5} = \frac{8}{10} = \frac{80}{100}$

Homework 2.4

1 a $\frac{4}{14}, \frac{6}{21}, \frac{8}{28}$ **b** $\frac{6}{16}, \frac{9}{24}, \frac{12}{32}$ **c** $\frac{2}{18}, \frac{3}{27}, \frac{4}{36}$ **d** $\frac{6}{10}, \frac{9}{15}, \frac{12}{20}$
2 a $\frac{16}{20}$ **b** $\frac{9}{21}$ **c** $\frac{12}{18}$ **d** $\frac{25}{30}$
3 a $\frac{4}{24}$ **b** $\frac{20}{32}$ **c** $\frac{10}{25}$ **d** $\frac{12}{27}$
4 $\frac{6}{8}, \frac{12}{16}, \frac{33}{44}$
5 $\frac{15}{24}, \frac{6}{16}$

Homework 2.5

1 a $\frac{7}{8}$ **b** $\frac{1}{4}$ **c** $\frac{2}{5}$ **d** $\frac{5}{6}$ **e** $\frac{8}{9}$ **f** $\frac{2}{9}$ **g** $\frac{4}{5}$ **h** $\frac{5}{8}$ **i** $\frac{1}{6}$ **j** $\frac{4}{9}$
2 a >   **b** >   **c** =   **d** =   **e** =   **f** >   **g** <   **h** =   **i** =   **j** <

Homework 2.6

1 a $\frac{3}{4}$, 75%   **b** $\frac{2}{5}$, 40%   **c** $\frac{7}{10}$, 70%
2 a 5%   **b** 30%   **c** 25%   **d** 40%   **e** 50%   **f** 45%   **g** 80%   **h** 99%   **i** 16%
3 a $\frac{1}{10}$ **b** $\frac{1}{5}$ **c** $\frac{19}{20}$ **d** $\frac{4}{5}$ **e** $\frac{16}{25}$ **f** $\frac{3}{20}$ **g** $\frac{1}{4}$ **h** $\frac{3}{50}$ **i** $\frac{3}{4}$
4 a <   **b** <   **c** =   **d** =   **e** >

Homework 2.7

1 a $\frac{13}{100}$ **b** $\frac{24}{100}$ **c** $\frac{73}{100}$ **d** $\frac{6}{100}$ **e** $\frac{30}{100}$ **f** $\frac{9}{100}$
2 a i £8   **ii** $9 \times £4 = £36$ **iii** $20 \times £4 = £80$
  b 6   **i** $3 \times 6 = 18$ kg   **ii** $12 \times 6 = 72$ kg   **iii** $35 \times 6 = 210$ kg
  c $3000 \div 100 = 30$ m   **i** 30, 120 m   **ii** $18 \times 30 = 540$ m   **iii** $40 \times 30 = 1200$ m
3 a 29.7   **b** 19.2   **c** $48 \div 100 \times 250 = 120$ **d** $3 \div 100 \times 265 = 7.95$

Homework 2.8

1 a 2 : 1   **b** 3 : 1   **c** 1 : 4   **b** 4 : 3
2 a 1 : 2   **b** 6 : 1   **c** 1 : 3   **d** 1 : 2   **e** 4 : 3   **f** 4 : 5   **g** 3 : 7   **h** 1 : 3
3 $9 : 15 = 3 : 5$
4 $8 : 24 = 1 : 3$
5 $25 : 55 = 5 : 11$

Chapter 3 Algebra 3

Homework 3.1

1 **a** 3 **b** 22 **c** 3 **d** 19 **e** 24 **f** 25
2 **a** 5 **b** 6 **c** 7 **d** 3 **e** 5 **f** 18
3 **a** 1 and 22, 2 and 21, etc. **b** 15 and 3, 20 and 8, etc.
  c 4 × 8, 2 × 16, etc. **d** 16 ÷ 4, 20 ÷ 5, etc.
4 **a** 8 **b** 4 **c** 7 **d** 10 **e** 9 **f** 2 **g** 7 **h** 4

Homework 3.2

1 **a i** 40 cm **ii** 48 m **iii** 24 cm **b** 15 cm
2 **a i** £12 **ii** £18 **iii** £36 **b** 10 leaves
3 **a i** £23 **ii** £25.50 **iii** £63 **b** 8 bags

Homework 3.3

1 **a** $4g$ **b** $3k$ **c** $9a$ **d** $13c$ **e** $3m$ **f** $5d$ **g** $11q$ **h** $9a$
2 $4a$ and $2a + 2a$, $8a - 3a$ and $2a + 3a$, $9a - 6a$ and $4a - a$, $2a + 6a$ and $10a - 2a$
3 **a** $4c + 3d$ **b** $p + 3q$ **c** $j + 3k$ **d** t **e** $5a + 3b$
4 $13a + 16b$ **b** $11m + 7n$ **c** $6a + 10n$ **d** $5p + 7q$ **e** $10c + 5d$

Homework 3.4

1 **a** 300 miles **b** 200 miles **c** 175 miles
2 **a** £18 **b** £14 **c** £10
3 **a** 50 s **b** 170 s **c** 230 s
4 9, 27, 25
5 12, 60, 67

Homework 3.5

1 **a** Subtract 5 from both sides, $x = 6$ **b** Subtract 7 from both sides, $x = 12$
  c Add 8 to both sides, $x = 21$ **d** Add 6 to both sides, $x = 30$
  e Add 10 to both sides, $x = 30$ **f** Subtract 14 from both sides, $x = 14$
2 **a** Divide both sides by 5, 5, 5, $x = 7$ **b** Divide both sides by 7, 7, 7, $x = 3$
  c Divide both sides by 2, $2x \div 2 = 24 \div 2$, $x = 12$ **d** Divide both sides by 8, $8x \div 8 = 32 \div 8$, $x = 4$
  e Divide both sides by 2, $2x \div 2 = 9 \div 2$, $x = 4.5$ **f** Divide both sides by 8, $8x \div 8 = 64 \div 8$, $x = 8$

Chapter 4 Geometry and measures 1

Homework 4.1

1 Second triangle – No sides the same – Scalene
  Third triangle – Two angles the same – Isosceles
  Fourth triangle – One angle is a right angle – Right-angled triangle

2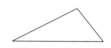

3 Any correct example, such as:

Homework 4.2
1 $a = 75°$, $b = 108°$, $c = 45°$
2 $a = 53°$, $b = 58°$, $c = 59°$, $d = 55°$, $e = 75°$, $f = 61°$
3 $a = 122°$, $b = 58°$, $c = 122°$, $d = 38°$, $e = 142°$, $f = 38°$, $g = 131°$, $h = 49°$, $i = 131°$

Homework 4.3
1 $a = 61°$, $b = 304°$, $c = 162°$
2 $a = 70°$, $b = 174°$, $c = 138°$, $d = 48°$, $e = 37°$, $f = 82°$
3 $a = 72°$, $b = 133°$, $c = 90°$, $d = 45°$

Homework 4.4
1 a $50°$ **b** $60°$ **c** $50°$ **d** $55°$ **e** $40°$ **f** $8°$
2 a $75°$ **b** $35°$ **c** $c = 80°, d = 20°$
3 a $107°$ **b** $105°$ **c** $55°$

Chapter 5   Statistics 1

Homework 5.1
1 a A table with categories, tallies and frequencies; chips (6), pizza (10), soup (12), sandwiches (2)
 b Students in other years may eat different foods
2 a Frequencies: 10, 9, 3, 3
 b Students in other years may watch a different amount of television

Homework 5.2
1 a 20, 20, 6, 10, 14, 10, 40 **b** cola **c** $\frac{1}{3}$ **d** 60% **e** 50%
2 a 7 **b** Wednesday **c** Friday **d** 8 hours **e** £19.25

Homework 5.3
1 a Frequencies are 2, 5, 6, 8, 4, 3, 2
 b Bar-line graph drawn to these values but follow through any incorrect frequencies
2 Bars drawn to correct heights

Homework 5.4
1 a £4 **b** 62 **c** 5.7
2 a 8 **b** 5 **c** 28
3 a Range 7, mean 9 **b** Range 7, mean 9.6 **c** Range 0.6, mean 0.6
4 a Mavis 20, Doris 22 **b** Doris – bigger mean

Homework 5.5
1 Pie chart drawn with following sectors: 0 goals – 1, 1 goal – 2, 2 goals – 3, 3 goals – 2.5,
 4 goals – 1.5
2 Pie chart drawn with angles: Action – 84°, Adventure – 54°, Racing – 150°, Fighting – 72°
3 Pie chart drawn with angles: Sweet – 120°, Computing – 64°, Book – 80°, Cosmetic – 40°,
 Other – 56°
Check that the sectors are labelled

Homework 5.6
1 Sun frequencies – 1, 9, 9, 3, 8, 7, 10, 0, 3, 2
 Guardian frequencies – 1, 6, 7, 9, 10, 5, 3, 3, 2, 2
 Check graphs are correctly drawn

Chapter 6   Geometry and measures 2

Homework 6.1
1 a mm   **b** cm³ or centilitres   **c** cm²   **d** grams
2 a 15 cm   **b** 4 m (3.6 m)   **c** 24 km   **d** 2 kg   **e** 9 litres
3 8 kg
4 45 litres
5 90 g flour, 150 ml milk
6 Speed 192 kmph, weight 1000 kg, tank 36 litres

Homework 6.2
1 a 48 cm²   **b** 26 cm²   **c** 35 cm²
2 120 cm²   54 m²   85 cm²   72 km²
3 a 23 cm²   **b** 56 cm²   **c** 62 cm²   **d** 90 cm²
4 a 4 cm   **b** 7 cm   **c** 9 cm   **d** 9 cm

Homework 6.3
1 a 6 cm²   **b** 6 cm²
2 a 7.5 cm²   **b** 6 cm²   **c** 9 cm²
3 a 9 cm²   **b** 35 m²   **c** 27 mm²
4 a 15 cm²   **b** 36 cm²   **c** 14 cm²

Homework 6.4
1 12 cm²
2 a 48 cm²   **b** 60 cm²   **c** 24 cm²   **d** 36 cm²
3 Any three parallelograms where base × height = 12 cm²

Chapter 7   Number 2

Homework 7.1
1 $10^5 = 100\,000$, $10^7 = 10\,000\,000$
2 a 1 000 000   **b** 10^6 **c** 10 000   **d** 10^4
3 a 7000   **b** 800 000   **c** 100, 300   **d** $12 \times 1000 = 12\,000$ **e** $18 \times 1\,000\,000 = 18\,000\,000$
4 a 650   **b** 3700   **c** 10 000, 77 000   **d** $4.3 \times 100\,000 = 430\,000$

Homework 7.2
1 a 523   **b** 991   **c** 1394
2 a 11.53   **b** 8.65   **c** 37.61   **d** 9.3   **e** 14.56   **f** 22.08
3 a 8.4 cm   **b** 6.26 m

Homework 7.3
1 a 351   **b** 313   **c** 162
2 a 1.59   **b** 3.27   **c** 15.15   **d** 5.2   **e** 1.84   **f** 74.62
3 1.16 kg
4 Yes, there is 0.66 MB of space left

Homework 7.4
1 a 276   **b** 2436   **c** 23.04   **d** 21.8(0)
2 a 378   **b** 55.2   **c** 25.12   **d** 230.4   **e** 5.37(0)   **f** 496.56
3 a 56.4 cm²   **b** 21.51 m²

Homework 7.5
1 a 13   **b** 17   **c** 21   **d** 1.6   **e** 0.38   **f** 2.2
2 a 34   **b** 4.3   **c** 1.37
3 a 19 *r* 1   **b** 14 *r* 3   **c** 15 *r* 3   **d** 1.5 *r* 0.2   **e** 1.3 *r* 0.02   **f** 2.6 *r* 0.3
4 a 5.7 cm   **b** 4.8 m

Homework 7.6

1 44.8

2 20.05

3 420 minutes

4 98 days

5 0.83 kg

6 £4.69

7 a £57.10   **b** Yes, the total is £59.99

Chapter 8   Algebra 4

Homework 8.1

1 a 4, 8, 12, 16, 20   **b** 9, 18, 27, 36, 45   **c** 12, 24, 36, 48, 60   **d** 18, 36, 54, 72, 90
  e 45, 90, 135, 180, 225

2 50, 55

3 88, 99

4 56, 70

5 66, 88

6 480, 540

7 32

8 20

9 90

10 Shade 21, 63, 36, 18, 9, 12, 99; T

Homework 8.2

1 a $1 \times 10, 2 \times 5$ **b** $1 \times 18, 2 \times 9, 3 \times 6$ **c** $1 \times 30, 2 \times 15, 3 \times 10, 5 \times 6$ **d** $1 \times 15, 3 \times 5$

2 a 1, 2, 4, 7, 14, 28   **b** 1, 2, 5, 10, 25, 50   **c** 1, 2, 4, 7, 8, 14, 28, 56

3 12

4 12

5 4

6 28

7 Shade 1, 9, 5, 48, 24, 10, 6, 15, 2, 8, 3, 16, 30; E

Homework 8.3

1 a 1, 2, 3, 4, 6, 12   **b** 1, 2, 4, 8   **c** 1, 2, 4; 4

2 a 1, 3, 5, 15   **b** 1, 5, 25   **c** 1, 5; 5

3 a 1, 3, 9, 27   **b** 1, 3, 5, 9, 15, 45   **c** 1, 3, 9; 9

4 a 5, 10, 15, 20, 25, 30, 35, 40, 45, 50   **b** 6, 12, 18, 24, 30, 36, 42, 48, 54, 60   **c** 30

5 a 3, 6, 9, 12, 15, 18, 21, 24, 27, 30   **b** 6, 12, 18, 24, 30, 36, 42, 48, 54, 60   **c** 6, 12, 18, 24, 30; 6

Homework 8.4

1 6, 10, 15, 21

2

3 a 2×17 **b** 3×13 **c** 3×17 **d** 5×19 **e** $3 \times 3 \times 5$ **f** $2 \times 3 \times 7$ **g** $5 \times 5 \times 2$

Homework 8.5

1 9; 25; 7×7, 49; 9×9, 81; 11×11, 121

2 64, twelfth, 100

3 $1 + 3 + 5 = 9 = 3^2$, $1 + 3 + 5 + 7 = 16 = 4^2$, $1 + 3 + 5 + 7 + 9 = 25 = 5^2$,
  $1 + 3 + 5 + 7 + 9 + 11 = 36 = 6^2$

4 c 900 **d** 1600 **e** 2500 **f** 3600 **g** 4900 **h** 6400 **i** 8100
5 Squares of 16 and 25 dots; 16, 25

Homework 8.6

1 $4 \times 4 = 16$, 16; $6 \times 6 = 36$, 36, 6; $8 \times 8 = 64$, 64, 8; $10 \times 10 = 100$, 100, 10; $12 \times 12 = 144$, 144, 12
2 a 7 **b** 5 **c** 11 **d** 9 **e** 1 **f** 8 **g** 10 **h** 2 **i** 3
3 $\sqrt{441}$, 21; $\sqrt{1225}$, 35; $\sqrt{256}$, 16; $\sqrt{361}$, 19; $\sqrt{676}$, 26; $\sqrt{729}$, 27
4 a 34 **b** 31 **c** 45 **d** 36 **e** 50 **f** 32

Homework 8.7

1 $3 \times 3 \times 3 = 27$; $5 \times 5 \times 5 = 125$; $7 \times 7 \times 7 = 343$; $9 \times 9 \times 9 = 729$
2 a 1331 **b** 1728 **c** 2197 **d** 2744 **e** 3375 **f** 4096
3 a 64 **b** 216 **c** Eighth **d** 64
4 a 17 576 **b** 10 648 **c** 6859 **d** 27 000 **e** 29 791 **f** 19 683

Homework 8.8

1 $3 \times 3 \times 3 = 27$, 27; $5 \times 5 \times 5 = 125$, 125, 5; $7 \times 7 \times 7 = 343$, 343, 7; $9 \times 9 \times 9 = 729$, 729, 9
2 a 3 **b** 5 **c** 10 **d** 2 **e** 6 **f** 4
3 a 9 **b** 8 **c** 6 **d** 5
4 a 18 **b** 1.5 **c** 0.5 **d** 17 **e** 14 **f** 22

Chapter 9 Statistics 2

Homework 9.1

1 a Impossible **b** Very likely to Certain **c** Very unlikely **d** Even **e** Very likely
2 a $\frac{1}{2}$ **b** $\frac{1}{4}$ **c** $\frac{3}{4}$
3 a $\frac{1}{6}$ **b** $\frac{3}{6}$ **c** 1 **d** 0 **e** $\frac{2}{6}, \frac{1}{3}$

Homework 9.2

1 $\frac{4}{9}$
2 $\frac{4}{8} = \frac{1}{2}$, $\frac{3}{8}$, $\frac{1}{8}$
3 $\frac{3}{10}$, $\frac{2}{10} = \frac{1}{5}$, $\frac{5}{10} = \frac{1}{2}$, $\frac{5}{10} = \frac{1}{2}$, $\frac{8}{10} = \frac{4}{5}$, 1, 0
4 $\frac{1}{2}, \frac{1}{2}$
5 $\frac{2}{11}, \frac{5}{11}, \frac{4}{11}, \frac{7}{11}$, 0
6 $\frac{12}{200} = \frac{3}{50}$, $\frac{8}{200} = \frac{1}{25}$, $\frac{20}{100} = \frac{1}{10}$

Homework 9.3

1 a Red 8, Blue 2 **b** 800 and 200 or 780 and 220
2 a Because all frequencies are near to 100
   b Because 2 has a frequency much higher than 100 and 5 is a lot lower
   c 200 for each or double table in **a**

Homework 9.4

1 a $\frac{7}{10}$
   b $\frac{32}{50} = \frac{16}{25}$
   c Second as it had more trials
2 a $\frac{12}{20} = \frac{3}{5}$, 0.6, Yes
   b $\frac{132}{200} = \frac{33}{50}$, 0.66, Biased because should be about 100 each

Chapter 10 Geometry and measures 3

Homework 10.1
1 Correct number of lines on each shape
a 4 b 8 c 1 d 4 e 2 f 1 g 1 h 1 i 1
2 a   b   c

Homework 10.2
1 a 2 b 6 c 8 d 4 e 2 f 2 g 2 h 8 i 6
2 a   b   c

Homework 10.3
Check the sketch

Homework 10.4
1 a C b E c H d F e B f I g J h G i D j A
2 a (–4, –3) b (0, –3)
3 a Z b W
4 a (–1, –0.3) b (0.1, –0.2)

Chapter 11 Algebra 5

Homework 11.1
1 a 8 + 12 = 20 b 50 – 5 = 45 c 16 –10 = 6 d 40 – 32 = 8 e 18 – 3 = 15
2 a 24 + 15 = 39 b 36 – 32 = 4 c 54 – 12 = 42 d 49 – 36 = 13 e 6 + 18 = 24
3 a 32 ÷ 8 = 4 b 5 × 6 = 30 c 20 × 7 = 140 d 5 × 9 = 45 e 9 × 6 = 54
4 a 8 + 12 + 9 = 29 b 20 – 5 + 3 = 18 c 6 × 5 + 7 = 30 + 7 = 37
  d 29 + 5 × 4 = 29 + 20 = 49

Homework 11.2
1 a 30 + 15 = 45 b 14 + 49 = 63 c 24 – 9 = 15 d 5 × 2 + 5 × 9 = 10 + 45 = 55
  e 6 × 6 – 6 × 3 = 36 – 18 = 18 f 2 × 6 + 2 × 9 = 12 + 18 = 30
2 a $3a$ b $8b$ c $10c$ d $7m$
3 a $6a + 12$ b $4b - 12$ c $9 \times c - 9 \times 6 = 9c - 54$ d $4 \times d + 4 \times 5 = 4d + 20$
  e $8 \times e - 8 \times 3 = 8e - 24$ f $5 \times f - 5 \times 3 = 5f - 15$

Homework 11.3
1 a Subtract 5, $3x = 15$, $x = 5$ b Subtract 7, $4x = 4$, $x = 1$
  c Subtract 7, $5x = 15$, $x = 3$ d Add 7, $4x = 32$, $x = 8$
  e Add 5, $6x = 30$, $x = 5$ f Add 11, $2x = 24$, $x = 12$
2 a Subtract 7, $5x + 7 - 7 = 32 - 7$, $5x = 25$, $x = 25 \div 5 = 5$
  b Add 7, $6x - 7 + 7 = 11 + 7$, $6x = 18$, $x = 18 \div 6 = 3$

Homework 11.4
1 a 25 minutes b 10 minutes
2 a 7.15 b 7.45 c 8.30 d 9.15
3 a i £1 ii £1 iii £2 iv £2 v £5 vi £5
  b i 1 hour ii 3 hours iii 6 hours
  c Because it looks like a set of steps

Chapter 12 Revision

Homework 12.1
1 a Half   **b** Less than a third   **c** More than a quarter
2 a i 22%   **ii** 44%   **b i** 30% (±2%)   **ii** 60% (±2%)
3 60%, 0.60, $\frac{60}{100}$, $\frac{3}{5}$ and $\frac{6}{10}$
4 $\frac{7}{12}$
5 £55.50
6 a 567   **b** 161

Homework 12.2
1 a 471   **b** 379   **c** 264   **d** 22
2 a 63   **b** 18   **c** 170   **d** 100
3 a $9 + 6 = 20 - 5$ **b** $15 - 3 = 4 \times 3$ **c** $5 - 2 = 15 \div 5$ *or* $5 \times 2 = 15 - 5$
   d $8 \div 4 = 4 \div 2$ *or* $8 \div 4 = 4 - 2$
4 £31.36
5 17 bins with £7 left over
6 £18
7 a 1.2   **b** 200   **c** 6   **d** 600

Homework 12.3
1 a £70   **b** 4 hours
2 a (10, 9)   **b** Because the first number must be even
3 a 24 or 12   **b** 15   **c** 49   **d** 2 or 11
4 a 36   **b** 81   **c** 8   **d** 125   **e** 4   **f** 8   **g** 4   **h** 3
5 a 10   **b** 1   **c** 20   **d** 1

Homework 12.4
1 a $y = -2$ **b** $y = 1, x = -\frac{1}{2}$
2 a $6x$ **b** $5y$ **c** £xy
3 a 2   **b** 4   **c** 16
4 a $0.5n$ and $n \div 2$ **b** Any valid expression such as $5n - 3n$

Homework 12.5
1 a 2 lines of symmetry, rotational symmetry order 2
   b 6 lines of symmetry, rotational symmetry order 6
   c 0 lines of symmetry, rotational symmetry order 2
2 a Scalene   **b** Isosceles   **c** Equilateral   **d i** true   **ii** false   **iii** false
3 a A(2, 3), B(4, −2), C(−5, 4), D(0, −5)   **b** (−1, −3)   **c** $(3\frac{1}{2}, -1)$
4 a 15 cm²   **b** 12 cm²   **c** 20 m²

Homework 12.6
1 a 13   **b** 4   **c** 18
2 a 7   **b** 11   **c** 2
3 a 13th January   **b** It is a leap year   **c** 20

Chapter 13 Statistics 3

Homework 13.1
1 a Not enough choices   **b** Leading question   **c** Offensive question
   d Confusing question, leading question
2 a People will be embarrassed, metre rule not accurate for measuring fingers
   b Take too long to collect enough data
   c Pensioners may not go on as many holidays, not a representative sample
   d Asking people who are going out to eat, biased sample

Homework 13.2
1 Frequencies are 4, 4, 6, 6
2 Frequencies are 7, 4, 7, 8, 4
3 Frequencies are 3, 7, 4, 2

Homework 13.3
1 a 8.5; no, two extreme values (30 and 42)
  b 25.5; yes
  c 30; no, two extreme values
2 a 8; yes **b** 28; no it is at one end of data **c** 4 or 7; no, no definite mode
3 a 8; no, mean is bigger than four of the data
  b 4; yes
  c 50; yes, extreme values cancel each other out
4 Mean = 2 kg, median = 2.2 kg, range = 1.2 kg
  2.4 kg is an extreme value
  In this case either could be used but mean uses all values

Homework 13.4
1 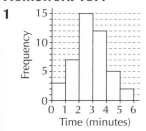 **2** 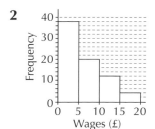 **3**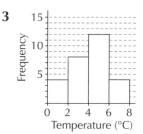

Homework 13.5
1 a 13, 13, 15, 19; 20, 22, 23, 23, 28, 29; 33, 36, 38
  b 52, 55; 61, 63, 66, 66, 68; 74, 78; 80

2 a
```
4 | 2  3  3  7  8
5 | 1  2  2  6
6 | 1  2
```
b
```
1 | 0  2  5
2 | 1  4  4  6
3 | 2  8
```
  Check key is representative of data

3 a
```
4 | 2  5  6  7
5 | 2  4  6  8
6 | 0  2  3  5  5
```
b
```
0 | 2  3  3  5  7  8
1 | 0  1  2  5  6
2 | 0  3  3  6
```
  Check key is representative of data

4
```
1 | 6  8
2 | 0  2  6  6  8
3 | 2  3  4
```
  Check key is representative of data

Chapter 14 Geometry and measures 4

Homework 14.1
Check construction
angle C = 80°, AC = 4.6 cm, BC = 6.2 cm

Homework 14.2
Check construction
Scalene

Homework 14.3
1 a Width = 4 cm, Length = 5 cm, Height = 2 cm   **b** 76 cm²
2 a Width = 5 cm, Length = 6 cm, Height = 4 cm   **b** 148 cm²
3 a 124 cm²   **b** 76 m²

Homework 14.4
1 a Width = 4 cm, Length = 6 cm, Height = 3 cm   **b** 72 cm³
2 a Width = 5 cm, Length = 6 cm, Height = 5 cm   **b** 150 cm³
3 a 125 cm³   **b** 36 m³

Chapter 15 GCSE Preparation

Homework 15.1
1 a 6   **b** 9   **c** 12   **d** 26
2 a 9   **b** 42   **c** 5   **d** 1
3 a 8   **b** 32   **c** 16   **d** 6   **e** 5   **f** 28   **g** 3   **h** 3   **i** 32   **j** 50   **k** 48   **l** 20
4 a $2 \times (5 + 7) = 24$ **b** $20 \div (2 + 2) = 5$ **c** $28 \div (4 + 3) = 4$ **d** $18 \div (3 + 3) = 3$
  e $5 \times (12 - 8) = 20$ **f** $(10 - 2)^2 \times 2 = 128$

Homework 15.2
1 £43.17, –£22.33, –£2.33, £122.47, –£46.91
2 a –13   **b** 8   **c** –6   **d** –2   **e** –9   **f** –1   **g** 12   **h** –16
3 a –20, –10, 0, 10, 20, 30, 40, 50, 60, 70, 80
  b –90, –75, –60, –45, –30, –15, 0, 15, 30, 45, 60
4 a –7   **b** –2   **c** 4   **d** 1   **e** –5   **f** –4

Homework 15.3
1 a 11, 22, 33, 44, 55   **b** 15, 30, 45, 60, 75   **c** 20, 40, 60, 80, 100
2 a 8, 14, 18, 24, 36, 48, 64, 90, 120   **b** 7, 14, 49   **c** 18, 36, 90
3 a 48   **b** 45
4 a 1, 2, 17, 34   **b** 1, 2, 4, 13, 26, 52   **c** 1, 2, 4, 5, 8, 10, 16, 20, 40, 80
  d 1, 2, 4, 5, 10, 20, 25, 50, 100   **e** 1, 2, 3, 4, 5, 6, 9, 10, 12, 15, 18, 20, 30, 36, 45, 60, 90, 180
5 1, 5

Homework 15.4
1 a 36   **b** 64   **c** 144   **d** 7   **e** 9   **f** 10
2 a 484   **b** 676   **c** 961   **d** 33   **e** 35   **f** 42
3 a 625   **b** 729   **c** 50 625   **d** 5832   **e** 19 683   **f** 78 125

Homework 15.5
1 a 2.15 litres   **b** 0.85 litres
2 a 11.42 kg   **b** 6.38 kg
3 £44.29
4 5 hours 49 minutes ≈ 6 hours

New Maths Frameworking Year 9
Assessment Tests

ASSESSMENT TEST 1

CHAPTER
1
2
3

Algebra **1 & 2**

Number **1**

Algebra **3**

Name: _____

Time allowed 50 minutes

1 Look at the numbers in the box then answer the questions.

60	120	220	330	
50	80	180	290	

    a Which two numbers added together make 200? _____

    b Which two numbers have a sum of 240? _____

    c Which two numbers have a difference of 110? _____

2 Complete these multiplication tables.

a

×	11	18	19
2			
5			95
8			

b

×	25	16	17
5			
8	200		
9			

3 A box of cakes contains 6 cakes. How many cakes will be in

    a 7 boxes? _____

    b 15 boxes? _____

4 Use the rule **multiply by 3 then subtract 1** to work out the next five terms in this sequence. The first term in the sequence is given.

1					

5 Work out the missing terms in these sequences.

a [   ] , 110, 90, 70, [   ] , [   ] , 10

b [   ] , 6 , 12, 24, 48, [   ]

6 In this question the letters a, b and c represent three numbers. Write down the value of each expression for the values of a, b and c given below.

| $a = 2$ | $b = 5$ | $c = 8$ |

a $a + 7$ _____

b $10 - c$ _____

c $2b + 3$ _____

d $a + b - c$ _____

7 Round each of these decimal numbers to one decimal place.

a 5.27 _____

b 6.65 _____

c 0.58 _____

8 Put these amounts of money in order of size, starting with the smallest.

a £3.66, £3.60, £3.06, £0.69   _____ , _____ , _____ , _____

b £4.52, £2.54, £5.42, £5.24   _____ , _____ , _____ , _____

9 Complete this table by filling in the equivalent decimals, percentages and fractions of the amounts given.

Decimal	0.4		
Percentage		75%	
Fraction			$\frac{1}{10}$

10 Fill in the missing values in these equivalent fractions.

a $\frac{2}{5} = \frac{}{35}$

b $\frac{3}{4} = \frac{24}{}$

11 There are 32 students in Class 9D. Three quarters of them have blue eyes. The rest have brown eyes. Write the ratio of **students with blue eyes to brown eyes** in its simplest form.

_____ : _____

12 In a box of 45 chocolates there are 18 soft-centred chocolates. The rest are hard-centred. Write the ratio soft-centred : hard-centred in its simplest form.

_____ : _____

13 Fill in the boxes to make these calculations correct.

a $9 + \boxed{} = 21$ **b** $45 \div \boxed{} = 5$

14 A florist charges for bouquets using the rule:

cost of bouquet = number of flowers × £2

a How much will a bouquet with 14 flowers cost? _____

b A bouquet cost £44. How many flowers were in it? _____

15 Simplify these expressions.

a $2a + 5a - 3a$ _____

b $4a + 3b - a + 6b$ _____

16 A tiler uses this formula to work out the cost of tiling a wall:

$C = 25 + \frac{1}{2}t$ **where C = cost in pounds**
t = number of tiles

a Use the formula to work out how much he would charge to tile a wall with 300 tiles.

_____

b He charges £125 to tile a wall. How many tiles did he fix?

_____

17 Solve the following equations.

a $x - 12 = 30$ **b** $8x = 24$

_____ _____

_____ _____

$x =$ _____ $x =$ _____

ASSESSMENT TEST 2

CHAPTER
4
5
6

Geometry and measures **1**

Statistics **1**

Geometry and measures **2**

Name: _____

Time allowed 50 minutes

1 Label each triangle with the appropriate description.

Scalene	Equilateral	Isosceles	Right-angled

a   **b**   **c**   **d**

_____ _____ _____ _____

2 Find the size of angles a, b and c in the triangles below.

a 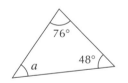   **b**   **c**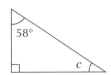

$a =$ _____ ° $b =$ _____ ° $c =$ _____ °

3 Find the size of angles a, b and c in the diagrams below.

a    **b**   **c**

$a =$ _____ ° $b =$ _____ ° $c =$ _____ °

4 Find the size of angles *a*, *b* and *c* in the quadrilaterals below.

a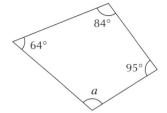

b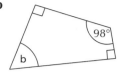

c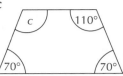

a = _____°   *b* = _____°   *c* = _____°

5 One angle of an isosceles triangle is 40°. Two different sets of angles are possible. What are they?

40° and _____° and _____°

40° and _____° and _____°

6 The two-way table shows some data about the number of boys and girls in a class and whether they are left- or right-handed.

	Boys	**Girls**	**Total**
Left-handed			
Right-handed			
Total			30

There are 30 students in the class altogether.

There are 16 girls in the class.

A quarter of the girls are left-handed.

3 boys are left-handed.

Complete the table.

7 The data in the frequency table shows the results of a student survey on favourite drinks.

Drink	**Frequency**
Coke	9
Milk	5
Fanta	3
Tea	4

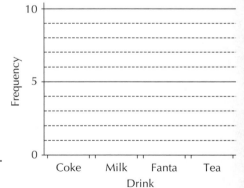

a Draw a bar chart to show this data using the axes on the right.

b How many students were surveyed? _____

8 The data in the frequency table shows the results of a survey on the methods of transport used by 20 students to travel to school.

Method of transport	Frequency
Walk	8
Bus	6
Car	2
Cycle	4

Draw a pie chart to show the information.

9 Find the mode, median, mean and range of these sets of data.

a 1, 3, 4, 4, 8
Mode _____ Median _____ Mean _____ Range _____

b 12, 14, 10, 12, 11, 13
Mode _____ Median _____ Mean _____ Range _____

10 Find the area of each of the following shapes.

a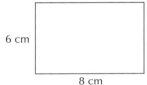
6 cm
8 cm

b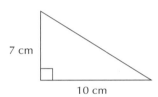
7 cm
10 cm

c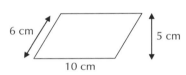
6 cm
5 cm
10 cm

Area = _____

_____ cm²

Area = _____

_____ cm²

11 This scale shows kilograms and pounds.

0	1	2	3	4	Kilograms

| 0 | 1 | 2 | 3 | 4 | 5 | 6 | 7 | 8 | 9 | 10 | Pounds |

a Approximately how many pounds is 4 kilograms? _____

b Approximately how many kilograms is 40 pounds? _____

ASSESSMENT TEST 3

CHAPTER

7

8

9

Number **2**

Algebra **4**

Statistics **2**

Name: _____

Time allowed 50 minutes

1 Work out each of these multiplications.

a $5.3 \times 1000 =$ _____

b $5.6 \times 100 =$ _____

c $6.7 \times 10^2 =$ _____

d $2.3 \times 10^3 =$ _____

2 Work out the answer to each addition. Remember to set out the question in columns first.

a $2.06 + 6.92$

b $2.57 + 9.9$

c $3.5 + 10.53 + 17.07$

3 Work out the answer to each subtraction. Remember to set out the question in columns first.

a $43.7 - 16.9$

b $57.5 - 27.8$

c $3.26 - 1.88$

4 Work out the answer to each multiplication. Remember to set out the question in columns first.

    a 5.9×6 **b** 41.2×8 **c** 9×7.05

5 Work out the answer to each division. Remember to set out the question in columns first.

    a $7.8 \div 6$ **b** $52.8 \div 8$ **c** $7.02 \div 9$

6 Write down the first **five** multiples of these numbers.

    a 7 _____   **b** 13 _____

7 Write down all of the factors for these numbers.

    a 18 _____ _____ _____ _____ _____ _____

    b 30 _____ _____ _____ _____ _____ _____ _____ _____

8 a List all of the factors of 12. _____ _____ _____ _____ _____ _____

    b List all of the factors of 20. _____ _____ _____ _____ _____ _____

    c What is the highest common factor of 12 and 20? _____

9 Circle the prime numbers in the list below.

| 2 | 5 | 9 | 11 | 15 | 17 | 21 | 23 |

10 Circle the square numbers in the list below.

| 2 | 4 | 8 | 9 | 10 | 16 | 20 | 25 |

11 Work out each of these square roots.

    a $\sqrt{49}$ = _____   **b** $\sqrt{81}$ = _____   **c** $\sqrt{121}$ = _____

12 Write down the answer to each of these.

    a 2^3 = _____   **b** 5^3 = _____   **c** 10^3 = _____

13 Work out each of these cube roots.

    a $\sqrt[3]{27}$ = _____   **b** $\sqrt[3]{64}$ = _____   **c** $\sqrt[3]{1}$ = _____

14 Work out the probability of each event, giving your answer as a fraction. Draw an arrow to show the position of each event on the probability scale. Don't forget to label each arrow **a**, **b** or **c**.

    a Probability of a flipped coin landing on Tails = _____

    b Probability of a rolled dice landing on a number less than 7 = _____

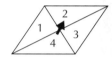

    c Probability of spinning 5 on this spinner = _____

```
├──────────┬──────────┬──────────┬──────────┤
0          1/4        1/2        3/4         1
```

15 A bag contains four blue counters and five red counters.
A counter is taken at random from the bag. What is:

    a the probability of picking a blue counter? _____

    b the probability of picking a red counter? _____

16 A box of crisps contains seven plain packets and five flavoured packets.
A packet is taken at random from the box. What is:

    a the probability of picking plain crisps? _____

    b the probability of picking flavoured crisps? _____

ASSESSMENT TEST 4

Geometry and measures 3

Algebra 5

Name: _____

Time allowed 50 minutes

1 Draw the lines of symmetry on each of the following shapes.

   a   **b**   **c**

2 Write down the order of rotation symmetry of each of these shapes.

   a   **b**   **c**

  Order _____   Order _____   Order _____

3 Make an accurate scale drawing of the shape sketched on the right using a scale of 1 cm = 2 m.

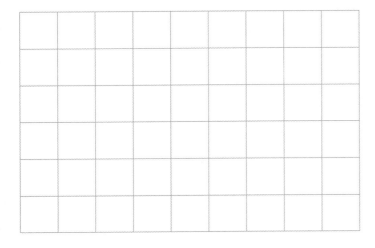

4 Write down the coordinates of each of the points marked by the letters A–H on the grid.

A(.......... , ...) B(.......... , ...)

C(.......... , ...) D(.......... , ...)

E(.......... , ...) F(.......... , ...)

G(.......... , ...) H(.......... , ...)

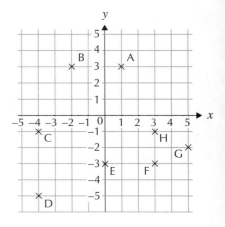

5 a Plot and label the points A(1, 4) , B(4, –2) and C(0, –4) on the grid.

b A, B and C are three corners of a rectangle, ABCD. Write down the coordinates of the fourth corner, D.

(.......... , ...)

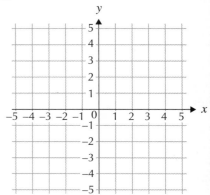

6 Work out each of these calculations.

a $35 \div 5 + 2$ = _____

b $35 \div (5 + 2)$ = _____

c $3 \times 9 - 3$ = _____

d $3 \times (9 - 3)$ = _____

e $(14 - 9) \times 8$ = _____

f $5 + 3^2 - 6$ = _____

g $(7 - 4) \times (8 + 3)$ = _____

h $(5 + 3)^2 - 6$ = _____

7 Expand the brackets by multiplying out.

a $5(a + 2)$ = _____

b $4(b + 6)$ = _____

c $3(c - 4)$ = _____

d $6(d - 1)$ = _____

8 Simplify each of the following.

a $4 \times 3a$ = _____

b $4 \times 6b$ = _____

c $2 \times 5c$ = _____

d $2 \times 7m$ = _____

9 Expand the brackets by multiplying out.

a $3(6a + 5)$ = _____

b $3(2b + 5)$ = _____

c $5(2c - 1)$ = _____

d $6(3d - 2)$ = _____

10 Solve each of these equations.

a $x + 6 = 13$

_____

$x =$ _____

b $x - 5 = 11$

_____

$x =$ _____

c $3x = 15$

_____

$x =$ _____

d $6x = 18$

_____

$x =$ _____

e $3x + 4 = 19$

$3x =$ _____

$x =$ _____

f $2x + 9 = 16$

$2x =$ _____

$x =$ _____

g $5x - 1 = 9$

$5x =$ _____

$x =$ _____

h $3x - 7 = 26$

$3x =$ _____

$x =$ _____

11 The graph on the right shows how a taxi driver works out the cost of the fare for a journey, depending on the number of miles travelled.

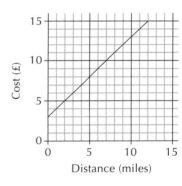

a Use the graph to work out:

i the cost of a 2 mile journey. _____

ii the cost of a 9 mile journey. _____

iii how far you could travel for £7. _____

iv how far you could travel for £13. _____

b What is the cost of a 15 mile journey? _____

ASSESSMENT TEST 5

CHAPTER 13 14

Statistics **3**

Geometry and measures **4**

Name: _____

Time allowed 50 minutes

1 Some students in Form 9C are planning a survey on sport and exercise. They decide to survey 30 students each.

John asks 30 boys who turn up for Soccer practice.
Mary asks 30 members of Form 7C.
Dave asks the first 30 students who come through the school gates in the morning.
Ethel asks 15 girls and 15 boys picked at random from the school register.

a Who do you think will get the most reliable results? Explain your answer. _____

_____

b Explain why each of the other students' methods will not give reliable results.

_____

_____

_____

_____

2 Frank measured the height (in centimetres) of 20 plants.

| 34.8 | 24.7 | 29.5 | 31.2 | 23.0 | 28.2 | 32.0 | 30.5 | 28.9 | 34.6 |
| 20.3 | 29.7 | 32.6 | 38.6 | 24.3 | 28.5 | 27.9 | 37.5 | 36.4 | 35.0 |

a Put these heights into the grouped frequency table.

Height (*h*) in cm	Tally	Frequency
$20 < h \leq 25$		
$25 < h \leq 30$		
$30 < h \leq 35$		
$35 < h \leq 40$		

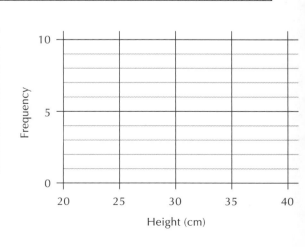

b Draw a frequency diagram to show this information on the axes on the right.

3 Work out the **median** of these sets of data.

   a 15, 16, 19, 21, 25, 42   _____

   b 7, 7, 3, 1, 4, 5, 7, 2, 1, 3   _____

4 Here are the heights, in metres, of seven children.

1.38	1.17	1.56	1.32	1.45	1.72	1.17

   a Find the **mode**, **median** and **range** of the heights.

   Mode _____   Median _____   Range _____

   b Why would you not use the mode as a measure of the average height?

   _____

5 Here are the weekly wages of 10 workers in a factory.

£100	£200	£200	£200	£200
£200	£300	£300	£300	£2000

   a Work out the **mode**, **median** and **mean** wage.

   Mode _____   Median _____   Mean _____

   b Which average do you think best represents the average wage? Give a reason for your answer.

   _____

   _____

6 Put the numbers below into a stem-and-leaf diagram. The stem is already given. Remember to add a key.

   a 34, 52, 28, 35, 42, 48, 40, 30, 34, 51
        23, 31, 28, 38, 28, 24, 53, 47, 31, 40

2	
3	
4	
5	

   b What is the mode? _____

7 a Using a ruler and a protractor, make an accurate drawing of the
triangle sketched on the right.

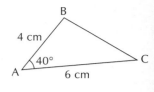

b Measure the side BC. _____ cm

8 a Using a ruler and compasses, make an accurate drawing of the
triangle sketched on the right.

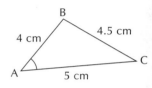

b Measure angle A. _____ °

9 Work out the surface area and volume of these cuboids.

a
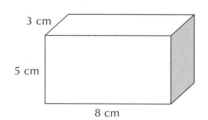

b
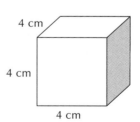

Surface Area = _____

_____

Volume = _____

_____

Surface Area = _____

_____

Volume = _____

_____

New Maths Frameworking Year 9
Assessment Test Answers

Assessment Test 1

Chapters 1–3

Question	Answer	Marks	Comment
1 a	80 and 120	1	
1 b	60 and 180	1	*Sum* means addition
1 c	220 and 330 *or* 180 and 290	1	*Difference* means subtract the smallest from the largest

2 a

×	**11**	**18**	**19**
2	22	36	38
5	55	90	(95)
8	88	144	152

Marks: 2 — 1 if 5 or more correct

2 b

×	**25**	**16**	**17**
5	125	80	85
8	(200)	128	136
9	225	144	153

Marks: 2 — 1 if 5 or more correct

Question	Answer	Marks	Comment
3 a	42	1	Calculation is 7×6
3 b	90	1	Calculation is 15×6
4	2, 5, 14, 41, 122	2	1 if 3 or more correct
5 a	130, 50, 30,	1	The term-to-term rule is 'subtract 20'
5 b	3, 96	1	The term-to-term rule is 'multiply by 2'
6 a	9	1	$a + 7 = 2 + 7 = 9$
6 b	2	1	$10 - c = 10 - 8 = 2$
6 c	13	1	$2b + 3 = 2 \times 5 + 3 = 13$
6 d	−1	1	$a + b - c = 2 + 5 - 8 = -1$
7 a	5.3	1	
7 b	6.7	1	Half way value rounds up
7 c	0.6	1	
8 a	£0.69, £3.06, £3.60, £3.66	1	
8 b	£2.54, £4.52, £5.24, £5.42	1	

9

Decimal	(0.4)	0.75	0.1
Percentage	40%	(75%)	10%
Fraction	$\frac{2}{5}$	$\frac{3}{4}$	$(\frac{1}{10})$

Marks: 3 — 2 if 5 correct, 1 if 4 correct

Question	Answer	Marks	Comment
10 a	14	1	Multiply top and bottom by 7
10 b	32	1	Multiply top and bottom by 8
11	3 : 1	1	24 students with blue eyes and 8 with brown eyes – 24 : 8 = 3 : 1
12	2 : 3	1	18 soft-centred means 45 − 18 = 27

hard-centred. 18 : 27, cancel by 9

13 a	12	1	Work out 21 – 9
13 b	9	1	Work out 45 ÷ 5
14 a	£28	1	Work out 14 × 2
14 b	22 flowers	1	Work out 44 ÷ 2
15 a	$4a$	1	
15 b	$3a + 9b$	1	$4a - a = 3a$, $3b + 6b = 9b$
16 a	£175	1	Work out $25 + \frac{1}{2} \times 300$
16 b	200 tiles	1	Subtract $125 - 25 = 100$, then multiply 100 by 2
17 a	42	1	Work out 30 + 12
17 b	3	1	Work out 24 ÷ 8

Total marks: 39

Mark boundaries

12 – 27	Level 3
28 – 39	Level 4

Assessment Test 2

Chapters 4–6

Question	Answer	Marks	Comment
1 a	Equilateral	1	
1 b	Right-angled	1	
1 c	Isosceles	1	
1 d	Scalene	1	
2 a	56°	1	The angles in a triangle add up to 180°. $180 - (76 + 48) = 56°$
2 b	55°	1	In an isosceles triangle the two base angles are the same. $180 - 70 = 110$, $110 \div 2 = 55°$
2 c	32°	1	In a right-angled triangle the two smaller angles have a sum of 90°. $90 - 58 = 32°$
3 a	71°	1	Angles on a straight line are 180°. $180 - 109 = 71°$
3 b	173°	1	Angles round a point are 360°. $360 - 90 - 97 = 173°$
3 c	50°	1	$3c + 210 = 360$, $3c = 150°$
4 a	117°	1	Angles in a quadrilateral add up to 360°. $360 - (64 + 84 + 95) = 117°$

4 b	$b = 82°$	1	As two angles are right angles this is just $180 - 98 = 82°$
4 c	$c = 110°$	1	$70 + 110 = 180$, and there is symmetry, so $c = 110°$
5	40 and 40 and 100, 40 and 70 and 70	2	Two angles are equal so 40 could be one of the equal angles or 40 could be the unequal angle

6

3	4	7
11	12	23
14	16	(30)

3   2 if 6 or 7 cells correct

1 if 4 or 5 cells correct

Fill in each cell of the table according to the given information

7 a

2   1 if 3 bars correct

7 b	21	1	Add up the frequencies in the table

8

3   2 if sectors correct but not labelled

2 if 2 sectors correct and labelled

1 if 2 sectors correct but not labelled

Each sector represents 2 students

9 a	Mode 4, Median 4, Mean 4, Range 7	4	1 mark for each
9 b	Mode 12, Median 12, Mean 12, Range 4	4	1 mark for each
10 a	48 cm²	1	Area of rectangle = base × height
10 b	35 cm²	1	Area of triangle = $\frac{1}{2}$ × base × height
10 c	50 cm²	1	Area of parallelogram = base × height Ignore the value of 6 cm as this is not the height
11 a	8.8 – 9 pounds	1	Read from the scale or know that 1 kg ≈ 2.2 pounds

11 b	18–19 kg	1	10 pounds is about 4.5 kg so multiply by 4

Total marks: 37

Mark boundaries
12 – 26   Level 3
27 – 37   Level 4

Assessment Test 3

Chapters 7–9

Question	Answer	Marks	Comment
1 a	5300	1	Move the decimal point three places right
1 b	560	1	Move the decimal point two places right
1 c	670	1	Move the decimal point two places right
1 d	2300	1	Move the decimal point three places right
2 a	8.98	1	Line up the decimal point $\quad\begin{array}{r} 2.06 \\ 6.92 \\ \hline 8.98 \end{array}$
2 b	12.47	1	Line up the decimal point and add zeros to make up the digits $\quad\begin{array}{r} 2.57 \\ 9.90 \\ \hline 12.47 \\ {\scriptstyle 1} \end{array}$
2 c	31.1	1	Line up the decimal point and add zeros to make up the digits $\quad\begin{array}{r} 3.50 \\ 10.53 \\ 17.07 \\ \hline 31.10 \\ {\scriptstyle 1\ 1\ \ 1} \end{array}$
3 a	26.8	1	Line up the decimal point $\quad\begin{array}{r} {\scriptstyle 3\ 12\ 1} \\ 4\!\!\!/3.7 \\ 16.9 \\ \hline 26.8 \end{array}$
3 b	29.7	1	Line up the decimal point $\quad\begin{array}{r} {\scriptstyle 4\ 16\ 1} \\ 5\!\!\!/7.5 \\ 2\!\!\!/7.8 \\ \hline 29.7 \end{array}$
3 c	1.38	1	Line up the decimal point $\quad\begin{array}{r} {\scriptstyle 2\ \ 11\ 1} \\ 3\!\!\!/.2\!\!\!/6 \\ 1.88 \\ \hline 1.38 \end{array}$
4 a	35.4	1	Line up the decimal point with the decimal point in the answer $\quad\begin{array}{r} 5.9 \\ \times\quad 6 \\ \hline 35.4 \\ {\scriptstyle 5} \end{array}$
4 b	329.6	1	Line up the decimal point with the decimal point in the answer $\quad\begin{array}{r} 41.2 \\ \times\quad 8 \\ \hline 329.6 \\ {\scriptstyle 1} \end{array}$

| **4 c** | 63.45 | 1 | Line up the decimal point with the decimal point in the answer | $\begin{array}{r} 7.05 \\ \times \quad 9 \\ \hline 6\,3.4\,5 \\ {\scriptstyle 4} \end{array}$ |

| **5 a** | 1.3 | 1 | Keep the decimal points lined up | $\begin{array}{r} 1.3 \\ 6\,\overline{)\,7.^{1}8} \end{array}$ |

| **5 b** | 6.6 | 1 | Keep the decimal points lined up | $\begin{array}{r} 6.6 \\ 8\,\overline{)\,52.^{4}8} \end{array}$ |

| **5 c** | 0.78 | 1 | Keep the decimal points lined up | $\begin{array}{r} 0.7\,8 \\ 9\,\overline{)\,7.0^{7}2} \end{array}$ |

6 a	7, 14, 21, 28, 35	1	Multiples are the times table
6 b	13, 26, 39, 52, 65	1	
7 a	1, 2, 3, 6, 9, 18	1	Factors are numbers that divide exactly
7 b	1, 2, 3, 5, 6, 10, 15, 30	1	
8 a	1, 2, 3, 4, 6, 12	1	
8 b	1, 2, 4, 5, 10, 20	1	
8 c	4	1	The HCF is the biggest number that divides exactly into 12 and 20

| **9** | 2, 5, 11, 17 and 23 should be circled | 2 | 1 if any non-primes are circled or only 4 primes are circled
Prime numbers only have 2 factors, 1 and themselves |

| **10** | 4, 9, 16 and 25 should be circled | 2 | 1 if any non-squares are circled or only 3 squares are circled. Square numbers are 1×1, 2×2, etc |

11 a	7	1	The square root is the number that multiplies by itself to give 49
11 b	9	1	
11 c	11	1	
12 a	8	1	Cube means multiply by itself three times, i.e. $2 \times 2 \times 2$
12 b	125	1	
12 c	1000	1	
13 a	3	1	The cube root is the number that multiplies by itself three times to give 27
13 b	4	1	
13 c	1	1	
14 a	$\frac{1}{2}$	1	Position must be marked on scale
14 b	1	1	A certain event has a probability of 1 Position must be marked on scale
14 c	0	1	An impossible event has a probability of 0 Position must be marked on scale
15 a	$\frac{4}{9}$	1	4 counters out of 9 are blue
15 b	$\frac{5}{9}$	1	
16 a	$\frac{7}{12}$	1	7 packets out of 12 are plain
16 b	$\frac{5}{12}$	1	$12 - 7 = 5$ packets out of 12 are flavoured

Total marks: 43

Mark boundaries

20 – 29   Level 3
30 – 43   Level 4

Assessment Test 4

Chapters 10 and 11

Question	Answer	Marks	Comment
1 a		1	
1 b	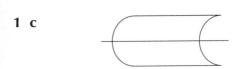	1	This shape does not have diagonal mirror lines
1 c		1	
2 a	6	1	Trace the shape and turn it around It will look the same 6 times
2 b	4	1	
2 c	3	1	
3	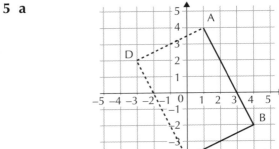	2	1 mark if 2 sides are correct The scale means each square is 2 m so, for example, 8 m is 4 squares
4	A(1, 3) B(–2, 3) C(–4, –1) D(–4, –5) E(0, –3) F(3, –3) G(5, –2) H(3, –1)	8	1 mark each Read across first, up second If all the coordinates are the wrong way round but otherwise correct give 4 marks
5 a	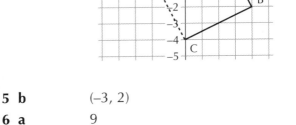	2	1 mark if only 2 points plotted correctly
5 b	(–3, 2)	1	
6 a	9	1	Divide first
6 b	5	1	Do the bracket first

6 c	24	1	Multiply first
6 d	18	1	Do the bracket first
6 e	40	1	Do the bracket first
6 f	8	1	Do the square first
6 g	33	1	Do both brackets then multiply
6 h	58	1	Do the bracket to get 8 first then square 8
7 a	$5a + 10$	1	Multiply a by 5 and 2 by 5
7 b	$4b + 24$	1	
7 c	$3c - 12$	1	
7 d	$6d - 6$	1	
8 a	$12a$	1	$4 \times 3 = 12$, $4 \times 3a = 12a$
8 b	$24b$	1	
8 c	$10c$	1	
8 d	$14m$	1	
9 a	$18a + 15$	2	1 mark for each term: $3 \times 6a = 18a$, $3 \times 5 = 15$
9 b	$6b + 15$	2	
9 c	$10c - 5$	2	
9 d	$18d - 12$	2	
10 a	7	1	$x = 13 - 6$
10 b	16	1	$x = 11 + 5$
10 c	5	1	$x = 15 \div 3$
10 d	3	1	$x = 18 \div 6$
10 e	5	1	$3x = 19 - 4 = 15$, $x = 15 \div 3 = 5$
10 f	3.5	1	$2x = 16 - 9 = 7$, $x = 7 \div 2 = 3.5$
10 g	2	1	$5x = 9 + 1 = 10$, $x = 10 \div 5$
10 h	11	1	$3x = 26 + 7 = 33$, $x = 33 \div 3 = 11$
11 a	i £5	1	Read from 2 on the bottom axis up to the graph and across
	ii £12	1	
	iii 4 miles	1	Read from 7 on the side axis across to the graph and down
	iv 10 miles	1	
11 b	£18	1	It is £3 for a basic charge then £1 a mile. $£3 + 15 \times £1 = £18$.

Total marks: 56

Mark boundaries

| 25 – 40 | Level 3 |
| 40 – 56 | Level 4 |

Assessment Test 5

Chapters 13 and 14

Question	Answer	Marks	Comment
1 a	Ethel – she has a random sample	1	In a random sample everyone has the same chance of being picked
1 b	**John** has a biased sample as they are all 3 keen on sport. **Mary** has a non-representative sample as they are all in Year 7. **Dave** may get a good sample but he may get large groups of friends with similar interests.		1 for each Samples should be non-biased and representative
2 a	Frequencies are 4, 6, 7, 3	2	1 if 3 frequencies are correct
2 b		2	Follow through the frequencies. 1 mark if 3 bars correct
3 a	20	1	
3 b	3.5	1	
4 a	Mode 1.17 m Median 1.38 m Range 0.55 m	3	1 mark for each In order the values are 1.17, 1.17, 1.32, 1.38, 1.45, 1.56. 1.72
4 b	It is one of the extreme values.	1	
5 a	Mode £200 Median £200 Mean £400	3	1 mark for each
5 b	The mode as this is the wage of half the workers.	1	
6 a	2 │ 3 4 8 8 8 3 │ 0 1 1 4 4 5 8 4 │ 0 0 2 7 8 5 │ 1 2 3	2	1 mark if only 2 lines correct or if key not given
6 b	28	1	Mode is most common
7 a	Check lengths and angles are accurate	3	1 mark for AC = 6 cm ± 1 mm 1 mark for AB = 4 cm ± 1 mm 1 mark for BAC = 40° ± 1°
7 b	BC = 3.9 cm	1	Measured to ± 2 mm
8 a	Check lengths are accurate	3	1 mark for AC = 5 cm ± 1 mm 1 mark for AB = 4 cm ± 1 mm 1 mark for BC = 4.5 cm ± 1 mm
8 b	59°	1	Measured to ± 1°
9 a	Surface Area = 158 cm^2 Volume = 120 cm^3	2	1 for each
9 b	Surface Area = 96 cm^2 Volume = 64 cm^3	2	1 for each

Total marks: 33

Mark boundaries

10 – 19   Level 3
20 – 33   Level 4

Published by Collins
An imprint of HarperCollins*Publishers*
77–85 Fulham Palace Road
Hammersmith
London W6 8JB

Browse the complete Collins catalogue at
www.collinseducation.com

10 9 8 7 6 5 4 3 2 1
ISBN-13 978-0-00-726808-5

British Library Cataloguing in Publication Data
A Catalogue record for this publication is available from the British Library

Commissioned by Katie Sergeant
Design and typesetting by Newgen
Edited by Karen Westall
Project managed by Sue Chapple
Proofread by Margaret Shepherd
Covers by Oculus Design and Communications
Illustrations by Nigel Jordan and Tony Wilkins
CD mastering by InFuze Ltd
Production by Simon Moore
Printed and bound by Martins the Printers, Berwick-upon-Tweed